Acting With Both Sides of Your Brain

Perspectives on the Creative Process

Acting With Both Sides of Your Brain

Perspectives on the Creative Process

RAMON DELGADO

Montclair State College

Holt, Rinehart and Winston
New York   Chicago   San Francisco   Philadelphia
Montreal   Toronto   London   Sydney
Tokyo   Mexico City   Rio de Janeiro   Madrid

Library of Congress Cataloging in Publication Data

Delgado, Ramon, 1937–

  Acting with both sides of your brain.

  Includes index.

  1. Acting. I. Title.

PN2061.D43   1986   792'.028   85-7611

ISBN 0-03-000104-8

CBS COLLEGE PUBLISHING
Holt, Rinehart and Winston
The Dryden Press
Saunders College Publishing

In memory of
Juana de Laban
and Constance Welch

Books and Plays by Ramon Delgado

The Best Short Plays 1981 (editor with Stanley Richards)
The Best Short Plays 1982 (editor)
The Best Short Plays 1983 (editor)
The Best Short Plays 1984 (editor)
The Best Short Plays 1985 (editor)

The Youngest Child of Pablo Peco
Waiting for the Bus
The Little Toy Dog
Once Below A Lighthouse
Sparrows of the Field
The Knight-Mare's Nest
Omega's Ninth
Listen, My Children
A Little Holy Water
The Fabulous Jeromes
The Jerusalem Thorn
Stones

Contents

Preface

Imagine my dismay a couple of years ago when at the end of a trying semester, one of my brightest acting students reflected somewhat regretfully, "Oh, the class was okay, but I didn't realize it was going to be so . . . well, physical!" As a typically left-brain dominated student, surrounded by the left-dominant academic world, she had expected a heavier dose of analysis, psychology, and motivational discussion. Throughout the semester she had skeptically tested my right-hemisphere exercises, and despite the one occasion when she appeared in the Dean's Office, costumed and clucking like a chicken, most of her work had been restrained and predictable.

The following year, however, the aftereffects of my efforts began to appear in her work. A new, exciting, open use of her imagination transformed her performances into interesting explorations of behavior. Furthermore, it was gratifying to hear her say how much she had learned the previous year, even though at the time she had not realized that the transformation was taking place.

At the time she was in class there was no single written source I could point to and say, "Read this, and understand the approach." Realizing the need, I resolved to fill the gap with an organized text that would help put in perspective those principles and practices which I and many of my colleagues use to develop the creative processes in the student performer.

Sources for This Approach

Brain Hemisphere Research

Recent research on right and left hemisphere brain functions provides a metaphor and possibly even a physical explanation for the dual nature of the performing experience. Investigations by psychologists and neurologists suggest that the creative, non-verbal functions of the right hemisphere of the brain are equally important to our balance as whole personalities as is the dominant left hemisphere of the brain, long believed to direct logical and verbal functions. If the dominant left hemisphere can be temporarily overridden, we can gain access to the creative right functions and a healthy balance can result.

It is this balance between the two hemispheres which creates the double awareness that the audience has of the performer as both actor and character. It is this balance which permits actors the simultaneous experience of emotional release and emotional control. Further study convinced me that the right-brain/left-brain approach was indeed a useful way of organizing the development of the creative processes. This general approach had been fragmentedly successful in random classroom experiences—but the progressive organization of the approach had been cohesively impossible until the recent research on the functions of the two brain hemispheres.

Traditional Influences

Ever since the 1930s when members of the Group Theatre introduced the theories and practices of Constantin Stanislavski to the United States, Stanislavski's influence has dominated the approach to realistic acting. But the realistic style, so well supported by Stanislavski's earliest work, is only one of many acting styles used today.

The theatricalizations of realism by Michael Chekhov and Eugene Vakhtangov as well as the epic theatre approaches of Bertolt Brecht and Peter Brook have had their influence on stylistic directions in the contemporary theatre. The improvisational approach for training and rehearsal has been advanced tremendously by workshop leader Viola Spolin. All of these viewpoints must be integrated into any viable training of theatre students if they are to perform effectively the variety of material written for the contemporary theatre. The astute theatre scholar, therefore, can find threads of each of these masters woven into the fabric of this text.

Professional and Personal Influences

The ideas developed in this text are grounded also in the work of former teachers and professional actors—from my years of study and exploration with Bruce Griffiths, Theatre Director at Stetson University; Charles Ritter, now at Ohio State University; Paul Baker, who for twenty-two years was artistic director of the Dallas Theatre Center, and his imaginative and capable assistant Mary Sue Jones; the late Juana de Laban with whom I studied movement at Baylor University; and the late Constance Welch, acting teacher at Yale University for four decades. The text also reflects many conversations about creativity with Jan McHughs and Robert Fish, and discussions on acting with Eelin Stewart-Harrison, all at Southern Illinois University in Carbondale. I also have gained valuable insights from recent classes and workshops with Apollo Dukakis, Maggie Abeckerly, James Campodonico, and Olympia Dukakis of the Whole Theatre Company in Montclair, New Jersey, and from colleague-actor Frank Caltabiano, with whom I learned under his direction, as his director, and as a fellow actor.

Additional thanks goes to my colleagues at Montclair State College, Gerald Ratliff, Ann Seidler, Diane Holub, and Ellen Kauffman, who have read and suggested improvements in the original manuscript. Other colleagues in the field, Beverley Byers Pevitts at Kentucky Wesleyan College, Robert Barton at the University of Oregon, Pauline Peotter at Portland State University, and director Roger H. Simon have also given valuable suggestions.

An acting teacher also learns from the students. During my twenty-five years of teaching acting, directing and creative writing, scores of students have graduated to find personal and professional applications of their creative processes in writing, art, music, and theatre. Their growth as students and their continued development after college have proven the validity of the approach here, an approach which has applications not only to acting but to the broader areas of creative communication.

My own creative work is a testimony to the validity of this approach. Using the creative approach presented here, my own plays have received awards and publications, productions under my direction have won raves in the American College Theatre Festival, and students of mine have appeared as regional and national winners of the Irene Ryan Acting Award.

The biggest secret to our successes, however, are not the specific exercises included here, helpful though they may be. The more important factor has been the discipline of single-mindedly pursuing our work with faith in each other and in our own individual creative processes, working together to express the inexpressible.

> We must treat ideas somewhat as though they were baby fish. Throw thousands out into the water. Only a handful will survive—but that is plenty.
>
> *Anne Heywood*

Organization and Use of the Text

This text is divided into five areas:

1. the Creative Perspective
2. the Human Perspective
3. the Perspective of Craft
4. the Perspective of Role Development
5. the Perspective of Genre.

An Appendix with scenes for analysis and practice follows the body of the text. I suggest that the five sections be pursued in the order presented, except for the scenes in the Appendix, which should be read early in the work on the actor's craft (Part Three). This permits the scenes to serve double duty—as examples for practical work on specific, basic techniques—before considering the additional problems of genre (Part Five). The use of the scenes from a genre viewpoint after the six levels of craft have been explored will help the students see the relative emphasis of each of the six levels as they apply to the various genres. This can re-enforce the learning of craft as the student begins to focus on the characteristics of genre. Greater appreciation for the context of the scenes will be possible, of course, if the plays from which the extracted scenes come are read in their entirety.

Adapting the Text

The material included here is designed for two semesters or three quarters of beginning work. A one semester program adaptation may include features from Parts One, Two, and Three if you select about one-third of the exercises and use one or two scenes from Part Five at the end of the semester. For a two semester program Parts One, Two, and the first two chapters of Part Three should be thoroughly explored in the first semester, leaving the rest of Part Three and the role development sections and scene work in Parts Four and Five for the second semester. For a year's program on the quarter system, use selected exercises from Part One, Part Two, and the first two levels of Part Three in the first quarter, ending the quarter with a monologue or a two-character scene; the rest of Part Three fills the second quarter; and Parts Four and Five, the third quarter.

Using the Exercises

Before tackling the exercises, the students should understand the basis for the approach used in this text. Some of the most useful observations of the right-brain/left-brain research as they apply the creative processes of acting are presented in the Introduction of Part One and Chapter One. Though I have minimized the theory to provide more room for the practical application, a basic understanding of the rationale for the organization of the exercises can be gained from these opening sections. If you wish to supplement the brain research material presented here, several of the books listed "For Further Reading" at the end of Chapter One can provide additional information and insights. From the Chapter One reading list one particularly good survey of brain lateralization studies and speculations is *Left Brain, Right Brain* by Sally Springer and George Deutsch.

The exercises grouped within each section of this text offer a latitude of varying difficulty. This choice was made to offer you as instructor the opportunity to select those exercises best suited to the level, sophistication, and needs of your own students. Undoubtedly, you will recognize in many exercises some elements you are already familiar with, but the organization and purposes offered here are connected to an overall plan for the progressive development of the student's creative processes through a right-brain/left-brain approach. Therefore, if you wish to substitute other exercises for any of those in the text, you might want to consider whether the purposes of the suggested exercises are served, so that all skills are covered in the student's progressive development.

There are several exercises for which you probably will want to provide step by step guidance to the students as they perform the exercises in class. Other exercises need only minimal suggestion on your part. Also, I urge you to do many of the exercises with the students so that you will have a more complete understanding of the experiences the exercises provide. (I have been doing exercises with the students for over twenty years, and make new discoveries every day.) And, of course, you can help students gain the most from discussions after performing exercises by drawing out their responses from them. So not only will the students benefit from the exercises, but their left-brains will learn what their right-brains have experienced.

One way to get the most mileage out of the text and more experiences for your students is to assign some of the exercises—particularly some of those in Chapters 2 through 5—for work outside of class. The students can then write out their answers to the discussion questions in the text, and you can use their written responses as the basis for class discussion. Other times you might have the students perform the exercises in class, then write out the answers to the discussion questions in their journals (as explained to them in the Introduction to Part One) or as an assignment to be turned in. If there are exercises that you think your students would perform better without reading about them prior to performing, you can have the students perform the exercises in class first, then assign text reading to re-enforce the points made through the performance of the exercises.

Developing Creative Performers

Many beginning performers, anxious to dig into "acting," begin work on scenes before they have worked on the basic components of sensitive communication, and as the seed that lands on shallow ground in the parable, their work, based only on a charming personality or an attractive appearance, flourishes rapidly only to shrivel when the scant nourishment is depleted. Deep roots in fertile soil are the stuff of creative endurance. Careful work on the exercises in Parts One, Two, and Three will develop those roots.

Attempting to verbalize about the innately non-verbal has been at times a frustrating experience, but like any memorable experience in the human expression we call theatre, I would not trade the stimulation of that experience for blissful ignorance. And if my work can help make your task easier, then we are all rewarded for the effort by both sides of our brains.

Your responses to this approach, your experiences in using it, and your suggestions for further refinement will be greatly appreciated. I hope to hear from you and to see your students using both sides of their brains on stage.

Lastly, I would like to express my thanks to the other creators of this work, to C. Spaccavento for the photographs of exercises and masks and Nancy Bartlett for graphic illustrations. The support at Holt, Rinehart and Winston from editor Anne Boynton-Trigg and assistant Jackie Fleischer has been terrific. And the production team members consisting of Theresa Bowers, Annette Mayeski, and Robert Kopelman have been models of efficiency.

Ramon Delgado
Montclair, New Jersey

Part One

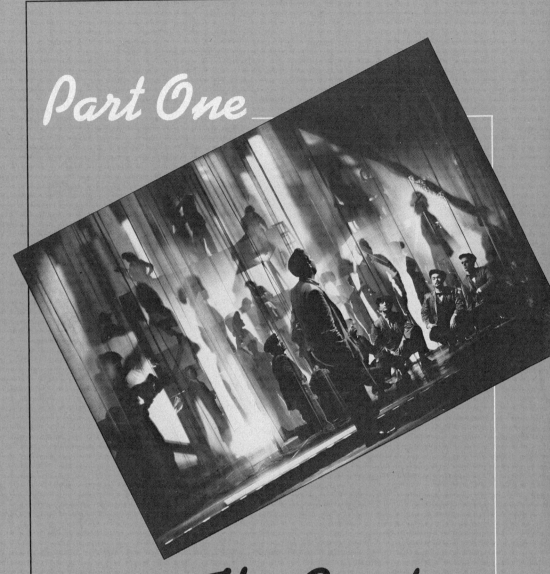

The Creative
Perspective

Introduction

Survey Both Hemispheres

There is no way to tell whether the patterns extracted by the right hemisphere are real or imagined without subjecting them to left-hemisphere scrutiny. On the other hand, mere critical thinking, without creative and intuitive insights, without the search for new patterns, is sterile and doomed. To solve complex problems in changing circumstances requires the activity of both cerebral hemispheres.

———*Carl Sagan*, Dragons of Eden

The Actor as a Two-headed Turtle

On the first day of class I show my own acting students a tattered clipping from the *New York Times* of a two-headed turtle. (See fig. 1.1.) It is a perfect image for any creative artist—a soft, sensitive nature, a tough outer shell, one head for creation and the other for self-criticism.

The recent research into left-brain/right-brain functions by psychologists and neurologists has confirmed the validity of this two-headed turtle image. For nearly a century the left hemisphere of the brain has been associated with verbal and logical processes. But it is only in the last three decades that serious attention has been given to the more elusive, nonverbal, and creative functions of the right hemisphere. The new research provides a key to unlock some of the mysteries of the creative processes involved in acting. This text focuses on the development of those processes.

The observations resulting from split-brain research also have helped me to resolve a problem raised many years ago during my own days as an undergraduate theatre major. My first two acting classes in a two-faculty department of a small liberal arts college were distinctly different. On the one hand, Teacher A required thorough written analyses of playscripts and characters, made heavy demands on logical justification for every expression of character behavior, and directed his preconceived, meticulously planned productions with an autocratic flair. On the other hand, Teacher B filled our class hours with sense awareness

Figure 1.1. Two-headed Turtle. How many other ideas does this image suggest about the experience or work of an actor? (Photograph: Courtesy of Staten Island Zoo.)

exercises, emotional improvisations, and both realistic pantomime and abstract movement work; his productions were directed with a spatial and rhythmic sensibility that brought order out of improvised chaos. At the time, I had no framework to reconcile the two approaches and floundered haphazardly from one extreme to the other in my own efforts to benefit from the obvious, though incomplete, successes of each approach.

Today, after 25 years of acting, directing, playwriting, and teaching, I believe I have found in the research on right-hemisphere/left-hemisphere brain functions a metaphor (if not an actuality) that places the delicate balance of the creative processes of acting in perspective. In these creative processes the river of imagination—the right-brain functions—flows through the banks of artistic form—the logical, left-brain functions. When the river is low, the dry banks expand; when the river is too full, the banks are flooded. Either extreme can be catastrophic; only the balance best serves the substance and the container.

Approaching the Exercises

In developing your own creative processes, try all the exercises you have time to work on. Many exercises begin simply on one level, and then are presented in a more complex version in later chapters. Note the differences between your experiences with similar exercises as you progress in your development.

Most exercises suggest that you examine your reactions to the discoveries you make. Discuss your observations with your teacher and your classmates. An unexamined exercise might as well go unperformed. The left hemisphere will never learn what the right hemisphere has experienced unless it makes the effort of assessing the progress.

If you have resistances to performing any of the exercises—and you may—see if you can discover why, and in the discovery, you may overcome the barrier. Not all exercises will benefit everyone equally. Discover why you respond enthusiastically to some exercises and not to others. Are you the only one in the class with that reaction? Why? When you approach a later exercise with a similar focus, does your reaction change? Why?

Within each chapter there are exercises that require right-hemisphere functions, exercises that use left-hemisphere functions, and exercises that integrate the two processes. When the exercises are arranged in this order, do the right-brain exercises first as presented in the text. If you attempt to do the left-brain exercises first, you later may find that the right brain will be too inhibited to put forth its best effort.

Approaching Your Creative Development

The approach to creative development in this text is nonjudgmental. There are no right and wrong ways to develop the creative processes. The one error you can make, however, is to continue frustrating and denying your right hemisphere the access to the rest of your consciousness that it needs to complete your sense of self. Development of the creative processes is a way of saying yes to your imagination, yes to your environment, yes to one another, yes to life itself.

Avoid the judgmental naysayers. They are guardians of the left-hemisphere processes, and if you let them, they will intimidate your right hemisphere before you can try the first exercise. The critics, the skeptics, the naysayers spell death to the creative processes, and indeed, many of them do not even recognize creativity the first time they observe it.

Also, beware the desire to achieve polished results instantaneously. In your initial efforts do not worry about final forms. The final form is a coffin, a perfectly shaped, perfectly respectable piece of craftsmanship, but it is designed to contain the bones of the dead. The Lebanese-born mystic Kahlil Gibran writes:

Life and all that lives is conceived in the mists, not in the crystal, and who knows but that the crystal is mist in decay.

Live in the mists, in your dreams, in your imagination. They are the source; everything else is refinement. Refinement, of course, is desirable if you continue your training for the stage, but initially the development of your creative processes should be your primary focus.

Keeping a Journal

You will find it helpful to keep a journal of your reactions to your work. The journal may be offered for your instructor's perusal or kept as a personal diary. In your journal you may wish to include the following items:

1. your reactions and resistances to exercises
2. your observations of the work of others presented to the class
3. your discoveries about yourself
4. your discoveries about characters in scenes you are working on
5. the reactions and observations made by your teacher and classmates to the work you present in class

The more written detail you include in your journal for each observation, the more likely you are to become aware of the value of your discoveries about your self and your work. Jotting down your instructor's comments on your own work and the observations of your classmates can be especially valuable in informing you if you have clearly and convincingly communicated the reality of your experiences in an honest way to others.

Keeping such a journal can be fun as well as enlightening. One interesting way of recording your observations is to draw a line down the middle of each page and record left-brain-related observations, discoveries, and conclusions on the left side of the page and right-brain imagery, metaphors, and sketches on the right. Sometimes you will have entries on only one side of the page, sometimes on both. If you date your entries, you will have a running record of when particular reactions or insights occurred and what triggered them. The more you learn about your own unique ways of thinking with both sides of your brain, the more use you can make of your creative processes.

Working on Scenes

When you progress to the work on scenes, it will be helpful to perform a single scene several times in class, each time with an altered circumstance to test yourself and the material along other lines. The classroom is your laboratory, your place to experiment with new discoveries, your space to test new ideas without embarrassment. Your classroom is the place to take risks of imagination.

Dealing with Frustrations

Along the way you undoubtedly will experience some frustrations now and then. That is to be expected. If you never have the feeling of failure in class, you probably are not growing; you are repeating the safe things you have been rewarded for in the past. You, like the two-headed turtle, must stick out your neck and stretch every fiber to move ahead.

If occasionally you are surprised that your right-brain functions become more accessible and your approach to performing becomes more creative, then my work here will have been well rewarded.

Chapter 1

Two Brains Are Better than One

The intellect is an organ composed of several groups of functions, divisible into two important classes, the functions and faculties of the right hand, the functions and faculties of the left. The faculties of the right hand are comprehensive, creative, and synthetic; the facilities of the left hand critical and analytic. . . . The left limits itself to ascertained truth, the right grasps that which is still elusive or unascertained. Both are essential to the completeness of the human reason. These important functions of the machine have all to be raised to their highest and finest working power, if the education of the child is not to be imperfect and one sided.

————*Sri Aurobindo*

Right-Brain/Left-Brain Research

This book focuses on the creative processes. It explores those special types of creative processes that are developed and refined for the purpose of sharing experiences with an audience in a theatre. The view expressed here recognizes the need to develop your intuitive, nonverbal, right-hemisphere brain functions as well as your analytical, logical, left-hemisphere brain functions. Both sides of your brain work together as a team, producing and coordinating the creative processes used in acting.

Occasionally a new theory appears on the scene, which, though still unproven, provides a fresh approach to former practices. The theory of right-/left-hemispheric functions of the brain is one of those discoveries. For more than 100 years psychologists have known that the left hemisphere of the brain is usually the verbally dominant half. But it is only in the past three decades that experiments on patients with a severed *corpus callosum* (the band of nerve fibers that connects left and right brain hemispheres) suggest the equally important functions of the dominated right hemisphere. The exact physical locations of those functions we call right-brain phenomena are at this point still unknown, but a primary value of the current research is to focus attention on the differences among the various functions of the brain. As Robert Ornstein of the Langley Porter Neuropsychiatric Institute in San Francisco has observed:

Split- and whole-brain studies have led to a new conception of human knowledge, consciousness, and intelligence. All knowledge cannot be expressed in words, yet our education is based almost exclusively on its written or spoken forms. . . . But the artist, dancer, and mystic have learned to develop the nonverbal portion of intelligence.[1]

The discoveries of psychological and neurological research have provided a springboard for emphasizing the need to develop right hemisphere specializations in Western society. Without utilizing right-brain functions, we operate at only half our capacity. As Milton Fisher pictures the problem:

Our two brains work together like a good doubles tennis team. Each of them can probably do everything required of a tennis player—serve, rally, volley, and so forth, but there is a tendency to specialize. Whenever the opportunity arises, they each take their own specialty. . . . Now, imagine one of the players is "mute." This player is like the right brain. The "mute" player sees many things his partner misses—and tries desperately to alert him, to warn him, to guide him—but if he can't get his partner's attention or make his message clear, the team will not succeed.[2]

In the last few years several books have been published that apply the principles of right-brain/left-brain discoveries to the fields of art, writing, education, and business. Some of these books are listed at the end of this chapter. If you wish to see how you can use this approach in other areas and make the most of both sides of your brain, you might want to take a look at some of the books listed and try the exercises in them as well as the exercises offered here.

Among the arts that can benefit from the awareness of right-brain/left-brain functions is the art of acting. For acting, like its many related forms of human expression, relies heavily, though not exclusively, on those abilities attributed to right-brain function, namely: nonverbal, visuo-spatial, spatial, simultaneous, analogic, Gestalt, synthetic, intuitive, and expressive processes.

The illustration (fig. 1.2.) shows the contrast between left-brain and right-brain functions as they relate to development of the creative processes of acting. You will note that the left-brain functions are verbal and logical; the right-brain functions are nonverbal, kinesthetic, spatial, and interpretive. In the creative processes of acting, creative and interpretive right-brain specialties combine with the logical, recognition abilities of the left brain to collate their abilities into an integrated performance that is both emotionally sensitive and intelligently controlled.

British actor Sir Cedric Hardwicke echos this view when he says:

On the stage he [the actor] becomes a dual personality. Outwardly he portrays the character he is supposed to represent. Inwardly the passions and emotions of his part occupy a kind of antechamber in his mind, while he remains in possession of the innermost room. . . . Great actors have raised this dualism to such heights of efficiency that, in the older days, they could count the house while playing the most taxing scene.[3]

Sri Aurobindo, the yogic philosopher cited at the beginning of this chapter, recognized at the turn of this century such right-brain/left-brain specialization, as

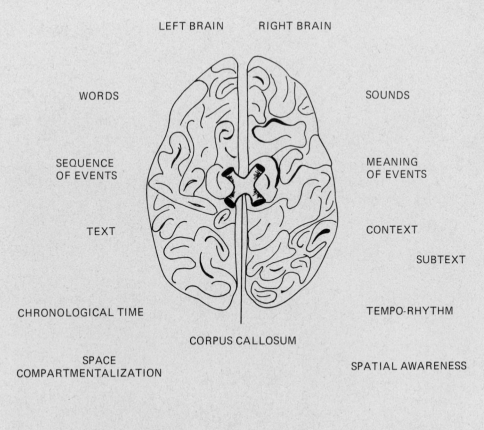

LEFT BRAIN   RIGHT BRAIN

WORDS   SOUNDS

SEQUENCE   MEANING
OF EVENTS   OF EVENTS

TEXT   CONTEXT

                                                   SUBTEXT

CHRONOLOGICAL TIME   TEMPO-RHYTHM

CORPUS CALLOSUM

SPACE   SPATIAL AWARENESS
COMPARTMENTALIZATION

IDENTIFICATION OF ROLES   INTERACTION OF ROLES

EVALUATES   CREATES

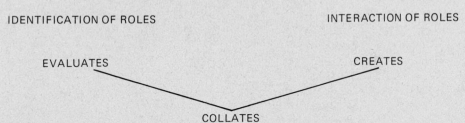

COLLATES

Figure 1.2.   Right-brain/Left-brain Functions. The various functions of each hemisphere of the brain are coordinated in the creative processes of acting.

well as the need to teach young people how such processes might be developed to complete the potential of the individual. In this recognition of the right-brain role we Westerners are far behind our Oriental counterparts, who for centuries have known the physical and spiritual benefits of cultivating the right-hemisphere functions.

The approach offered here also deals directly with a problem common to young performers, that of intellectualizing a characterization rather than manifesting it. By working through exercises that the verbal, logical, left hemisphere cannot or will not perform, we put those critical, intellectual functions to rest, allowing the nonverbal, rhythmic, Gestalt functions of the right brain to emerge and develop. Actor Ben Kingsley, Academy Award winner for his portrayal of Mahatma Gandhi, recognizes this need: "I use my voice and body to explore character, rather than my intellect. I'm sort of like a performing horse; I will run and run at a fence and finally leap over it."[4] (See fig. 1.3.)

Figure 1.3.   Ben Kingsley as "Edmund Kean." Mr. Kingsley, a versatile actor both on stage and in film, adapts his appearance, voice, and behavior to the needs of the character and situation. (Photo © 1983 by Martha Swope. Used by permission.)

Training the Whole Person as Performer

The ability to be sincere onstage—that is talent.

————*Konstantin Stanislavsky*

With the whole person in focus, this book presents a sequential program of both right-brain and left-brain exercises designed to develop your creative processes for acting. The same communication skills that serve you in daily life lie at the heart of effective stage performances. These skills include establishing rapport, clarifying intentions, economizing effort, avoiding unintended messages, observing and listening, maintaining openness, and interacting through response. For use in the theatre, however, these skills must be adapted, refined, raised to a highly sensitive degree of expression, and amplified for an audience.

Therefore, there are no "born actors," even though some bodies and nervous systems may be more suitably adapted than others for the rigors of professional training and the hardships of making a living in the theatre. Whatever your professional ambitions and potential, initially you should pursue the development of your overall creative abilities.

Creative Growth

Paul Baker, for more than 20 years artistic director of the Dallas Theater Center and widely recognized for his outstanding contribution to theatre education, sums up the type of growth the program of this text promotes:

> To some few, growth is the discovery of a dynamic power of the mind. There is a long period of intense study, criticism, and self-examination. Directions are not easily found; words do not come easily; the growth process is of little immediate interest to anyone else. . . . It is fed by ideas and sensations from nature, books, works of faith, bodily movement. . . . It has no formula. . . . It works and slaves; engulfs whole ideas; absorbs; performs surgical operations on pat formulas; laughs heartily at mediocrity and opens new worlds of insight. This mind is at home in any period, in any place where genius has produced lasting works.[5]

Creative Doodling

Much of your creative growth will be exploratory in nature and random in intention, a type of mental and physical doodling. Often exciting and absorbing ideas begin with just such randomness. The poet Robert Frost took the "road less traveled" and tells us "that made all the difference." The computer theorist Douglas Hofstadter drew such a lesson from an ant hill:

> Anteater: . . . I take a stick and draw trails in the moist ground, and watch the ants follow my trails. Presently, a new trail starts getting formed somewhere. I greatly enjoy watching trails develop. As they are forming, I anticipate how they will continue (and more often I am wrong than right).[6]

Even for this serious scientist, fooling around is part of the creative process.

Eliminating Inhibitions

The first major goal in developing the whole of your creative processes is to eliminate those inhibitions, resistances, and tensions that left-hemisphere-dominated, Western society has imposed. Insofar as possible, many of the right-brain exercises will return you to the naive potential of your childhood before language inhibited your sense of wordless wonder and before culture incarcerated your vision with preconceived notions.

You cannot achieve total success in this effort, of course, for you cannot escape the world that made you, any more than you can escape the body and mind that perceive and operate in that world. But with application and discipline you can find new discoveries within yourself and share these with the "yet unknowing world."

The exercises in the first part of this text are designed for this purpose—to open, to release, to sensitize you to the environment, to yourself, and to others. Without such sensitivity you will miss the richest depths of experience, and you cannot share with others, either in life or on stage, a depth that does not exist. To deepen your life, deepen your art; to deepen your art, deepen your life.

The Scope of Acting Skills

If we have a talent and cannot use it, we have failed. If we have a talent and use only half of it, we have partly failed. If we have a talent and learn somehow to use all of it, we have gloriously succeeded, and won a satisfaction and triumph few individuals ever know.

———*Thomas Wolfe*, The Web and the Rock

The development of acting competency demands work in three areas:

1. the creative process (developing sensitivity and imagination)
2. the craft of acting (how to understand a script, develop a character, and design a performance)
3. the physical techniques of voice and body usage

Though recognizing the need for development of all three areas, this text concentrates on the first two areas—the creative process (in parts 1 and 2) and craft (in parts 3, 4, and 5). It assumes that if you have goals for success in the professional theatre, you will pursue collateral work in voice, diction, singing, dance, fencing, and gymnastics to develop your physical instrument to its maximum expressiveness.

You may find it disconcerting to discover that the creative process is consciously shaped by the craft process. Even the great Russian teacher Konstantin Stanislavsky had such nonplussed students:

I explained to him [Tortsov—the alter ego for Stanislavsky] how crushed I had been to find that inspiration had been replaced by theatrical calculation.

"Yes . . . by that too," admitted Tortsov. "One half of an actor's soul is absorbed by his super-objective, by the through line of action, the subtext, his inner images, the elements which go to make up his inner creative state. But the other half of it continues to operate on a psycho-technique. . . . An actor is split into two parts when he is acting."[7]

Once having opened the lid to your creative potential and having overcome your resistance to craft, you will not be satisfied until you have given your creative abilities the chance to fly.

Summary

In the introduction to this section and in this chapter you have surveyed the major differences between the nonverbal functions of the right brain and the verbal and logical functions of the left brain. You have been introduced to the approach to creativity taken in this text, to your need to overcome inhibitions, to experiment, and to take risks. You have looked at the scope of acting skills and become aware of the need for developing your creative processes, the craft of acting, and your physical and vocal techniques in order to develop as a performer.

Notes

1. Robert Ornstein, "The Split and Whole Brain," *Human Nature* 1 (1978): 76-83. Cited in Sally Springer and George Deutsch, *Left Brain, Right Brain.* (San Francisco: W.H. Freeman, 1981).
2. Milton Fisher, *Intuition.* (New York: E.P. Dutton, 1981), p. 11.
3. Sir Cedric Hardwicke, *A Victorian in Orbit.* (Garden City, New York: Doubleday, 1961), p. 292.
4. Cited by Judy Klemesrud, "Ben Kingsley Leaps from 'Gandhi' to 'Kean,'" *New York Times*, 18 September, 1983, p. H 3.
5. Paul Baker, *Integration of Abilities: Exercises for Creative Growth.* (San Antonio: Trinity University Press, 1972), p. 17.
6. Douglas R. Hofstadter, *Godel, Escher, Bach: An Eternal Golden Braid.* (New York: Basic Books, 1979), p. 315.
7. Constantin Stanislavski, *Building A Character.* Translated by Elizabeth Reynolds Hapgood. (New York: Theatre Arts Books, 1949), p. 167.

For Further Reading

Ball, William. *A Sense of Direction.* New York: Drama Book Publishers, 1984. Ch. 2.
Downey, Bill. *Right Brain . . . Write on!* Englewood Cliffs, N. J.: Prentice-Hall, 1984.
Edwards, Betty. *Drawing on the Right Side of the Brain.* Los Angeles: J.P. Tarcher, 1979. Chs. 1, 3, 12.
Fincher, Jack. *Human Intelligence.* New York: G. P. Putnam's Sons, 1976. See esp. Ch. 2.
Gorelik, Mordecai. "The Divided Actor." *The Cue* 61, no. 2 (Spring/Summer, 1983): 6-7.
Pines, Maya. "The Human Difference." *Psychology Today* 17, no. 9 (September 1983): 62-68.
Restak, Richard M. *The Brain.* New York: Bantam, 1984. Ch. 6.
————. *The Brain: The Last Frontier.* New York: Warner, 1979. Ch. 10.
Rico, Gabriele Lusser. *Writing the Natural Way.* Los Angeles: J.P. Tarcher, 1983. Ch. 4.
Springer, Sally P., and George Deutsch. *Left Brain, Right Brain.* San Francisco: W.H. Freeman, 1981. Chs. 2, 10.
Wonder, Jacquelyn, and Priscilla Donovan. *Whole Brain Thinking: Working from Both Sides of the Brain to Achieve Peak Job Performance.* New York: William Morrow, 1984.

Chapter 2
The First Dip into Both Sides

. . . our more primitive capability, our largely unused right brain, is beginning to function again as it so often does in less "civilized" societies. Perhaps this "metaphoric mind" can come to know a universe which is nonlinear, in which the terms time and space come to have very different meanings.

————*Carl Rogers, in* Explorers of the Mind

You are about to begin a journey you may not have taken since you were a child, a journey into an undefined territory. Part of this exploration will take you to the territory of your inner world. If you struggle through that subterranean stratum, you will eventually emerge on the other side and see the light with both sides of your brain. Then you will understand the reaction of Tony Award–winning actress Jessica Tandy, who at age 74 reflected on beginning rehearsals for Amanda (fig. 2.1.) in a revival of Tennessee Williams's *The Glass Menagerie*:

> It's difficult to talk about something you are going to do . . . I'm scared, in a way. . . . you just do it and hope you will measure up. . . . I'd like to continue working as long as I can stand up. I don't want to get rusty.[1]

Another part of your exploration will be your contact with the outer world. The actor Charles Laughton used to visit acting classes at Baylor University and the Dallas Theatre Center. On one occasion he said it was not until he was past his 50th birthday that his voice and body would respond to his inner impulse as sensitively as he wished. It is that inner impulse and your ability to express it through your voice and body that we are going to explore in this process. Then you can spend the next 30 years working to perfect your responsiveness.

Dress comfortably, come ready to work. We are going to start a marvelous adventure with the two hemispheres of your brain, and we are going to begin making connections with the body and voice they control.

Figure 2.1. Jessica Tandy with John Heard, and Bruce Davison in *The Glass Menagerie*. Miss Tandy finds every role an exciting, new challenge. Here as Amanda, she flirts coyly with Laura's "gentleman caller" as she recounts her own courtship days in this revival of Tennessee Williams' American classic. (Photo © 1983 by Ken Howard. Used by permission.)

Warm-up Exercises

A few physical and vocal warm-ups are a good way to prepare yourself for the maximum benefit of all the exercises in this text. Such warm-up exercises help relax your body, increase your alertness, and begin sensitizing you to physical and vocal skills that you may refine later. These warm-ups also can be used to tune up your body and voice for class, rehearsals, or performances. As you read further in the text, you will find other exercises you may wish to substitute for some of these from time to time.

Doing Physical Warm-ups

The neck and stomach are two spots where tension tends to focus in the actor. Each area can be relaxed by an easy right-brain exercise.

A. Slow Head Rotation. You will relieve most of the unnecessary neck tension by an extremely slow rotation of the head. Let the weight of the head lead the head slowly forward. Then rotate the head in a circle in slow counts of eight for each quarter of the circle, very slowly stretching out the muscles of the neck as the weight of the head leads the rotation. The count should be as follows:

```
forward—2—3—4 (Let your head fall forward into position.)
left—2—3—4—5—6—7—8
back—2—3—4—5—6—7—8
right—2—3—4—5—6—7—8
forward—2—3—4—5—6—7—8
```

Repeat a second time. Then reverse:

```
right—2—3—4—5—6—7—8
back—2—3—4—5—6—7—8
left—2—3—4—5—6—7—8
forward—2—3—4—5—6—7—8
```

B. Trunk Rotation. With this exercise you can help relieve the tension in the stomach area and lower rib cage. Bend the knees slightly. On a count of eight lower the head and spine forward, the arms dangling loosely in front of you. Then on a slow count of four with the upper trunk, arms and neck dangling forward as loosely as an unstringed puppet, rotate the trunk:

```
left—2—3—4
back—2—3—4
right—2—3—4
forward—2—3—4
```

Repeat three times. Then reverse the direction:

```
right—2—3—4
back—2—3—4
left—2—3—4
forward—2—3—4
```

Repeat the exercise three times.

C. Human Jukebox. For your last physical warm-up, turn yourself into a human jukebox by bouncing up and down on your toes, and jiggling your entire body, including the arms, fingers, neck, and head. Shake out any remaining tension. As you jiggle, sing a simple song such as "Row, Row, Row, Your Boat," "Three Blind Mice," or "Happy Birthday." Relax the jaw as you sing. You are not concerned with articulation in this exercise but with relaxation. Let the vibrations travel all over the body. Feel the song in your fingertips, in your stomach, in your buttocks, in your legs and toes. Vibrate with the sounds. With a large group, you may divide into teams and sing the songs as rounds.

Doing Vocal Warm-ups

A. Sustained Vowels. Breathe deeply using the abdominal muscles. Take the air into the lungs in four equal portions, and release it in four equal portions.

in—2—3—4
out—2—3—4
in—2—3—4
out—2—3—4

Then with the mouth closed and the lips touching each other lightly, start vocalization, sending an open-throated hum through the oral cavity and out the nose. Relax the jaw and move from the "m" sound of the hum to an open sustained "ah." Sustain the vowel until just before you run out of supported breath, then let the sound fade out. Repeat the process with the other vowels and diphthongs, starting each one from the closed mouth hum:

Vowels:
M-m-ah
M-m-oo
M-m-uu
M-m-ee
M-m-eh
M-m-ih

Diphthongs:
M-m-ae
M-m-ai
M-m-ou

B. Responsive Lips. Loosen the lips by vibrating them vigorously:

1. vocalizing, as with the sound of a motor boat
2. with air only, lips loose as with the sound of a horse
3. with air only, lips tighter as with a "Bronx cheer"

C. Flexible Tongue. Loosen the tongue through the following:

1. a hum
2. open to "Ah"
3. **La**-la-la-la, **La**-la-la-la, **La**-la-la-la, **La**-la-la-la
      (Emphasize the first "La" in each group.)

D. Resonant Consonants. Run through the three nasal consonants:

1. M-m m-m
2. N-n n-n
3. **Ng**-ng-ng-ng, **Ng**-ng-ng-ng, **Ng**-ng-ng-ng, **Ng**-ng-ng-ng
      (Emphasize the first "Ng" in each group.)

E. Paired Consonants. Repeat the other consonant sounds vigorously in pairs:

1. p-b, p-b, p-b, p-b
2. t-d, t-d, t-d, t-d
3. k-g, k-g, k-g, k-g
4. f-v, f-v, f-v, f-v
5. s-z, s-z, s-z, s-z
6. sh-zh, sh-zh, sh-zh, sh-zh
7. ch-dg, ch-dg, ch-dg, ch-dg

F. Crisp Articulation. Run through a variety of consonant pair combinations with each of five vowel sounds between the consonants. First spell out the letters as separated, then pronounce the word. With each new word, repeat the previous words. Start with a slow tempo. Then pick up the tempo gradually until you are articulating as rapidly as possible.

1. b-a-d, bad
   b-e-d, bed; bad, bed
   b-i-d, bid; bad, bed, bid
   b-o-d, bod; bad, bed, bid, bod
   b-u-d, bud; bad, bed, bid, bod, bud
2. t-a-p, tap
   t-e-p, tep; tap, tep
   t-i-p, tip; tap, tep, tip
   t-o-p, top; tap, tep, tip, top
   t-u-p, tup; tap, tep, tip, top, tup

Try the same exercise with w-a-b, k-a-t, and other combinations. Some combinations produce surprises. Be careful, for example, with f-a-k.

These right-brain physical and vocal warm-ups will help relax you and tune up your physical instrument for class, rehearsals, or performance.

Right-Brain/Left-Brain Exercises

Once upon a time an artist hurried to fill his canvas before the sunset faded from the sky. A critic stopped to look over his shoulder at the canvas. Puzzled, the critic complained, "I'm sorry, but I fail to see all those colors in the sky."

The artist smiled, "I know, but don't you wish you could?"

Right-Brain Exercises

Work in a quiet atmosphere. Prepare yourself for the right-brain exercises by reading them over first. Then round up the materials you will need (paper, crayons, scissors, miscellaneous scraps, a container, and glue) before you tackle the details of each exercise.

For all right-brain exercises, here and elsewhere, you should be as relaxed as possible. For the present, the warm-up routine introduced above will suffice. Then move rapidly from one exercise to the next within each section without previously planning any effect.

Expressing Attitudes in Color

A. Course Expectations. Use crayons, pastels, or watercolors to splash a sheet of paper with colors that express your expectations and hopes for this approach to the development of your creative processes.

B. Course Apprehensions. Color a second sheet expressing your apprehensions or skepticism toward the approach. After you have completed the two sheets, place them side by side.

FOR YOUR JOURNAL OR FOR DISCUSSION
1. Do you perceive a pattern on either sheet? On both sheets?
2. What provides the pattern? Do the colors? The shapes?
3. While you were using the colors to express your expectations and apprehensions, were you aware of any verbalized thoughts going through your mind?
4. Have you ever thought purely in color or in images before? When? Do you ever dream in color?

Expressing Attitudes In Lines

A. Course Expectations. Now with only one color, draw lines—thin lines, fat lines, curved lines, angular lines—to express your expectations for the course.

B. Course Apprehensions. Draw lines on another sheet of paper to express your apprehensions. Place the sheets side by side.

FOR YOUR JOURNAL OR FOR DISCUSSION
1. How do the lines on one sheet differ from the lines on the other?
2. Which pattern of lines do you like better? Why?

Expressing Attitudes in Tempo-rhythms

A. Course Expectations. Be sure you are in a quiet place. Close your eyes. Now clap out a rhythm pattern at a tempo that expresses your expectations for your acting course. Repeat it. Repeat it a third time.

B. Course Apprehensions. Create a tempo-rhythm for your apprehensions about the course. Repeat it. Repeat it a third time.

C. Alternate Tempo-rhythms. Alternate the tempo-rhythm of your expectations with the tempo-rhythm of your apprehensions. Try different patterns:

A B A
B A B
A A B B A

FOR YOUR JOURNAL OR FOR DISCUSSION

1. Have you ever heard this pattern before? If so, where?
2. For what environments do you think this rhythm seems appropriate?
3. What types of occupation might have this rhythm?
4. Shakespeare's Richard II says, "So it is in the music of men's lives. . . ." Cite two characters in a play you are familiar with who have contrasting tempo-rhythms. What kinds of music would suggest each of their lives?

Expressing Attitudes in Textures

A. Performance Satisfaction. Clip scraps of textured material such as paper, fabric, string (consider discarded wrappers in your trash can). Paste the scraps on a piece of paper or cardboard, arranging them to express your satisfactions about your last experience in front of a group.

B. Performance Frustration. Use the same technique with textures to express your frustration about your last experience in front of a group.

FOR YOUR JOURNAL OR FOR DISCUSSION

1. When you are working with textures, is there any difference in your sense of touch and your way of thinking from the time you worked with colors?
2. Can you think of two characters in the same play that would have very different textural qualities? Describe their differences in terms of texture.

Expressing Attitudes by Combining Image-making Elements

Combining the visual elements you have experimented with (color, line, texture), decorate a container that has an inside and outside surface (such as a box, a cube, a cylinder). The inside surface represents the way you feel about yourself and your undeveloped creative processes; the outer surface represents the way you perceive others think about you. You might want to return to this exercise at the end of the year and see how much you have changed in both aspects.

You will benefit more from this exercise if you present it to the class for their reactions. Offer it for their reactions without responding one way or the other to their observations, but rather absorb the consensus of their views. Afterwards jot down their reactions and your responses to their reactions in your journal.

FOR YOUR JOURNAL OR FOR SELF-ANALYSIS
1. Are you comfortable in showing this project to the class to let them see your self-perception? If not, why not?
2. If you are open enough to share your project with the class, do others interpret your expression in a way that agrees or disagrees with your own interpretation?

Left-Brain Exercises

Expressing Attitudes in Metaphors

A. Expectations. Make a list of metaphors that represent your expectations and hopes for the class.

B. Apprehensions. Make a list of metaphors that represent your apprehensions or reservations toward the approach to the class.

Expressing Attitudes in Adjectives

A. Expectations. Make a list of adjectives to describe your expectations toward the course.

B. Apprehensions. Make a list of adjectives to describe your apprehensions toward the course.

FOR YOUR JOURNAL OR DISCUSSION
1. Make a list of infinitives and objects that express your personal goals for this class as, for example, "to develop self-confidence on stage."
2. In a brief paragraph describe your physical reactions before, during, and after you made your last appearance in front of a group. (Note: Not your feelings but your physical reactions.) What, if any, changes would you like to make in the future for this experience?

Integrated-Brain Exercises

Pantomiming Metaphors

Perform a realistic or stylized pantomime of the metaphors on your list from the left-brain exercise "Expressing Attitudes in Metaphors." You may use nonverbal sounds but no words.

Using Gibberish

Choose one item from the list you made of goals for this class. Close your eyes. Visualize yourself accomplishing this goal. Then use gibberish or non-verbal sounds as you perform this goal in your own working space.

Using Dance

Develop a one- or two-minute free-form modern dance based on the two rhythms developed in the exercise on attitudes in tempo-rhythms.

Using Poetry

Make a poetic expression about your self-perceptions.

A. Write a short poem in free or traditional verse to express the way you feel about your inner self as in the exercise with image-making elements.

B. Write a brief poem to express your perception of others' view of you.

Using Song

Develop improvised tunes for your two poems. Then sing or talk-sing them to the class.

Using Furniture and Props

Use two chairs, a table, and an apple or a glass of water (or both) to share the two sides of your personality (based on the right-brain exercise with image-making elements). Use one chair for seating one side of your personality, the other chair for the other side. Begin the exercise by sitting in the chair of your right-brained personality. Explore how that side of your personality deals with the water or apple. Then switch chairs, and explore how the left side of your personality deals with the water and apple.

FOR YOUR JOURNAL OR FOR DISCUSSION

1. If you present this exercise to the class, discuss the differences between the two sides that your classmates perceived.

2. If you do the exercise only for your own exploration, record your own perceptions of the differences in your behavior in your journal.

Summary

In this chapter you have been introduced to the stimulating value of warm-up exercises. You have taken initial steps into nonverbal, right-brain exercises that expand your understanding of your self by preventing the left brain from dominating your perceptions and behavior. Then you added left-brain exercises to help define your new experiences. Lastly you integrated the functions of both sides of your brain to provide an artistic balance to your explorations and expression.

Notes

1. Interview by Carol Lawson, "Broadway," *New York Times*, 29 July 1983, p. C 2.

For Further Reading

Baker, Paul. *Integration of Abilities: Exercises for Creative Growth*. San Antonio, Texas: Trinity University Press, 1972. "Preface," "First Exercise."
Cory, Irene. *The Mask of Reality*. New Orleans: Anchorage Press, 1968. Ch. 3.

Part Two

The Human Perspective

Introduction
Examine Your Equipment

The full range of our potentials has never been consciously discovered by us and lies as yet unused, but can be brought to life and gradually unfolded. . . . There are *no ungifted people!* If we believe we are ungifted, we will find on closer examination that we are only *hindered*, and hindrances can gradually be shed when we get insight into what has held us back, and we can give ourselves new chances—what I call a fresh learning.

———*Charlotte Selver and Charles Brooks, in* Explorers of Humankind

Unless you have studied acting before, you may think the development of the creative process of acting consists only of improvisations and scene work, some of the things you will find in parts 3, 4, and 5 of this text. So that you don't plunge recklessly ahead into those areas without absorbing the principles contained in part 2, a word of explanation about the purpose of this part of your development as creative performers is in order.

The three chapters in part 2 are designed:

1. to increase your sensitivity to yourself, to your environment, and to your fellow performers
2. to eliminate unnecessary tensions and habitual mannerisms which years of social conditioning may have inflicted on you
3. to provide you with a starting place, a "zero line" from which to begin your creative work as an actor
4. to help you recapture the freshness with which you viewed yourself, the world, and others before you were entangled in the prescribed perceptions of your culture
5. to show you a way to renew your creative resources continually despite the pressures on you which tend to distract your attention and dissipate your time and energy

In the first chapter in this section you will find exercises that increase your awareness of your own body and help you gain greater access to your innermost being. You should spend several weeks on the exercises in this first chapter.

In the second chapter in part 2 you will extend your contact to both the outside world and the stage environment. A week or two on this work is helpful.

The third chapter in this preparation phase leads you to explore relationships with your classmates as you examine the nature of the dynamics of interpersonal communication, the raw stuff at the heart of dramatic character behavior. You will want to spend at least a couple of weeks with these exercises.

You should return to many of the exercises in these three chapters throughout your work. Repetition will expand and deepen your sensitivity to your self, your environment, and your classmates, both as people and as performers.

Chapter 3

Touching Both Sides of Your Brain

With the power of both halves of the brain available to you and the myriad of possible combinations of the separate powers of the hemispheres, the door is open to your becoming more intensely aware, more capable of controlling some of the verbal processes that can distort thinking. . . .

In observing your own brain at work, you will widen your powers of perception and take advantage of the capabilities of both its halves. Presented with a problem, you will have the possibility of seeing things two ways: abstractly, verbally, logically—but also holistically, wordlessly, intuitively.

———*Betty Edwards*, Drawing on the Right Side of the Brain

A Lesson from the Decapods

The Decapods are aquatic crustaceans: shrimp, lobster, crayfish, and crabs. As they mature from larval stage to adulthood, they outgrow the confines of their external skeletons by molting, that is, by splitting out of their old shells to enlarge their potential for further growth. With each successive molt, additional appendages with new specialties appear, until the individuals have all the capabilities of previous generations of shrimp or lobster, crayfish or crabs. But during the times of transition—the periods immediately after a molt when the outgrown shells have been discarded—the creatures are highly vulnerable to predators. But the Decapods cannot grow unless they take the risk, unless they shed their tight outer shells and become vulnerable until new protection offering new capacities forms around them.

So it is with the creative processes of acting. To grow we have to deal continually with the encrustation of old behaviors that have protected us for a certain period of our lives. We have to break down the barriers of tensions and fears and burst forth from previous limitations into unknown dimensions of behavior. If we wish to develop the ability to convey the demeanor of a character with behavior unlike our own, we must relinquish old ways of thinking about ourselves and the emotional tensions that accompany them. If we are to move freely, to have access to our inner impulses,

28

to encourage the outward flow of action and reaction, we must free ourselves from the physical tensions that have become a part of our daily lives.

The first exercises useful in breaking through those rigid patterns of mental and physical behavior are for relaxation and meditation.

Relaxation and Meditation

At the outset the most valuable skills the creative performer can develop are the abilities to relax the body and to form thoughts and images in either a random or an organized fashion. These two skills are interrelated and together comprise what Dr. Herbert Benson has described as "the relaxation response."[1] This response is a meditative state of restful alertness in which the body is relaxed comfortably, and the mind is allowed to focus on whatever thoughts or images may surface. When you are in this state, your brain produces a predominance of alpha waves, which frequently have been associated with creativity.

Four elements promote the state of restful alertness that characterizes this response: a quiet environment, a comfortable position, a point of concentration, and a passive attitude.

1. A quiet environment is helpful. When you are learning the process, you should begin in a quiet spot free from distractions. After a little practice, however, you will find that you will be able to evoke the response in any environment.

2. A comfortable position aids the process. You will initially learn to relax lying down on your back. But you may achieve similar results sitting comfortably in a chair or even in the familiar cross-legged "lotus" position used by the yogi.

3. A point of concentration is necessary. In the meditation exercises you will find a variety of possible points for concentration. You may find either a single device or a combination of devices more effective. In my own use of meditation, which I have been practicing for more than 14 years, the combination of a color device and a sound device is most effective.

4. A passive attitude is important. Any effort to force an effect will work against positive results. Whatever point of concentration you find effective for yourself will remain at the center of your attention only briefly during the entire time of your practice. You must allow other images, thoughts, and feelings to come and go, returning to the point of concentration without effort from time to time.

In addition to the benefits meditation may have on your creative processes, it may also benefit your health by lowering your stress level and blood pressure.

If you have any doubts regarding the effectiveness of this approach to the development of your creativity, you might study the differences in performances by the actress Shirley MacLaine before and after she started practicing meditation. Since she began the discipline of meditation, the variety, complexity, and depth of her performances are astonishing.[2]

The following relaxation exercises will meet the first two requirements for attaining the state of restful alertness—a quiet place and a calm state. Then you will be ready to develop the attitude and concentration of the last two components of restful alertness through the meditation exercises.

Relaxation Exercises

Direct Relaxation through the Body   Physical relaxation is necessary before the mental creative processes can be released. The two exercises that follow use a direct approach to place your body in a state of relaxation and receptiveness for the subsequent meditation exercises.

Progressive Relaxation

A mat or rug will aid your comfort for this exercise in progressive relaxation. First, lie down on your back and close your eyes. (See fig. 3.1.) Bend your knees slightly to eliminate any strain on your lower back. The parts of your body should be relaxed in the order given below. Repeat each phrase silently to yourself for each part of the body as you perform the suggested action:

"I am tensing my _____ (part of the body).
I am wiggling my _____ (part of the body).
I am relaxing my _____ (part of the body).
Hello, _____ (part of the body)."

The parts to be named are as follows:

toes	stomach	neck
feet	rib cage	jaw
ankles	fingers	tongue
calves	wrists	cheeks
knees	lower arms	nose
thighs	upper arms	forehead
buttocks	upper back	eye muscles
lower back	shoulders	scalp

After you have tried this exercise in class, continue to practice it on your own, whispering the instructions to yourself or repeating them silently. Experience the extreme state of physical relaxation brought about by this process. Which areas, if any, seem difficult to relax? You should spend extra time tensing and releasing any problem areas you discover.

After you have performed this exercise a few times, move on to the following enhancement, which adds a mental image (a right-brain function) to your state of restful alertness.

Ocean Float

Immediately after performing the progressive relaxation exercise, with your eyes still closed, imagine that you are lying on a warm beach with your feet pointed toward the water. Gentle ocean waves cover and float each part of your body (from the list in the previous exercise), one part at a time.

Figure 3.1. Progressive Relaxation Circle. Performing this relaxation exercise with heads together in the center of a circle increases the rapport of the group through a shared experience.

When your entire body has been floated, slowly open your eyes, then very slowly, maintaining the floating sensation, rise to a seated position, then to a standing position.

As you stand comfortably, close your eyes, and imagine that you are a piece of sea kelp, floating slowly and rhythmically to and fro, the water-space around you supporting every part of your body. Now open your eyes, and float randomly and freely with your classmates, circling in and out among them without touching them or reacting to them. (See fig. 3.2.) Visualize as many things as you can of the underwater environment.

Next, form a circle with your classmates, and maintain the floating sensation, as the entire group floats slowly around in the circle.

DISCUSSION

1. How vivid were your images?
2. What differences did you feel between the progressive relaxation and ocean float exercises?
3. How did the water feel compared to the beach sand? Texture? Temperature?
4. What sensations did you have when you moved randomly and freely among your classmates?
5. Which aspects of these two exercises (including this discussion) do you think are from right-brain functions and which from left-brain functions?

Indirect Relaxation through the Air Sea Though we cannot see the air we breathe, we are constantly swimming in a vast sea of it, inhaling pieces of it to

Figure 3.2. Ocean Float. The more relaxed and random the movement in the ocean float, the more images you will imagine as you sway through the imaginary water.

burn our fuel, dispelling other gases back into the air sea. We share this air sea not only with other people but with all life on the planet. Respect for the air is vital to our well-being and the well-being of the rest of life.

For the performer the most immediate threat of air contamination comes from tobacco smoke. Any performer who smokes on a regular basis is harming not only his or her breathing and vocal apparatus but is contributing to the pollution of the air sea of others. Actors no less than singers should protect the health of their voices by foregoing smoking. As you perform the following exercises expand your awareness of the value of the air sea we share.

Following Your Breath

A. Resting with your back on the floor, exhale the air from your lungs. Then slowly inhale, measuring your breath intake in four equal segments, pausing between each segment. Inhale:

one—one-quarter of your capacity filled
two—one-half of your capacity filled
three—three-quarters of your capacity filled
four—filled to capacity

Reverse the process on exhalation. Exhale:

one—one-quarter empty
two—one-half empty
three—three-quarters empty
four—empty

Then relax and breathe normally for a moment.

B. Perform the exercise a second time, focusing on the breath itself as it comes in through the nose, down the throat, through the trachea, the bronchial tubes, and into the lungs. Inhale in four equal amounts. Follow your breath.

Exhale in four equal amounts. Follow your breath.

DISCUSSION

1. At which points can you feel the temperature of the air?
2. At which points can you detect any sound of the air as it passes from your nose to your lungs?

C. Perform the exercise a third time, focusing on the movement of the muscles that allow the air to enter the lungs. Inhale: one, two, three, four. Exhale in four equal amounts.

DISCUSSION

Which muscles did you feel contracting and releasing as you inhaled? As you exhaled?

D. If you did not experience muscles working all the way down to the base of your abdomen, try the exercise again, concentrating on the muscles of your lower abdomen and lower back.

Supporting Your Breath

The efficient use of the muscles of the abdomen and lower back is important not only to energy flow and flexibility in movement but also to the proper support of your voice as a performer. If you have any difficulty with this exercise, you should discuss plans to work on the problem with your teacher or with a vocal instructor.

Stand in front of a chair, then lean over the chair seat, supporting the upper part of your body with your arms. (See fig. 3.3.) In this position perform exercise A again, focusing on the muscles of the stomach and lower back.

Following Your Sound

Standing in a state of restful alertness, start a hum. Place the buzz of the hum to tickle the roof of your mouth. Then lower the head forward slowly, dropping the apparent vibration of the hum to the throat. Continue leaning over forward with the vibration of the hum moving lower in the body with the loosening of each new vertebra. The vibrations move from throat to shoulders, to upper rib cage, to mid-rib

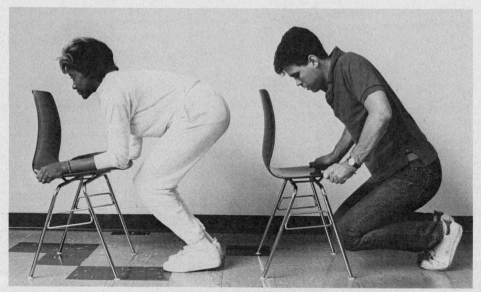

Figure 3.3.   Chair Breathing. Supporting your body with your arms over the seat of a chair will force deep breathing with your abdominal muscles. Your knees will rise on inhalation and lower on exhalation.

cage to lower rib cage to lower back and buttocks. Sense the vibrations all the way down.

Maintain the vibrations in the lower part of the body as you slowly straighten up, vertebra by vertebra. Repeat the exercise a couple of times until you can send the vibrations to the lower part of the body immediately without leaning over. Repeat the exercise, focusing on the location of the vibrations as they move through the body. Go through the following sequence.

1. Try the same exercise on "M-ah."
2. Repeat with "O-oh."
3. Now without leaning over, sustain the words "No—go." Repeat four times.
4. Expand the phrase to "No, I won't go," sustaining each word.

DISCUSSION
1. How did the sounds seem to change as the vibrations moved lower in the body?
2. If the voice is produced through vibrations of the vocal folds in the larynx, what is the point in finding vibrations lower in the body when sound is produced?
3. When the sensation of vibrations was lower in the body, was your throat tense or relaxed? What are some reasons for maintaining an open, relaxed throat when you speak?

(You will work on more detailed development of these concepts in chapter 7, "The Level of Words," in part 3.)

Taking a Space Walk

The concept of the air sea in the first breath exercise is developed further in this exercise. Not only do we breathe from the same air sea, but the air sea also helps to support us in space. The air sea has substance, it has weight, all the more evident on hot, muggy days, when the moisture in the air presses on us uncomfortably. In the following exercise allow the air sea to support you. Give up your sense of body weight to the substance of space. (You will work with this concept of space as substance in many future exercises, so begin now to experience the reality of the air sea.)

You and your classmates work singly in your own working space. You are in a space shuttle. Your body is in a condition of weightlessness. You have reached your destination, a space satellite that must be repaired. The antenna is bent and must be straightened out. The solar batteries must be replaced. Everything goes well until a piece of space debris gets in your way. Use "swoosh!" sounds to simulate your mini-rockets on your individual space carriage.

DISCUSSION

1. What was the difference in the focus of your energy and attention after the interruption of the debris?
2. If your attention was focused on the task "to repair the satellite," what happened to that goal when you had to deal with the debris?
3. Can you focus on two tasks at once? Can an audience?

(You will work more with the concept of goals in chapter 6, "The Level of Actions," for this is a basic principle in the craft of performance.)

Meditation Exercises

Now that you know how to relax the body through the relaxation exercises, you are ready to learn how to open the creative processes of the mind. Learning to meditate, which is an easy and natural process, is one of the best ways to focus the energy and power of the mind and spirit. As Charles Marowitz, director of London's Open Space Theatre, observes, "It is no accident that actors study Yoga, Transcendental Meditation and other 'spiritual' disciplines, all of which have clear affinities to acting."[3]

Before you attempt to meditate, you should lie or sit comfortably in a quiet environment. Then you should prepare your body through the progressive relaxation exercise you have learned. You will be presented with several possible points of concentration to begin your meditation. You may find that one method is most effective for you, though all methods are usable for most people.

To benefit most from meditation, a session of 15 minutes in the morning—either before breakfast or mid-morning when your stomach is not full—and 15 minutes mid-afternoon should be enough. If you must time yourself, you may open one eyelid slowly to check your watch. After a little practice, you will know by the condition of your rested body and mind when 15 minutes is up.

When you come up from the depths of meditation, do so slowly, giving yourself a couple of minutes to leave the deeper restful state so that you bring with your return to normal awareness as much as of the restful alertness as possible. If you continue the practice over several years, you will find that your normal awareness will become more like the state of meditation achieved initially.

Meditating with Color

Choose any three colors in the spectrum that move from warm to cool, as for example, peach, magenta, blue.

1. Close your eyes and visualize the colors with the following words as you deepen your relaxed state:

peach . . . . . peace
magenta . . . . meditation
blue . . . . . bliss

2. Begin counting from 20 backwards, pausing at every three numbers to revisualize the colors and words:

20, 19, 18, peach . . . peace
             magenta . . . meditation
             blue . . . bliss
17, 16, 15, peach . . . peace,
             magenta . . . meditation
             blue . . . bliss, etc.

By the time you have reached the count of 10, you will be in a meditative state.

3. At the count of 10 allow the mind to entertain whatever thought or image it moves to, occasionally returning to your colors and words whenever the mind has the opportunity. You do not force concentration on anything; you allow attention to wander wherever it will go. Each time you return to this experience you will find it quicker and easier to reach the state of restful alertness. You will be fully conscious of sounds around you, though they may seem either magnified or distant. Loud noises like the ring of a telephone can be very jarring, so when you meditate at home, you might want to remove yourself to a location where you will not be disturbed.

Meditating with Sound

Choose a nonverbal sound such as the universal "om." Repeat the sound silently several times. Then visualize the word. Examine the letters. Allow the letters to change size, to change color, to change into different styles of print. Repeat the sound silently several times. Return to the changing visual impression. Then follow step 2 as in the color focus earlier, counting backwards from 20 to 10, returning your attention to the visualization of the word and the silent repetition of your sound after every third number.

Meditating with Images

Choose a visual image that has a particularly peaceful significance to you—a beach, a forest, a field. Close your eyes and picture the entire scene. Breathe in the smells of the image, hear the sounds of the scene. Then focus your attention on one small item from that scene. For example, if you have visualized a beach, focus on a sea shell. In your imagination take the shell in your hand. Observe the color, the texture, the shape. Put the shell back on the sand. Move your focus from the shell to the overall scene again and then back to the shell. Put the shell to your ear and listen to the sound of the sea. Once more return the shell to the sand, and shift your focus again to the overall scene and finally back to the shell. Then follow step 2 as in the color focus earlier, counting backwards from 20 to 10, returning your attention to the shell after every third number.

Meditating with Touch

Find a smooth pebble, small enough to fit comfortably in your hand. Hold the pebble in either hand and feel the texture. Look at the colors of the pebble. Then close your eyes and visualize all the colors you have found in the pebble. Invent for yourself a story about where the pebble originated.

Imagine the following:

1. Did glaciers bring the pebble down from northern regions?
2. Did Indians walk over it before the Europeans discovered North America?
3. What will happen to the pebble when you have finished with it?
4. Will the pebble go back where you found it?
5. Will someone else use it for a similar purpose?

Now follow step 2 as in the color focus earlier, counting backwards from 20 to 10, returning your attention to the pebble after every third number.

Typical Experiences with Meditation

When you begin meditating, here are some of the experiences you might encounter.

1. Your tear ducts may loosen up and let out released tension with a few teardrops.
2. Small muscles, especially of the appendages, may twitch as years of stress and tension are being released. The phenomena will cease in a few days.
3. You may require less sleep. (Don't meditate after 6:00 or 7:00 P.M. unless you intend to stay up late.)
4. Your dreams may become more vivid. If you formerly dreamed only in black and white, you may begin to dream in color.
5. You may exerience a heightened sense awareness—stronger smells, keener vision, more acute hearing, and greater taste discrimination.
6. You may find your energy level is higher and your concentration deeper.

7. You may even have some extrasensory experiences such as mental telepathy or clairvoyancy.

Can meditation be dangerous? Only if you drive with your eyes closed. The worst experience I ever had with meditation was one time when I sneezed while meditating. The vibrations went through my entire body so intensely that it felt as if someone had sent me through a food processor.

Record any unusual phenomena from your meditative experiences in your journal. Discuss your experiences in meditation with your classmates.

DISCUSSION
1. Are your classmates's experiences the same as yours or different?
2. Can you find reasons for any differences?

Opening the Flow: Imagination and Energy

In this section you will find two types of exercises. The first type, imagination exercises, stretches the powers of your image-making ability, both mentally and physically. The second type, energy focus exercises, sensitizes you to the flow and focus of energy in your body and encourages freedom from habitual tensions.

Imagination Exercises

To gain the most benefit from this group of exercises, you should warm up first with at least one relaxation exercise and an eight to ten minute period of meditation.

Evolving from Primordial Slime

In biology class you probably learned that during embryonic development, the fetuses of higher forms of life develop through phases that resemble embryonic states of more primitive forms of life (or, as the biologists say, "ontogeny recapitulates phylogeny"). In this exercise you will "recapitulate" the evolutionary development of higher life forms.

Everyone lies down in a random pattern on the floor with a working space as wide as both arms can reach. As you change from one life form to the next, make whatever physical adjustments you need to adapt yourself to the form. You may use nonverbal sounds if you wish. For each form, experience the natural environment of the creature first. Then find an activity appropriate to your new life form that you can perform alone. The life forms to evolve through are as follows:

blue-green algae
jelly fish
slug
snail
lizard
pterodactyl

tree shrew
chimpanzee
Homo erectus
Homo sapiens
Homo futurus (man of the 21st century)

DISCUSSION

1. For many students this exercise is a profound experience. Did you discover any new attitudes toward life forms by performing this exercise?
2. Share with the class through performance images created of 21st century humans. To what extent do you believe that we can shape our own development, as individuals and as members of a society?

Stepping Outside Your Skin

In this exercise you are going to reveal facets of yourself that you usually keep hidden. You will need to find your own working space within your classroom. You and your classmates will work only for your own openness and development. This exercise is not to be presented for the viewing of others but rather to help you get in touch with your deeper, inner self, so that you may have greater access to that self in your creative work.

Place yourself in a state of restful alertness. Now find something within your self that you never or rarely share with others. This aspect of your self may be positive or negative. Imagine that your skin is like a space suit, which you can remove to reveal the inner aspect you have selected. A zipper is located down your back, starting at the top of your skull. With one hand, grasp the handle of the zipper and pull it down to the base of your spine, step out of your skin and explore, with movement and nonverbal sounds or with single words, the nature of the aspect you have revealed.

Then, while you are outside your skin, find an activity, skill, or occupation, you would like to perform well. In your own working space perform the activity.

When you have finished, reenter your discarded skin and zip yourself back up. In discussing your experiences with your classmates neither reveal what aspect of your self you released nor mention the activity you performed, but rather follow the questions suggested below.

DISCUSSION

1. What physical adjustments did you find yourself making? Weight changes? Energy levels?
2. What tensions were released? Muscularly? Vocally?
3. What were your experiences in returning to your skin after performing the exercise?
4. After returning to your skin on completion of the exercise, were there any lingering aftereffects of the "inner you" on your external behavior?
5. How do you think your experience in this exercise can help you when you begin to work on characters from a play?

Creature Selves

Humans share many traits with other living creatures. This exercise affords an opportunity to examine some of the similarities and differences between yourself and other creatures. It also will help you overcome any inhibitions about behaving in unaccustomed ways.

Unlike the previous exercise, this one is to be performed for others in the class. Class members should choose different categories from the list below, so that a variety of "creatures" may be presented.

Suggested categories are as follows:

feathers
smooth hide
furry coat
scales
lived in water
hopped
glided through the air

Each person begins with the following statement:
"If I had (category), I probably would be a _____."
(Pantomime the specific response rather than say it.)

When the class guesses the correct creature, the performer continues:
"If I had (category), I would prefer to be a _____."
(Pantomime the specific response.)

After everyone has performed the exercise, discuss the following points.

DISCUSSION

1. What similarities do you and your classmates share with the creatures performed?
2. What things can the creature do that are difficult or impossible for you?
3. What things can you do that are difficult or impossible for your creature?
4. Describe the behavior of someone you have observed that reminded you of another creature.
5. Can you think of any characters in plays whose behavior might be compared to the behavior of other creatures?

Energy Focus Exercises

The group of exercises in this section are designed to help you become aware of the flow of energy in your body and its origin, direction, and point of termination. In later chapters we will apply these awarenesses to your performance of actions and development of characterization.

Flowing with Mercury

Stand freely in a circle with your classmates, allowing for a circle of space around yourself large enough to accommodate the full expanse of your reach from a stationary position. Begin the exercise with imaginary drops of mercury on the fingertips of your right hand. Encourage the "mercury" to flow easily through the joints of your fingers, through your wrists, up your arm, through your elbow, across your shoulders to your left arm, wrist, and fingers. Then work the mercury back up your left arm, through your shoulder and down your spine, zig-zagging across your chest and back to your spine as it spirals downward through every vertebra. As the mercury reaches your pelvis, direct it first to your right leg, down your thigh, through your knee, down your calf, through your ankle, into your foot and toes. Then work the mercury up from your right toes back to the pelvis, across to the left leg. Repeat the process used on your right leg.

Then reverse the process by coaxing the mercury back up the left leg, back up the spine and into your neck. Bend your head forward as you encourage the mercury to roll around in your head. Then work the mercury toward your right shoulder, down your right arm, and back to the starting point of your right fingertips.

The second time you perform this exercise, vary the temperature of the mercury, so that it will chill every part of your body as it flows through.

The chilled mercury should be followed immediately with a third variation with imaginary rays of sunshine, which warm up every muscle and joint that the chilled mercury has cooled.

DISCUSSION
1. Where were the areas of tightest resistance to the flow of mercury? How do your tightest areas compare to those of your classmates?
2. What sensations did you have when the temperature was altered—first by the chilled mercury, then by the rays of sunlight?
3. Who are some characters from plays that might have an extremely loose flow of energy? Who are some characters that might have a restricted flow of energy?
4. Have you observed either patterns of unrestricted energy flow or restricted energy flow among your classmates or instructors?

Experiencing the Gravity Center

In the last exercise you experienced the flow of energy. In this exercise you will deal with the focus of energy and the adjustments the body may make to accommodate a different focus.

First, you will focus on your gravity or power center. With you and your classmates in a circle, imagine a warm ball of energy located about two inches below your navel. Rays of energy extend downward into your thighs and legs, giving them power to move. Rays of energy extend upward through your spine and trunk to support the

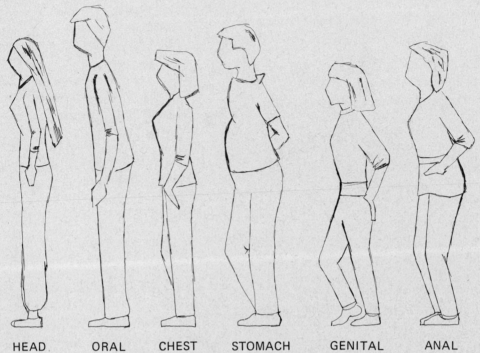

HEAD   ORAL   CHEST   STOMACH   GENITAL   ANAL

Figure 3.4.   Centers. Each different focus of energy creates a different center which produces a different alignment or silhouette. The centers represented here are from left to
right: 1) head, 2) oral, 3) chest, 4) stomach, 5) genital, 6) anal.

upper body, the arms, and the head. Moving clockwise in the circle, stride forward,
encouraging the energy center to propel you. After you have completed the circle
twice, pause, then imagine that the rays from the energy ball are extending a few
inches in front of your body. Then move slowly clockwise into the space the energy
ball has projected ahead of you.

DISCUSSION
1. What, if any, effect did the energy ball have on your posture or walk?
2. How was the sense of your overall energy level affected by this focus of energy?

   Modify and repeat this exercise with a book balanced on your head.

3. What differences did you perceive when you balanced the book on your head?

Developing Other Centers

   Though theoretically a person could "center" energy in any part of the body, six
other locations will be sufficient to establish clear distinctions. (See fig. 3.4.) In addition to the gravity center, other common centers of energy focus are as follows:

1. the head center
2. the oral center
3. the chest center
4. the stomach center
5. the genital center
6. the anal center

Here is a brief description of these centers starting at the top of the body and working down. If you focus energy in 1) the head center, the forehead leads the head in front of the body, causing the neck to jut forward and the body to appear to follow behind. If you focus energy in 2) the oral center, the chin is tipped up and forward so that the mouth becomes the focus. Energy focused in 3) the chest center lifts the chest up and forward as in a military posture. Energy focused in 4) the stomach center relaxes the stomach muscles, so that the area protrudes forward, pushing the shoulders and the pelvis backwards for counterbalance. Energy focused in 5) the genital center causes the stomach muscles to tighten, and the pelvis rocks forward. With energy focused in 6) the anal center, the buttocks are tightened, the trunk tips back slightly, and the knees are bent slightly.

The group should spread out, each person with a chair in his or her own working space. Focusing on one center at a time, imagine a warm ball of energy in the selected center; sit, stand, walk around the chair, maintaining the focus of energy in the chosen center.

After the class members have worked their way through all the centers, consider the following points.

DISCUSSION
1. What physical adjustments in posture and walk did you make with the energy focus at different centers?
2. How was your attitude affected when the focus was at different centers?
3. Have you observed people in your daily life who seem to have energy focused at the centers you have just explored?
4. What are some particular behavior patterns or personality traits you might associate with the different centers?
5. Can you think of characters in plays who might have a particular relationship with one of the centers you have explored?

Cultivate your awareness of centering, for you will return to it in chapter 8 as a technique for developing characterization.

Using Circles of Influence

Begin this exercise with the chest-centered focus of energy you explored in the previous exercise. You should work individually in your own chair and your own working space. Sitting quietly in the chair, encourage the ball of energy in your chest to expand in all directions—upward, downward, backward, and forward. Then let the warmth of the energy expand a few inches beyond your skin.

Experience yourself as a warm glow of light radiating in all directions but still contained within an imaginary shell the shape of your body a couple of inches outside of your body. As you rise and move forward, the shell moves forward; as you move to fill the front of the shell, it continues to precede you. Walk around the chair with this sensation. Next, return to a seated position in the chair with the shell and radiation inside the shell preceding you.

Now expand the distance between you and the shell to a distance of about a foot and a half by encouraging the extension of the radiation from your expanded energy field. While you imagine the larger shell, rise, walk around the chair, and return to a seated position.

Try eliminating the shell and project your radiation to a diameter the reach of your arms (about five or six feet). Rise from the chair, walk around it, and return to a seated position.

DISCUSSION

1. What differences did you experience as your energy moved from the smaller space to the larger?
2. What changes did you find in your awareness of the space surrounding you as your energy expanded from the smaller area to the larger?

If your classroom can be darkened, try the same exercise without light, or try it in your own room in the dark.

3. What differences, if any, do you experience between performing the exercise in the light and in the dark?

Conscious of Self, Not Self-conscious

The concept of a conscious being is, implicitly, realized to be different from that of an unconscious object. In saying that a conscious being knows something, we are saying not only that he knows it, but that he knows that he knows it, and that he knows that he knows that he knows it, and so on, as long as we care to pose the question.
———*J. R. Lucas*

In the last group of exercises you focused on the flow and focus of energy through your body. In the exercises in this section your focus will be on the muscles through which that energy flows and on the skeleton animated by those muscles.

Contraction and Expansion Exercises

All movement throughout the body, both the visible and the internal movement, is composed of the alternating rhythm of contraction and expansion. Muscles that move each articulated joint and that compose some of the internal organs of the body are arranged in opposing pairs, which balance one another in their tension. When one set of muscles contracts to move the skeleton, the opposite set expands to accommodate the movement.

Martha Graham, the great innovator of modern dance, based her exploration of human movement on this principle of contraction and expansion (that she termed "release").

> The release is the moment in life when you inhale; the breathing going out, when you exhale is the contraction. It's the first and last moments in life and it's used as technique, to increase the emotional activity of the body—so that you're teaching the body, not teaching the mind.[4]

(Miss Graham's use of "mind" refers to left-brain functions.) We will explore the use of contraction and expansion in the next two exercises.

The Sponge

Imagine that your body is a sponge that is dipped in water. Experience expansion in your chest, in your stomach, in your legs, your feet, your arms, your hands, your neck, your jaw, your head. Become a swollen, bloated sponge. (See fig. 3.5.) Explore:

How much space can you fill in this condition?
How wide a stance? How large a reach?

After you have filled as much space as possible (expanded in as many directions as you can), imagine that the water is being squeezed out of you. Reduce yourself into as tight a space as possible. Fold in your hands and arms, collapse your ankles and knees, contract your stomach and chest. How small a space can you occupy?

Repeat both the expansion process and the contraction process a second time. Then relax.

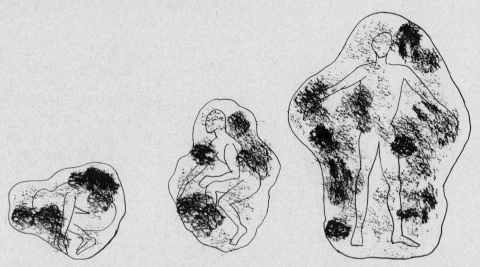

Figure 3.5.   Sponge: Contraction and Expansion. As well as exercising most large muscles of the body, the sponge exercise is helpful in developing awareness of the flow of energy from the trunk outward and from the extremities inward.

DISCUSSION

1. Where did you discover muscle groups that you were not accustomed to stretching when expanding?
2. Where did you discover muscle groups that you were not accustomed to stretching when contracting?
3. Where did you observe muscles working in opposition to each other—one contracting, one expanding—while doing either phase of the exercise?

Sunflower Seed

Compact your body and appendages into as small a space as possible, like the contraction phase of the sponge exercise. Imagine that you are a sunflower seed encased in a tough outer hull. You are planted into the moist, warm ground. The soil is patted firmly over you. The cool, spring rains fall on your back. The life inside you begins to push against the hull.

When the hull can contain you no longer, you burst out of the hull, splitting it with an expansion of your stalk (your back). Then you work your way through the soil, reaching up and out to bask in the warm sunlight, stretching from east to west (left to right) as you reach out toward the sun. As the sun sets, the energy drains from your face, arms, and upper body. You rest quietly, waiting for another day.

Repeat the sunflower seed exercise, focusing on what your muscles are doing to fulfill the function of the seed and plant as suggested in the action of the narrative.

DISCUSSION

1. Under what circumstances might a character in a play assume a closed position like the seed?
2. Under what circumstances might a character in a play reach out for full physical expansion?
3. Under what circumstances might a character in a play feel the energy draining out of the upper part of the body?
4. How do tensions in the muscles and the silhouettes created by pairs of contracting and expanding muscles relate to mental attitudes and emotional behavior?

Notice how contraction and expansion are used in character behavior in the scene from *Curse of the Starving Class* in figure 3.6.

Points of Concentration Exercises

The next two exercises will help you develop your image-making ability. This is one of the most powerful right-brain functions a performer can develop, for an image created in the performer's imagination can leave indelible impressions on members of an audience, affecting them for many years after they have seen a performance.

Figure 3.6. *Curse of the Starving Class* by Sam Shepard. Notice how one actor's body is expanded in space while the other actor, in contrast, has contracted. (Photograph: Joe Meyer. Courtesy of Montclair State College, Major Theatre Series. Set and lights: John Figola; costumes: Joseph F. Bella.)

Constance Welch, who for most of four decades headed the acting program at the Yale School of Drama, used to tell her classes of an afternoon she spent in New York City with the great actress Lynn Fontanne. As the two women were walking past an exclusive shop on Fifth Avenue, Miss Fontanne stopped and stared at a lovely shawl in a display window. In a twinkling the actress assumed in her body the flow and folds of the shawl. She had created the impression of the shawl through the power of her image-making ability and the responsiveness of her body to the image in her mind.

Recently I witnessed a similar experience with the performances of Alvin Epstein and Rand Mitchell in Samuel Beckett's *Ohio Impromptu*. At the end of this extraordinary short play, the performers took on the quality of a Rembrandt painting. The experience was as if three dimensions became two, and the image of two elderly religious pilgrims had become frozen in time on a canvas stage. The illustration here from a college production of *The Crucible* (fig. 3.7) has a similar quality achieved through side lighting, picture composition, and a variety of body positions in the physicalizations of the characters.

In the next three exercises you will practice visualizing an image, transforming yourself into an image, and developing multiple images for a character in a scene. The discussion questions for each of these exercises may be found after the third exercise and should be explored after all three exercises have been performed.

Figure 3.7. *The Crucible* by Arthur Miller. The body adaptations of each actor suggest that each is externalizing a clearly imagined internal image. (Kentucky Wesleyan College. Set and lights: Phil Sommer; costumes: Vivian Parks, Mark Walker.)

Visualizing: Rosebud

A. Sitting quietly with a partner, place yourself in a state of restful alertness. Close your eyes. Your partner will direct your imagination to create a rosebush.

"This is a sturdy, flourishing rosebush full of lovely olive green leaves tinged with maroon. Several buds appear on long, thorny stems. Focus on a single bud. The bud is swelling as you study it. Notice the serrated sepals covering the bud. Reach out and touch the sturdy stem. Feel the prick of the sharp thorns.

"As the rosebud swells, you begin to see the color of the flower. It is a vibrant, velvety red, rich and deep. The swelling petals force open the covering of sepals, and beautiful, tightly wrapped petals break through. But even as you watch, the rose opens wider—to a full-blown, sweet-smelling rose.

"Leaning forward and inhaling deeply, smell the delicious fragrance. But the rose continues to open, and you can see the pistil and stamen inside the middle of the petals where the base of the petals changes from red to pink to white. The color of the petals begins to darken, turns inky; the petals shrivel and fall away from the exposed center. One by one the petals crumple and fall off, leaving only the hard green nub of a rosehip as a reminder.

"But now there is another bud about to open. You turn your attention to this new flower. As the rose bursts open you marvel at its brilliant yellow color. What—a rose of a different color on the same bush? Why not? In the imagination there are no rules except those we wish to impose."

B. Reverse roles, and guide your partner through a similar image-making process, but vary the flower and the colors.

Transforming: Abstraction to Recreation

Bring to class any small portable object, for example, a stuffed animal, a light bulb, a shoe, a ballpoint pen, a toothbrush, or a cup. On a scrap of paper jot down answers appropriate to your object for the following questions.

1. What is the size of your object relative to others of its kind?
2. What is the color of your object?
3. Is the surface smooth or textured? Shiny or dull?
4. Is the silhouette regular or irregular? Rhythmical or arrhythmic?
5. What is the strength of the object?
6. What weaknesses does the object have? How could it be damaged or destroyed?

Look over your answers. Close your eyes, and put yourself in a state of restful alertness. See if you can visualize a blank, featureless puppet made of modeling clay. With your answers as a guideline, shape the features of the puppet in your imagination. What does the profile look like? The posture? Watch the puppet walking around, sitting, standing, performing a simple activity. What do the features of the face look like? How is the head carried? What gestures does the puppet make? Perform for the class the activity the way you visualized the puppet performing it.

Celling: Sense Images

Read one of the scenes from those included in the appendix. Use a character from the scene for this exercise. Select a metaphor or image that captures the dominant impression you have of the character solely from your reading of the scene. (We are not concerned here with a valid interpretation of the character for the whole play but rather with developing a technique for creating images for any character.)

In the middle of a sheet of paper write the metaphor or image you have chosen. Draw a cell around your metaphor. Surround the cell with five other (empty) cells. Connect each of these cells to the cell in the middle with a line. Within each new cell write a label designating experiences for each of the five senses (that is, sounds, sights, textures, tastes, and smells).

Surround each of the "sense cells" with at least three additional cells, and connect these cells to the sense cells with a line. Now go back to your central image or metaphor. As quickly as possible, without taking any time to evaluate your responses, fill in all the cells with images for sounds, then for sights, tastes, smells, and textures. (See fig. 3.8.)

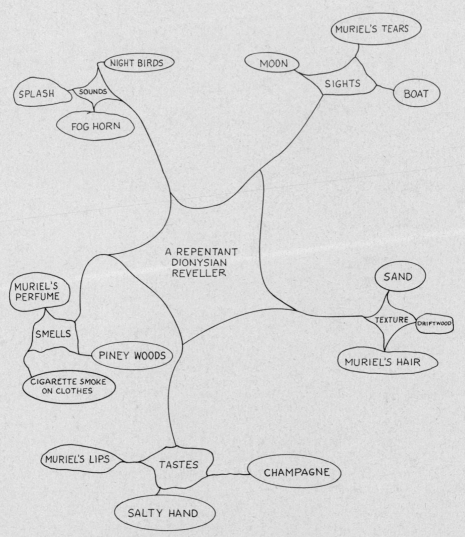

Figure 3.8.   Celling Technique. The example here was created for the character of Richard Miller in the scene from *Ah, Wilderness!* in the Appendix.

After you have filled in all the cells, close your eyes, and imagine the character from the scene performing activities that use as many of the sense images you have written down as possible. (Please note: you are not following stage directions given by the script but giving free reign to your image-making, right-brain functions to improvise activities that capture the essence of the character.)

Show your character performing the activities to the class, using as few words as possible. See how close the class can come to perceiving your original image or metaphor.

DISCUSSION (for all three image-making exercises)
1. How would you evaluate your own success in developing an image in your own mind?
2. How would you evaluate your own success in perceiving an image created by a classmate?
3. Where do you think that the image of a character exists? In the playscript? In the performer's mind? In the performer's body? In the director's interpretation? In the mind of the audience? In the body of the audience? To what extent in each of the above?

Exercises for Tempo-Rhythms

Our use of time and our participation in time contribute to the total rhythm of life. All of us contain internal organs that produce tempo-rhythms—the heart, the glands, the breathing complex. Each action we perform and each emotional state has a different tempo and rhythm, which interacts with our environment and with other people.

Because of the importance of tempo-rhythms as right-brain functions in the creative process you will return to practice them frequently throughout your study, so work on these beginning exercises thoroughly. Later tempo-rhythm exercises assume your familiarity with the awareness of tempo-rhythms found here.

Discovering Tempo-Rhythms from the Body

A. While sitting comfortably, breathe normally. Focus on your breaths, on the flow of air in and out of your lungs, on the rise and fall of your abdominal muscles as the rib cage is enlarged for fresh air and compressed when the used air is expelled. Then clap your hands together at the moment when your lungs are empty, just before your breathing muscles reverse the process. Clap when your lungs are full, just before you start to release the breath. Listen to the slow tempo and steady rhythm created by your clapping.

B. Stand up and either run in place or run around the room in a circle with your classmates. As you run, clap your hands each time a foot hits the floor. Then clap only when your right foot hits the floor. Next clap only when your left foot hits the floor.

C. Return to your seat and repeat exercise A. Notice the faster tempo of the breathing and clapping. Notice how the tempo gradually slows down as the body's oxygen balance is gradually restored.

Creating Tempo-Rhythms with Images

A. Close your eyes and imagine a situation in which you would have a cause for excited celebration (for example, a ball game, a visit from a long-lost friend, winning a million dollars in a contest). Visualize what you would do physically and vocally (but without words) to express your excitement. Then, simultaneously with your classmates, open your eyes, stand up and do what you visualized, making the noises to reinforce your movement.

Now return to your seat, and, one person at a time, clap out the tempo-rhythms of the actions just performed.

B. Again close your eyes. Visualize a situation in which you would be very depressed (for example, the illness of a relative, the death of a pet, a disappointing grade, a special person you asked to go somewhere turning you down). After you have taken a few minutes to visualize the specific details of the situation, open your eyes, stand up, and perform what you visualized doing, using nonverbal sounds if you wish.

Return to your seat and individually clap out the tempo-rhythms that you discovered in your expression.

C. Again close your eyes. This time imagine a situation of great warmth (such as, hugging a loved one, receiving praise from a parent or teacher, giving a gift to a dear friend). Open your eyes and with nonverbal sounds perform (as a solo) the action you visualized.

Return to your seat and individually clap out the tempo-rhythms that you discovered in your performance.

DISCUSSION

1. In each exercise how did your breathing change?
2. How did the tempo-rhythms differ from one another?
3. What mental impressions of the imagined and performed incident did you have as you clapped the tempo-rhythms?

D. Each person claps a tempo-rhythm based on an imaginary situation of any nature for the class to listen to. Members of the class should guess both the general emotional tone of the event and, if possible, the specific event clapped.

DISCUSSION

What connections have you now made between visualization of images, tempo-rhythms, and performing?

Summary

Through performing the exercises in this chapter you have used right-brain functions to explore your ability to relax your body, to achieve a state of restful alertness through meditation, to free your imagination to experience different states of behavior, and to open the doors to your inner self.

You have also become familiar with the right-brain awareness of the flow of energy within your body, the focus of energy in various centers, the muscular rhythms of expansion and contraction, the techniques of developing your concentration through image making, and the expressiveness shaped through tempo-rhythms.

The discussions that followed each exercise were opportunities for your left-brain functions to examine and evaluate the experiences initiated and monitored by your right-brain functions. In the next chapter you will bring this new sense of awareness of yourself into a relationship with your environment.

Notes

1. Herbert Benson, M.D., *The Relaxation Response*. (New York: William Morrow, 1975), see esp. Ch. 7.
2. Shirley MacLaine makes several references to her meditation experiences in her book, *Out on a Limb*, (New York: Bantam, 1983).
3. Charles Marowitz, *The Act of Being: Towards a Theory of Acting*. (New York: Taplinger, 1978), p. 103.
4. Cited by Anna Kisselgoff in "Martha Graham," *New York Times Magazine*, 19 February 1984, pp. 54–55.

For Further Reading

Benson, Herbert. *The Relaxation Response*. New York: William Morrow, 1975.

Chekhov, Michael. *To the Actor*. New York: Harper & Row, 1953. Ch. 2.

Gunther, Bernard. *Sense Relaxation: Below Your Mind*. New York: Macmillan, 1968.

Rico, Gabriele Lusser. *Writing the Natural Way*. Los Angeles: J.P. Tarcher, 1983. Ch. 2.

Rosen, Gerald M. *The Relaxation Book*. Englewood Cliffs, N. J.: Prentice-Hall, 1977.

Chapter 4
Touching Your Environment

We learn in different ways. Of our assorted brains, some are left-dominant, some are right-dominant, some are neither. Some of us learn better by hearing, others by seeing or touching. Some visualize easily, others not at all. Some recall odometer readings, telephone numbers, dates; others remember colors and feelings. Some learn best in groups, others in isolation. Some peak in the mornings, others in the afternoon.

No single educational method can draw the best from diverse brains. Findings about the specialties of the two hemispheres and the tendency of individuals to favor one style or the other also helps us understand why we differ so much in how we see and think.

—————*Marilyn Ferguson*, The Aquarian Conspiracy

Environmental Awareness

We become aware of our environment through the senses—sight, sound, smell, touch, and taste. In daily life we ignore many of the sense impressions that constantly bombard us, habitually overlooking things that once were unfamiliar and fascinating.

Observe an infant tasting and touching objects in the playpen. For the baby, to know is to smell, to chew, to rub against. Watch a dog make the rounds of its territory, sniffing and licking at both the familiar and unfamiliar new smells and tastes of the neighborhood. Have you ever watched a goose sticking her neck out in all directions on a farm or in a zoo? No matter how often she has surveyed the terrain, to the goose every day is a new world! Like the child, like the dog, like the goose, your sensuous awareness is waiting to be tapped daily.

To increase your sensitivity toward your environment and the elements in it, you should focus on one type of sense impression at a time. The exercises in this chapter are designed for your class to work on as a group but without individuals interacting, except in the discussions that follow each exercise.

Out of Sight, into Mind

As you grew from childhood into adolescence, you learned to depend on sight at the expense of the other senses. What you saw you did not have to investigate further with the other senses. To rediscover what you have forgotten, you will perform the first environment exercises, right-brain exercises, without the use of sight.

Sensing the Life Environment

First, sitting still, close your eyes. Let your ears reach out to catch as many sounds as you can pick up inside the room. Then listen for sounds beyond the room, outside the windows or doors. Can you perceive a tempo-rhythm from these sounds? Tap your foot or a finger to the tempo-rhythm you hear.

Then turn your attention to any smells you can pick up in the room. Humans do not have a highly developed sense of smell, but perhaps you can detect someone's cologne or aftershave lotion or the smells of jackets, shoes, or of materials used in the construction of the room. Silently think of words that might describe the smells.

DISCUSSION
1. What sounds did you hear inside the room? Outside the room?
2. Clap the tempo-rhythm you responded to. Why do different people clap different tempo-rhythms in response to the same sounds?
3. How do you describe the smells you experienced? (Do not simply label them by name, but describe them with adjectives.)

Could your difficulty in describing smells have anything to do with the fact that our sense of smell is relatively unimportant to us? Did you realize we have fewer words for describing smells than for any other sense?

Experiencing the Environment Blindfolded

A. Bring to class a cloth to be used as a blindfold. (This exercise works best in an open space where tables, chairs, and other pieces of furniture have been scattered randomly about the room, but it may be performed in a regular classroom if necessary.) Working with a partner, secure the blindfold over your partner's eyes. Now place your partner's dominant hand (right or left) on your left upper arm. Guide your blindfolded partner around the room, avoiding bumping into other people or objects. At several points during the journey on a prearranged signal you should pause wherever you are.

When you receive the signal, you lead your partner to the nearest object—chair, table, desk, railing, curtain. Your blindfolded partner then reaches out with the nondominant hand first to find and feel the object. He or she should focus on the shape, the textures, the temperature, and the wetness or dryness of the object. Your partner should then reverse hands and repeat the touching process.

Figure 4.1. Blind Exploration. What new awarenesses do you discover through the other senses when you are deprived of sight?

Then place your partner's nondominant hand on your right upper arm and return him or her to the original seat.

Reverse positions and repeat the exercise, so that you have a similar blindfolded experience. After everyone has finished the exercise, discuss your experiences.

DISCUSSION

1. Describe new observations you made about objects in the room as a result of being blindfolded.
2. Were there any differences in being led by the dominant and nondominant hand?
3. Were there any differences in touching objects with the dominant and nondominant hand?
4. Do you know which side of your brain controls the left side of your body?[1]
5. What are some things you can do easily with your dominant hand that you cannot do as well with your nondominant hand?

B. Try the same exercise outdoors, and compare your experiences with those you had indoors. (See fig. 4.1.)

Determining Environmental Tempo-Rhythms

Close your eyes and imagine the sounds you might hear in another environment. Determine a tempo-rhythm for the environment. Clap the tempo-rhythm for your classmates.

Suggested locations:

your room in the morning
busy airport

exclusive restaurant
disco
church or synagogue
library
student hangout
post office
barber shop or beauty salon
theatre lobby before a show

DISCUSSION

1. What places are suggested to class members by the tempo-rhythm you clap?
2. Did they come close to the atmosphere of the location even if they didn't guess the exact location?
3. Discuss scenes from plays you are familiar with that might have widely differing tempo-rhythms.

Tastes and Smells

Tasting

Everyone in the class brings in one item with a distinct taste (either a food or nonfood item, but no drugs or poison please!). Each person places an item at random in his or her work space. Begin at your own contributions. Close your eyes and taste the item (but do not eat it!). On an agreed-upon signal, open your eyes, move to another station, and repeat the procedure. After you have experienced the entire range of items, the class sits in a circle.

One person at a time, without revealing which item he or she is referring to, uses adjectives to describe the flavor of that item; then the person gives a metaphor from another sense area to describe the same item. For example, "It was very bitter. If it were a sound it would be like a slow funeral march."

DISCUSSION

1. Can class members guess the item described?
2. If there are disagreements over the appropriateness of descriptions and metaphors, how can these differences be understood?
3. Were any class members aware of physical reactions to the items other than on the tongue? Lips? Eyes? Throat? Rest of the body?

Smelling

Everyone in the class brings in two items with a distinct odor (one pleasant, one unpleasant, as for example, cologne and iodine). They repeat the procedure used with taste, moving from item to item. Then they describe the odor in adjectives and give a metaphor from another sense area. Example: "This item was faintly sweet. If it could be touched, it would be like the caress of wet tissue paper over the lips." (To use the metaphor "like violets on a forest floor" would not be an acceptable response, for the idea is to transfer the impression entirely into another sense area.)

DISCUSSION

1. Can class members guess the item described from the adjective and metaphor given?
2. Were any class members aware of physical responses in reaction to the smell? Noses twitching? Lips smiling or scowling? Throat? Eyes? Rest of the body?
3. Do you think it is more difficult or less difficult to describe and find metaphors for smell than it is for taste?

Sense Circles

Each class member brings in one object that stimulates one of the five senses. It is designated in advance which class members will bring in objects from each category, so that all five senses are represented. Five concentric circles are chalked (or imagined) on the floor. (See fig. 4.2.) The objects are placed at random within the circle for their category. Ignoring everyone else, each person moves freely from circle to circle, responding to each of the objects found in the space.

DISCUSSION

1. Which objects produced the most negative reactions? How were the negative reactions expressed when you encountered the objects?
2. Which objects produced the most positive reactions? How were the positive reactions expressed when you encountered the objects?
3. Can you think of characters in plays who might use any of the objects brought in? How would the characters' reactions to the objects be different from your own?

Atmospheric Weight: Body Tension

In chapter 3 you began to experience the reality of space as a substance. Here, we are going further with that concept by using additional images to help eliminate body tension and develop the imagination with experiences in different environments. We shall work on four tension levels and sensations: floating, flying, molding, and radiating. You will find it helpful to work on floating and flying initially. Then after you review the first two, add molding. Review the three, and lastly, add radiating.

Floating

Water Lilies

Form a large circle with your classmates. Close your eyes and imagine that you are standing in a pool with the water level up to your armpits. You are transformed

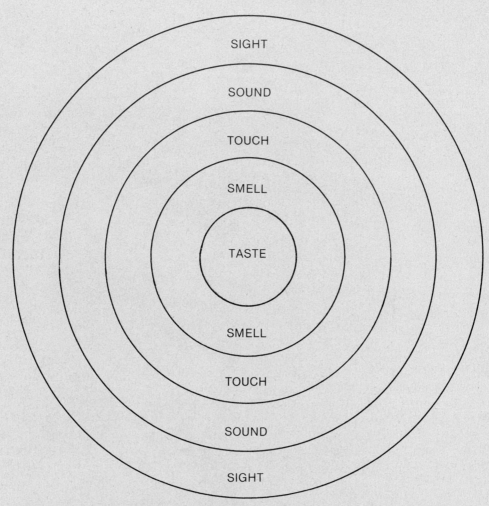

Figure 4.2.   Sense Circles. The floor plan arrangement for a "Sense Circle" can be drawn with chalk, or imaginary boundaries can be established.

into a water lily. Your arms and hands become the lily pad and your head the blossom. Your arms and hands float on the surface of the water. Your head rolls back to capture the warm spring sun. Sway gently to and fro, left and right, as gentle currents rock you in the water. Now slowly raise your head forward and let your arms come down to your sides.

DISCUSSION
1. Alma in Tennessee Williams's *Summer and Smoke* says, "I feel like a water lily on a Chinese lagoon." How does a water lily feel?
2. What differences (if any) did you detect between the lower part of your body and the upper part? Is it possible to experience different tensions in different parts of

the body at the same time? How much does this have to do with your imaginative control of your body and how much with your attitude toward the space?

3. Which viewpoint is more effective for you: "My body is floating in space," or "The space is floating my body"?

Magic Carpet

Sit on the floor or a mat. In your imagination mark the outline of a small rectangular carpet on which you are sitting. Hold on as the carpet takes off; experience both the lift (the inertia upwards) and the pull of gravity downwards as you take off. Now you are high in the air gently floating above the Middle East. What do you see below?

> minarets?
> people worshiping?
> outdoor market places?
> farms?
> oil fields?
> battlefields?
> demonstrations?

Choose an environment from the ones you imagine, and land in the middle of it. What sounds and smells do you find that are unfamiliar? How are the colors of buildings, clothes, and the earth different? Can you adjust your physical behavior so that you are not recognized as a foreigner? Working in your own space, perform in pantomime a simple activity appropriate to the environment, an activity like purchasing some food or joining in worship. Return to your magic carpet and float home. Land gently. Did you bump?

DISCUSSION

1. How were your physical experiences different while floating on the carpet compared to your experiences in the foreign environment?
2. What physical adjustments did you make to disguise your identity and try to pass for a native?
3. What sights, sounds, smells, tastes, and tactile experiences did you discover on your trip?

Flying

Soaring Like an Eagle

The class forms a circle. One person is designated the leader. The leader begins flying, arms extended, soaring like an eagle. Playing follow-the-leader, the rest of the class imitates the leader, pausing where the leader pauses, landing where the leader lands, pouncing where the leader pounces.

Buzzing Like a Bee

Furniture is placed randomly about the working space. The class begins clustered tightly together like worker bees in the center of the working space. The boundaries of the bee hive are marked either with chalk or with imaginary lines. Morning dawns. The bees leave their hive and "buzz" audibly about the space searching for honey. Each piece of furniture is a bush where honey may be gathered by audible "slurps." After the first bush, each bee must brush off the pollen at the next bush before collecting more honey. After all the bushes have been visited, the bees return to the hive and deposit their honey. Then they settle down for a refreshing supper of beebread and honey.

DISCUSSION
1. What physical adjustments did you make to "soar like an eagle"?
2. What physical adjustments did you make to "buzz like a bee"?
3. How is the sensation of flying (eagle and bee) different from the sensation of floating (water lily and magic carpet)?
4. What do you know about the environments of the eagle and the bee? What aspects of the environments are the same as ours? What aspects are different?
5. What do you know about the social lives of the eagle and the bee? What aspects of their social lives are the same as ours? What aspects are different?
6. How do the five senses affect the lives of eagles and bees?
7. How many kinds of food can you name that eagles eat?[2]
8. Does anyone in the class know how many species of bees there are?[3]

Molding

In contrast to floating and flying, which emphasize lightness and fluidity, molding emphasizes weight and strength. In the first exercise, on building a body, you will deal with space as an object that may be molded, while in the next three using honey, jello, and molten lead, you will be in direct contact with the weight of space.

Etienne Decroux, a French mime and teacher, tells students that we "cut space with movement" and "break silence with sound." Use these exercises to experience and explore the substance of space.

Building a Body

The class forms a circle. Each person imagines that the space within the circle contains a pile of fresh, moist clay. Move globs of "clay" from inside the circle to the outside of the circle behind you. There you will mold a statue of an idealized human being, yourself as you would like to be. Start with the feet, the legs, the thighs, and move on upwards to the head. Mold in the facial features you would like to see.

After you have finished your idealized body, walk behind the "sculpture" and cut a slit down the back from head to buttocks. Step inside the sculpture. It is flexible and supportive. Move around inside the sculpture. Sit. Stand. Look in an imaginary mirror. Admire the strength and beauty of your "idealized self."

When the activity is completed, step out of the sculpture, and return to the circle for discussion.

DISCUSSION
1. As you worked on the exercise, what changes (if any) did you notice in your behavior or reactions?
2. What physical adjustments did you observe as you went from your everyday self to the idealized sculpture?
3. Psychologists have said that most people tap only about 10 percent of the potential of their mind power. In your journal you might examine what percentage of your mind power potential you think you are now using.

Honey

Place chairs, tables, other furniture at random in your working space. You and your classmates will scatter yourselves about in the space. Imagine that the entire space has the consistency of honey (a by-product of the bee exercise, no doubt!). Then on an agreed-upon signal move from one object to another, sitting and rising as you go. As you move forward, feel the resistance of the honey space in front of you and experience the honey space fill in behind you. Try moving backward; feel the same resistance behind you and the honey space filling in on your anterior side.

DISCUSSION
1. What did you experience internally when the external space became honey?
2. How is this experience different from "Floating"? From "Flying"?

Jello

Repeat the procedure from the honey exercise in a space filled with half-congealed gelatin dessert. Each time you move, you set up vibrations, which in turn bounce back to affect you. This effect is like a spatial echo. A slow, undulating movement should be experienced. Try this to music. Debussy's "Prelude to 'The Afternoon of a Faun'" would be a useful selection.

DISCUSSION
1. How does either the movement or the music affect your emotional responses?
2. This exercise should help you experience not only your effect upon space but the effect of space upon you. Discuss this experience and any remembered experiences in which you were aware of the effects of space on your behavior.

Molten Lead

Repeat the procedure for the honey exercise. The atmosphere this time has the consistency of molten lead (without its heat please!). As you mold through the "lead," notice what happens to the tempo of your movement, to the amount of energy and weight you must use to press through the heavy atmosphere. On an agreed-upon signal, quickly transform yourself into a flying image (eagle), a floating image (water lily). Be sure to end this session with an experience of flying or floating. Otherwise, you may carry over the heavier, molding experience past the exercise.

DISCUSSION
1. As space becomes more real for you, do you find your imagination affected in any way?
2. Can you think of any characters or scenes from plays in which the leaden weight of space might be useful?

Designs in Space

This exercise adds the skill of observation to the experience of molding in space. You and your classmates stand in a circle. The space inside the circle is the consistency of semi-congealed gelatin. One person tunnels to the center of the circle where he or she molds with the body an impression of a form in space. After the impression has been made, the person backs out of the tunnel to his or her original place in the circle.

The second person then burrows into the center, finds the form left in space, and adjusts his or her body into that space. The second person then backs out of the first person's form and creates a new impression in a different area of the space. The third person finds the impression of the second person, fills it, then creates a new form, and so on. Each person repeats in space the form created by the previous person before initiating his or her own form.

If the group is small enough, each person can then repeat all previous forms before initiating a new one, but a large group might use all the space before getting around to everyone in the circle.

DISCUSSION
Did it affect your ability to remember the form in space by thinking of the space as having substance, or did you simply imitate the body position of the previous person?

Try the exercise a second time. Concentrate on the empty form left in space by the previous person rather than on imitating his or her body position.

DISCUSSION
Referring back to the Decroux concept at the beginning of this section on molding, which is easier to think of as having substance—space or silence?

Radiating

A living organism is an electrically sensitive body involved in ongoing information and energy exchanges with surrounding bodies and systems. Its complex electrical and biological self-regulating system interacts with the electrical and magnetic environment.

————*I. F. Dumitrescu*

After floating, flying, and molding your way through space, you have now reached the fourth tension level: radiating. At some point in your life you have met a person who seemed magnetic, a person with compelling charm, a politician or performer with charisma. What is it that sets such people apart? Intelligence? Usually not. Physical beauty? Rarely. Neither Mahatma Gandhi nor Mother Theresa would have won a beauty contest, yet both held the attention and interest of people in an uncanny way. Lofty ideals and charming manners? Adolph Hitler could not be noted for either, yet his sway over people was legendary. Moral uprightness? Rasputin was not an outstanding moralist, but he wielded fantastic power over the last Russian tzar.

What about entertainers? The Beatles? Charles Laughton? Judy Garland? Bruce Springstein? Barbra Streisand? Michael Jackson? Prince? The attraction that such people have for an audience cannot be laid simply to talent, or skill, or hard work. There is an additional "stuff" that such people have cultivated or discovered that gives them a magnetic edge over the ordinary performer.

Let me suggest a few characteristics that all of these people exhibit and then point you in the direction of an approach you may try in order to develop whatever latent magnetism you possess. One characteristic these people share is a sense of mission, a total dedication of effort toward chosen goals. This sense of direction and certitude generates energy and channels it in the direction of specific goals. In other words, make up your mind and "go for it."

A second common characteristic is industry. The charismatic individual works longer and harder than the average person. The confidence that a sense of mission supplies also provides the energy to achieve.

A third characteristic is belief in the rightness of one's mission, even if it is morally obtuse by majority values.

Fourth, all of these people, at least in public, appear to radiate with a generosity of themselves, a sharing of common humanity in a magnified way.

Although you may not consider yourself like these magnetic people who possess all four characteristics, radiation is within your immediate grasp, and even an elementary achievement of it is well worth your effort. Though earlier in the century Michael Chekhov used exercises somewhat similar to those given here, it was not until mid-century experiments with Kirlian photography that people were able to see what the Russian director had worked on instinctively. The Soviet scientist Semyon Kirlian invented a method of electric photography that records the aura of radiation that surrounds all living things. Some of the most extraordinary Kirlian photographs are those of psychic healers and mystics, whose halos extend impressively beyond those of the average person when their psychic energy is generated. (See fig. 4.3.)

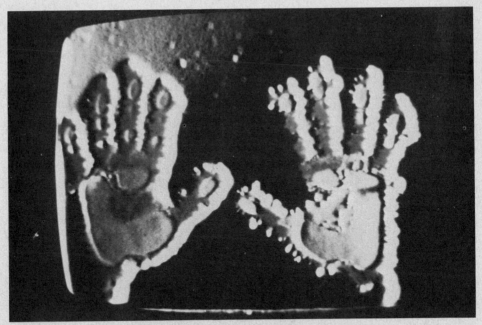

Figure 4.3. Kirlian Radiation. Contrast the radiation emanating from the hands of a swami healer at repose on the left, and on the right while sending healing rays. (Photograph Courtesy of Dr. Ioan Florin Dumitrescu. Permission for reprinting from *The Body Electric* by Dr. Thelma Moss. [J. P. Tarcher, Inc. 1979.])

In this first radiation exercise you will experience your own radiation and then extend the circle of your radiation further into your environment. The fewer clothes you wear for radiation exercises, the easier it will be to experience your own radiation, and later the radiation of others. You will still be able to feel some effect even while wearing regular street clothing, but not as much as when you wear a leotard and tights.

In the next chapter you will extend the experience of radiation to a partner and a group. Through these radiation exercises you may find yourself discovering unusual abilities you did not know you possessed.

Self-scanning

After you have performed a molding exercise, stand quietly, raise your arms, and touch together the fingertips of both hands with palms held flat in front of your face. Then scan your body, using your palms as if they were an x-ray scanner. (See fig. 4.4.) When you reach the base of the trunk, go down the right leg, then return to the groin and go down the left leg. Separate your hands and scan the right arm and hand with the left palm; then the left arm and hand with the right. Reach your hands behind you and scan as much as you can reach of your backside.

Figure 4.4.   Self-scanning. As you "take" a self-scan, can you detect warmer and cooler spots around your body? Are these locations associated with areas of greater or lesser tension?

Scan the entire body a second time and experiment with the distance of your palms from your body. See how far you can go from the body and still pick up the warmth. See if there is any detectable warmth at three inches, four, five, or six.

DISCUSSION
1. Where did you sense the greatest warmth? The coolest areas?
2. How far were you able to go beyond your body and still feel the warmth?

Body Halos

Start from a sitting position. Imagine that the warmth encircling your body is a glowing light. Project the light as far as you can in front of your body. Project the image of yourself rising from your seat and walking forward. As you sense your halo self surging through the space in front of you, move into the area the halo created. Move slowly, steadily, never exceeding the extent of the halo effect. Work only for yourself at this time. You will use this experience in encounters with your classmates in future exercises.

DISCUSSION
1. What, if anything, happened to your posture?
2. How did this experience feel different physically from your experiences with float-

ing, flying, and molding? Differences in weight? In flow of energy? In tension level?
3. Can you think of any experiences in life when your body felt as it did in the radiation exercise?
4. What characters in plays can you think of who would be enhanced by radiation or who have moments of radiation?

Environments Compared

Babbling-on

This exercise combines your observations about your activities with the ability to recreate those observations and share them with your classmates. It also uses: 1) your memory of past actions, 2) your awareness of present attitudes, and 3) your ability to project your imagination into the future.

Prepare your response in pantomime to the verbal introduction supplied below. Do not use words in presenting this exercise to the class. If you would like to use sounds, make nonverbal sounds or use nonsense syllables.

"When I got up this morning, I ___(pantomimed activity)___"
"At the present time, I would like to ___(pantomimed activity)___"
"After this class I'm going to ___(pantomimed activity)___"

Class members may respond after each presentation, reflecting on the following elements.

DISCUSSION
1. Which actions were most clear and believable?
2. Which actions were most unclear, blurred, or over-exaggerated?
3. Is there any difference in the clarity of actions from the past (before class), present, and future (after class)?

Exploring Stage Geography

This integrated-brain exercise is designed for the proscenium stage, but if your future performing experience is most likely to be in the round, you can use the terms for the stage areas as they are labeled in your theatre in the round.

In the drawing in figure 4.5 you see the nine basic areas of the proscenium stage. Your awareness of the location of these areas should become as automatic as your awareness of right and left in daily life. First, stand facing the audience on a proscenium stage or the equivalent in your classroom. Extend your left arm toward your left. That is "stage left." Extend your right arm toward your right. That is "stage right." Point toward the audience. Did you have to point down? That is "downstage." (Not because the audience is generally lower. Can someone in the class explain the origin of this antiquated term?)

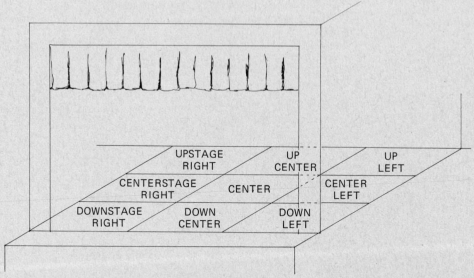

Figure 4.5. Stage Areas. The traditional divisions of stage areas are a convenient way to communicate the location of a character on stage; more importantly, the area itself may suggest certain qualities to the actor and audience.

Make a 180 degree turn. Your back is now toward the audience, and you are facing "upstage." Now move from area to area on stage, creating a whispered monologue for yourself as you locate your changing positions on stage. (For example: "I am standing center stage. I am crossing downstage and right to pause in the down right area. Now I am moving left through the down center area to the down left area.") Be sure that you have paused in every area of the stage before returning to your starting point.

Repeat the exercise visiting the areas in a different order, but this time see if there are any differences you sense in being in a different part of the stage. Some directors believe that certain stage areas are better locations for playing certain types of scenes. Can you find any physical reasons for playing love scenes in one area as opposed to another, or fight scenes in one area as opposed to another?

DISCUSSION
1. What differences (if any) did you experience between the downstage and upstage areas?
2. What differences (if any) did you experience between the left and right sides of the stage?

Expanding Your Space

Now that you are familiar with the basic geography of the stage, you can combine this awareness with your growing ability to radiate. Sit in any one of the nine basic areas. Recapture the halo of light you experienced earlier. Think of your performing space as being limited by the halo. Now extend in your imagination the boundaries of the halo to a radius of about five feet. (It may help you to extend your arms at shoulders height.) Turn around slowly. The radius turns with you. Move toward the next closest stage area. The radius precedes you and moves into the next area.

Try this exercise on your own in different environments—in your room, outdoors, in a restaurant. Keep working on this experience. You will come back to it in different forms later.

DISCUSSION

1. Can you perceive a difference in the extension of your radiation from the immediate area of your body to the larger circle? How?
2. Are there physical differences when you extend the radiation? Differences in energy level?

Stage Environment Transformed

In the next two exercises you are going to transform the stage environment through your imagination into other locales. In your working space you need to have ready access to chairs and tables, so that interior settings may be set up as you and your classmates develop the locations. Again, you are working for your own sense of reality with an environment. Any awareness of other performers at this time is only an acknowledgment of their existence, not the establishing of a performing relationship.

Discovering the United States

The class sits in a circle. Any member of the class may begin the exercise by moving into the center and performing an activity that establishes a particular environment in one of the three following categories: city, suburban, countryside. As soon as other individuals recognize the environment, they enter the circle, and without interacting with anyone else, begin another appropriate activity.

Suggested environments are as follows:

city: museum, park, department store, chain fast-food place, bus station, talent agency
suburban: grocery store, filling station, health club, church or synagogue, athletic stadium
countryside: farm, dairy, general store, post office, grain elevator, oil rig

DISCUSSION

1. Which activities were most clear? Did the clarity come from the nature of the activity itself or from details of performance?
2. Which activities have you actually experienced and which have you only seen in the media or read about?

3. Is there any difference in your own belief in the honesty of your performance between those activities actually experienced and those only seen in the media?
4. What about any differences in the believability of your classmates in activities they have experienced versus those they have only watched?
5. Are the boundaries to what we can convincingly perform limited by our personal experiences?

Expanding the Fantasy

In the next two exercises you may be relying on your imagination more than on experience or observation. In doing so, you will have to be even more careful that the details of your activities and behavior are clear, accurately performed in space, and completely executed.

Discovering the World

Follow the procedure for "Discovering the United States" except that the environment is a foreign country. The person establishing the environment should choose a specific place or type of place that will be recognizable to the rest of the class. Remember, even if activities are similar, behavior may be different.

Suggested countries are as follows:

China, Australia, El Salvador, The Netherlands, India, Iceland, Siberia, Sri Lanka, Ethiopia, Greece, Switzerland, Israel, Iran, France, Spain

DISCUSSION
1. What environmental and behavior characteristics identified the country for you?
2. How does understanding the way environmental conditions are dealt with in other cultures increase our ability to relate to people from those cultures?

Discovering the Past

Follow the procedure for "Discovering the United States." Instead of contemporary environments use historical ones. The person establishing the time and place should pick an activity readily identified with a particular era. Your behavior adaptations may have to be based more on imagination than on observation in this exercise, for though you may have seen historical behavior enacted in the media, you have few ways of knowing how authentic it was.

Suggested periods and events:

Spanish Inquisition
Roman festival
medieval plague
Elizabethan theatre
Neanderthal hunt

African tribal wedding
Viking exploration

DISCUSSION
1. Which of the historical times were most familiar to you? Why?
2. Which of the historical times were least familiar? Why?
3. Which of the times and places seemed most like experiences of today's world?
4. How do you think environments and human behavior have changed in the last hundred years?
5. How do you think environments and human behavior will change in the next hundred years?

Summary

The environmental work in this chapter started with the connections of your five senses to the outside world. You then dealt with space as substance, treating it in different ways with differing tensions. You familiarized yourself with the stage environment, then transformed the stage space into other locations. Now that you have some grasp of your inner world and your environment, you are ready to reach out to others in the next chapter.

Notes

1. The right side of your brain controls the left side of your body.
2. The *Encyclopaedia Britannica* lists fourteen.
3. The *Encyclopaedia Britannica* says more than 12,000!

For Further Reading

Chekhov, Michael. *To the Actor.* New York: Harper & Row, 1953. Ch. 1.
Krippner, Stanley. *Human Possibilities.* Garden City, N. Y.: Doubleday, 1980. Ch. 8, "The Electrical Photographs of Semyon Kirlian."
Moss, Thelma. *The Body Electric.* Los Angeles: J.P. Tarcher, 1979. Ch. 10.
Spolin, Viola. *Improvisation for the Theatre.* Evanston, Ill.: Northwestern University Press, 1963. Ch. 4.

Chapter 5
Touching Others

When we leave someone, we say "See you later," never touch, or taste or smell you later. . . . the greatest avoid/dance concerns the largest organ of the body: the skin. Young monkeys deprived of touch and closeness suffer from a lack of relatedness; even their physical growth is stunted.

——*Bernard Gunther*, Sense Relaxation: Below Your Mind

Touch Is a Many Splendored Thing

People of all cultures use both conscious and unconscious signals to send messages to one another through space and silence. The spatial distances themselves play a part in conveying the message and the response. In this chapter you will explore both nonverbal and verbal communication with your classmates as well as some of the messages sent by the different distances people place between themselves and others.

When you start working on scenes, you will frequently find that you must share close contact and feelings with performers who are not your most intimate friends. You may have to reveal dark sides of your nature, such as anger and lust, that you usually do not display in public. You may have to become vulnerable to the vicissitudes of love. You may have to display the fool that you usually become only when your guard is down.

You even may have to portray character behavior that you thought was alien to your nature. You may need to perform a murderous intention, a violent action, or a romantic aggression. Merely pretending to behave in these extreme ways will not convince anyone. You will have to reach down deep inside, find a connection within yourself for every character action, and bring it to the surface to be shared with your fellow players on stage and with the audience.

You may also have to touch people physically in ways in which you are unaccustomed. Society has developed taboos against touching that you may have to overcome to free yourself from your cultural chains. As Desmond Morris points out in *Manwatching*, his beautifully illustrated book on human action and gesture,

Each of us has a sense of body-privacy, but the strength of this varies from person to person, culture to culture, and relationship to relationship. . . . Only lovers and parents with babies have completely free access to all parts of the body. For everyone else there is a graded scale of body-contact taboos.[1]

None of the exercises in this text demand that you trot around in the buff. But building a bridge between your inner life and the inner lives of your classmates may be even more risky. The protection that you have in taking such risks, however, is the understanding that the context of using your inner life is that of a formal exercise in which you are protected by the "rules of the game." Later, when you work on characters in scenes, you will be protected by the illusion the fiction encourages you to create. A performer frequently uses reality to create an illusion, and sometimes, as you will see later, the performer uses an illusion to create an illusion.

So let us move on to connecting your reality with the realities of others.

Seeing Each Other without Words

Many of life's most profound experiences are wordless moments: the death of a loved one, the birth of a child, moments of ecstatic love, the departure of a dear friend. At such times, mere words are totally inadequate to express the turmoil, the sense of loss, the joy, the longings that come from sincere relationships with relatives and friends who are close to you. Words intellectualize your relationships and raise an unnecessary barrier between your inner experiences and those of others. Therefore, first you will use right-brain, nonverbal approaches to avoid the objectivity and censorship of the left-brain, verbal functions. Then in the discussions that follow each exercise, you will use the verbal, left-brain functions to understand and structure your discoveries into more complex experiences. Lastly, you will perform interpersonal improvisational exercises that integrate right-brain and left-brain creative processes.

In the rush of everyday activities we rarely take the time to look carefully at one another. In the third act of Thornton Wilder's *Our Town*, Emily, during the disillusionment of reliving her 12th birthday, cries out in pain for her mother to look at her as if she really saw Emily. Now dead, Emily longs to have filled the brevity of life with genuine human contact. In the next several exercises you are going to take the time to look at one another from different angles, with different senses, so that when you begin working on scenes, your knowledge of your classmates will be the greater. You will sharpen your awareness of the responses you evoke from your partners, and you will learn the need to change tactics as the relationships change.

Identifying People while Blindfolded

Like all exercises in this section, no words are used. Bring to class that blindfold you used when you were examining your environment. You will need it now to begin to discover one another. It will be helpful to mark the boundaries of a large, circular working space with rope attached to chairs, so that you do not wander afield. After

Figure 5.1. Blind Identification. While performing this exercise, what details trigger your identification of your classmates? How do your attitudes toward one another change through the process of identification?

you have defined your area, everyone in the class puts on the blindfolds. Wandering at random through the space, you stop with each person you encounter. Touching their face, their arms, their body, you explore them until you recognize who they are. When you identify them, give their hands a squeeze, and continue moving until you meet another person. (See fig. 5.1.) Continue the exercise until you have encountered everyone in the class. (You might count the class before you start the exercise to be sure you find everyone!)

An excellent variation of this exercise is to perform the activity crawling across the floor, if the floor is clean enough and safe to crawl on.

DISCUSSION
1. What things helped you identify the others in the group?
2. How did you feel about touching others and being touched by them?
3. How did the absence of speech and sight change your perception of others in the class?

See Yourself as Others See You

O wad some Pow'r the giftie gie us
To see oursels as others see us!
It wad frae mony a blunder free us,
     And foolish notion.

————*Robert Burns*

The exercises in chapters 3 and 4 with flying, floating, molding and radiating helped increase your awareness of habitual body tension. The next exercise will increase your awareness of habitual mannerisms and, by calling them to your attention, aid you in eliminating them.

Stealing Gestures

The class stands in a circle. Anyone in the circle may begin by making a gesture (hand, facial, or total body gesture) that another member of the class uses habitually. As the others in the group observe the gesture, they, too, imitate the gesture until everyone is doing the same thing. Only then is the original model identified.

Next, someone else starts a gesture copied from another class member. The process is repeated until everyone in the class has been imitated and identified.

DISCUSSION
1. What gestures were called to the attention of class members who were not aware of them?
2. What did the copied gestures appear to communicate to others? Were such messages intended?
3. Can you or others in the class provide any insights into the origins of any of the gestures copied?

Radiating with Others

A. At this point you will expand your experience with radiating to include your classmates. The class stands in a circle. One person begins the experience by stepping forward to face another person in the circle. The first person begins by placing turned-out palms with middle fingers of each hand touching one another a few inches from the face of the other person. The palms are used as sensors to detect the warm rays. Then the first person feels the radiation as the palms work down the rest of the second person's trunk, arms and legs. Adjust the distance from the palms to each person, so that the palms are as far from the person as possible without losing the radiation. Some parts of the body will be warmer, some cooler. After completing the experience with one class member, the first person works clockwise around the circle, experiencing the radiation of each person in the circle.

After the first person reaches the third person in the circle, the second person in the circle repeats the process with the next person and so on around the circle, each person following in line until everyone in the circle has sensed the radiation of every other person.

DISCUSSION
1. Could you detect any differences in tension at those points where bodies seem cooler?
2. What were the differences in the distance of your hands from the bodies of different individuals?
3. Were your reactions the same as those of other people for the same individual, or

did different people find different distances for the same person? If there were differences in distance for the same person, what variables might account for them?

B. After everyone has completed and discussed the above exercise, the class re-forms the circle. This time, any two people from opposite sides of the circle move to the center and radiate a silent message. Movement may be used, but no words. The message may be one of support or one of challenge. No order of participation is designated. Individuals move on impulse to the center, two at a time, until all have participated. (See figs. 5.2, 5.3.)

DISCUSSION
1. How did you decide when you should move to the middle of the circle? How did others decide when they should move?
2. Compare messages between pairs. How did the messages intended compare with those received?
3. What nonverbal clues were you aware of when you performed this exercise?

Grokking

Two decades ago Robert Heinlein wrote the popular science fiction novel *Stranger in a Strange Land* in which he introduced the word *grok*. This is a wonderful addition to our language, for it covers a meaning that earlier needed many words to explain. *Grok* means to understand in a comprehensive and compassionate way, to see things from the perspective of another person, to place oneself in such empathy that the two people become as one in thoughts and feelings, and beyond that to comprehend the relationship of both individuals to the universe of which they are but single expressions. *Grokking* means knowing and accepting not only the uniqueness of the individual but the oneness of the totality of existence.

This exercise will help you to *grok* your classmates. First, the class stands in a circle. One member of the class comes out of the circle to stand in front of another class member. The *grokker* grasps both hands of the *grokkee* and looks at the person— face, eyes, body. The *grokker* adopts in so far as possible the tension level of the person, his or her stance, posture, manner of holding the shoulders, neck, facial expression. (See fig. 5.4.)

As *grokker* you should attempt to penetrate beneath the surface. Discover as much as you can nonverbally the reasons for the person's posture and tensions. If your own body maintained those tensions and posture all the time, how would you feel inside? Squeeze the person's hands or give the person a hug and move clockwise to the next person in the circle. Repeat the process.

After the first *grokker* has moved on to the third person in the circle, the first person *grokked* begins the process with the person to the right, moving around the circle in the path of the first person. The process continues until all have completed the circle. Take plenty of time with this exercise. With a group of 12 it can take 30 to 45 minutes just to complete the circle.

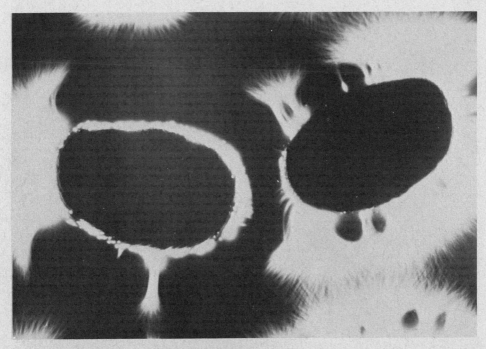

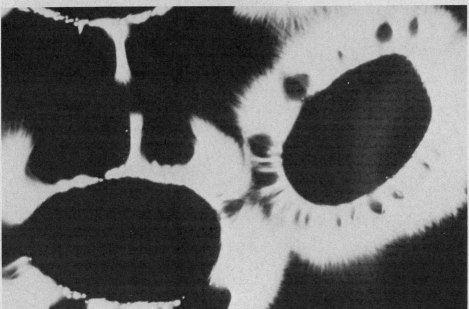

Figure 5.2, Figure 5.3. Kirlian photographs of the fingertips of role-playing individuals show retreating emanations of dislike and advancing emanations of attraction—visual evidence of the changes in radiation for different relationships. (Permission for reprinting from *The Body Electric* by Dr. Thelma Moss. [J. P. Tarcher, 1979.])

Figure 5.4.   Grokking. With a small group, instead of using a circle, you can face one another in pairs. By adopting the expressions and tensions of others, how much can you penetrate beneath the surface to discover their inner experiences?

DISCUSSION

1. Did you find any unexpected physical outcome in completing this exercise? In energy expended?
2. How much are you able to verbalize about what you *grokked*?
3. What were some of the things you discovered about other class members?
4. How do you feel now about the others in your class?
5. How has your attitude about what you are willing to share of yourself been changed by this exercise?

Monkey See, Monkey Do

Now that you are more keenly aware of the presence and differences of others in your group, you are going to try a variety of right-brain exercises to sharpen your powers of observation and imitation.

Aristotle, the classical Greek critic and theoretician, suggested that *mimesis* (the imitation of an action) is at the heart of drama. This recognition implies that the ability to imitate the behavior of others is a valuable tool among the skills of your creative processes. The first two imitative exercises are included to loosen you up and help overcome any inhibitions you still may have. Then you will work on some realistic mirror exercises to sensitize you to social roles and individual behavior patterns.

Imitating Animal Activity

***

Kittens and Puppies

The class divides into two equal groups: kittens and puppies. One kitten pairs off with one puppy. For this exercise you should imitate the animals as closely as possible. Partners tease and play with each other as if with an image in front of a mirror. First, the kittens initiate the action, which the puppies imitate. Then, the puppies begin the action, which the kittens imitate. They find as many ways as they can to be playful.

DISCUSSION
1. Did you find any difficulties in performing this exercise? Any lapses in concentration? If so, why?
2. What were the things you and your classmates did to play with the mirror image?
3. In what kinds of plays can the playful attitude and the reciprocal action be useful to you as a performer?

This exercise can be helpful in keeping your attention on your partner on stage if you have a tendency to play to the audience, a poor habit that many young performers must shed in order to become more involved with the relationships between characters.

***

Serpents and Mongooses

A. In this activity you and a partner will find ways to disagree within the restraints of the images you use. The class divides into two equal groups. The members of one group become cobras, the others become mongooses. The class then pairs off—one cobra to one mongoose. The creatures are in adjacent glass cages, so they may come close to each another but not touch. Either person begins to challenge or threaten the other from within the restraints of the images—cobras behaving like snakes, mongooses like mammals. The challenges are immediately answered with responses from the partners. They find as many ways to threaten and challenge as they can. Partners reverse roles and repeat the activity.

DISCUSSION
1. What were the things you found you could do to challenge or threaten your partner?
2. What observations can you make about the tempo-rhythm of each behavior pattern? Did you maintain different tempo-rhythms or did you move in the same tempo-rhythm, or were there changes from the beginning of the exercise to the end?

3. How was your behavior affected by your awareness that you could not touch the other person?

B. Try the exercise again with a different partner. This time threaten your partner without attempting to match action for action. Concentrate on maintaining your own tempo-rhythm.

DISCUSSION
What differences did you find when you maintained distinct tempo-rhythms?

Imitating Human Activity

Sharing Chores

A. The class divides into pairs, a male and female in each pair if possible (though the activities in this section may be performed by either sex). Each pair chooses a simple activity from one of those suggested below or selects one of its own observation. One person in the pair initiates the activity, and the other person mirrors the actions as closely as possible. They do not reveal what activity is being performed. They let the discovery of the action be part of the exercise. After the first activity has been completed, the second person initiates a different action, and the exercise is repeated. Suggested activities include the following:

>   making the bed
>   washing clothes
>   washing dishes
>   making bread
>   vacuuming a room
>   repairing a bicycle

DISCUSSION
1. How long did it take you to recognize the activity?
2. What did you discover about different ways of performing the same activity?
3. Why was an activity performed differently from the way you might have done it?

B. Now, with the same partner, repeat each of the activities, not as a mirror imitation, but as a cooperative effort, each helping the other to accomplish the task. Use only movements and facial expression to communicate, no words.

DISCUSSION
How were you able to assist each other without delaying the process or without getting in each other's way?

Imitating the Opposite Sex

Partners of the opposite sex try the mirror exercise with activities that are usually performed by only one sex. For example, the girls initiate applying evening makeup with the boys imitating them. Then the boys initiate shaving with the girls imitating. Each performs this activity slowly enough for the partner to follow. They do not generalize. They take their time to get in all the details.

DISCUSSION
1. What did you learn about the behavior of your partner?
2. Did your partner handle the details of the activity in ways that suggested anything to you about his or her attitude toward putting on makeup or shaving?
3. How would you feel if you had to perform the grooming rituals of the opposite sex every day?

Communication with Space

The way we use spatial distance between ourselves and other people suggests something about our relationships. The cultural anthropologist Edward T. Hall has observed the use of four major divisions of distance:

1. intimate distance—requiring direct physical contact
2. personal distance—from 1½ to 4 feet apart
3. social distance—with subdivisions of "close" from 4 to 7 feet and "far" from 7 to 12 feet
4. public distance—"close" at 12 to 25 feet and "far" at 25 feet to out of vision range.[2]

Using Distance

With a partner, assume the spatial footage for each one of these distances in turn. Discover a relationship that might exist at each distance.

DISCUSSION
1. How did the distance itself limit or assist the particular relationship you found for each type of distance?
2. How are the five senses and radiation affected by the various distances?
3. Because of the influence of film and television, many young performers tend to act all scenes in "personal space." Why could this tendency be a problem on stage?

Structured Improvisations

Though you have performed many imaginative activities up to this point, you have not been required to develop your actions into more formally structured improvisations. Structured improvisations draw upon the right brain for spontaneous expression and on the left brain for organization. In this way structured improvisations are given a form similar to the dramatic development of scenes in a play. This similarity makes structured improvisations valuable aids in the development of your dramatic imagination as well as steps toward working on scenes from playscripts. Like scenes from plays, structured improvisations should have a beginning, a middle, a climax, and an ending.

The beginning establishes a problem to be solved or presents a conflict to be resolved. The middle tests the possible solutions or develops the conflict. The climax, as the point of highest tension or greatest interest, presents decisive action or a new revelation to resolve the problem, or it presents the overwhelming power of one side of the conflict over the other. The ending restores balance to the situation or characters or indicates the future restoration of balance. In the suggested situations that follow, see if you can shape the actions into a structured improvisation with these four sections.

The first group of structured improvisations should be performed without words. They are divided into the tension levels you have already worked on: floating, flying, molding and radiating.

With the second group of improvisations you should add words. The topics in the second group are divided into three groups.

1. situations of disagreement in which there are conflicts to develop
2. situations of agreement in which there are problems to be solved
3. radiation situations which can be explored for their celebrative power

Your class may divide into groups to work on the same situations; then each group can present its version to the rest of the class. With this approach, the different solutions and tactics should be compared. Alternately, each group may work on a different exercise and present it to the class to show how solutions and tactics were developed for each problem. In either approach, your class should discuss alternate possibilities to the problems confronting the characters in each situation.

Nonverbal Structured Improvisations

Floating Improvisations

Recovering Sunken Treasure

In the first of these right-brain improvisations three divers descend to the bottom of the ocean to recover a sunken treasure. While underwater, disagreement breaks out over ownership of the treasure. What can each diver do to try to gain exclusive ownership of the treasure?

Planting the Flag on Mars

Three space explorers, each from a different country, land on Mars at the same time. Each explorer attempts to plant his or her country's flag on the planet first. How can each explorer foil the intention of the rivals?

DISCUSSION
1. What tactics were successful for accomplishing the goals in each situation?
2. Did the floating mode become a help or an obstacle to goals in either situation?

Flying Improvisations

Skydiving

Two (or more) groups of five or six make geometric figures as they "fly" through the air. The group with the most interesting or unusual designs is supposed to win a competition. When one group sees another group outmaneuver it, it attempts to form a more complex design.

Racing on the Beach

Overturned chairs, blocks, or other obstacles are used to simulate rocks and tree trunks on an isolated beach. Two fraternities have picked the same afternoon for a party. The challenge to a relay race is issued, and the two groups start racing over the obstacles in their paths. A rolled up newspaper serves as a fish, which the first person in each line must carry to the turn-around mark and back where he or she hands it to the next runner. The next runner takes the fish, runs, and returns with it, and so on. The first group to finish the relay race wins. The losing group must treat the winners to their favorite beverage.

DISCUSSION
1. What difficulties did you experience in maintaining the flying sensation and attempting to accomplish the goals at the same time?
2. Identify the obstacles in each situation. How do obstacles make a situation more interesting?

Molding Improvisations

Building a Snowperson

Before starting the improvisation two groups of three to five people agree among themselves on a famous personality to use as a model for a snowperson. One of the three becomes the core around which the snow is molded. As the snowperson takes shape, the person beneath the snow gradually assumes characteristics of the famous person. The observers may guess who the snowperson is. The group whose work is guessed first continues to go on to a second round with challengers from the observers until everyone in the class has participated. The group that survived the longest number of rounds is declared the winner.

Washing a Famous Statue

The class divides into groups of three. Two groups at a time are each given the task of washing a different famous statue. It may be a large or a small statue. The groups may select the statues from their own memory, or people may bring pictures of famous statues to class for this exercise. When members of an observing group guess the correct statue of either competing set of washers, they replace the group whose statue is guessed and begin washing their own statue until it is guessed. The exercise continues until all have participated.

DISCUSSION
1. What details made the correct guesses possible?
2. When do you think complete details are more important and when do you think only suggested details are more important in performance?

Radiation Improvisations

Guiding an Action

The class is divided into pairs. One partner in each pair decides on an action the other person should carry out—a single, simple action such as tipping over a chair, placing a waste basket on top of a table, writing one's name on a blackboard. The actions are to be real (not pantomimed), so they should be performable with objects in the room. The sender visualizes the action desired and gives gestures of encouragement or discouragement, but the sender cannot directly imitate the action. After every pair has a turn, roles are reversed so that senders become receivers and receivers become senders.

DISCUSSION
1. Which people seemed to be better senders? Which better receivers?
2. In what ways did different receivers discover the desired action? Facial clues? Gestural clues? Were any images transmitted from mind to mind?

Healing the Sick

One person is designated "saint." Everyone else in the class creates an internal illness that is not visible externally. The saint radiates healing power individually to each "infirm" person, who then recovers. This exercise should be performed several times with different saints and different infirmities.

DISCUSSION
1. What infirmities did the "saints" detect? How do these match the imagined illnesses?
2. Did any of the "infirm" feel anything physically when they were "healed"?

Visiting from Outer Space

One person is designated "visitor from outer space." The visitor has beamed down to earth in human form and is passing on the secret of happiness to individuals by the laying on of hands. The uninitiated have various attitudes: scoffing, curious, skeptical, derisive, autograph seeking, self-serving. But as each individual finally submits to the initiation, understanding is achieved, and respect for the visitor and one another prevails.

DISCUSSION
1. What physical adjustments were made when the initiation took place?
2. What impressions were received of what the secret was?

Structured Improvisations with Words and Movement

In the next two groups of improvisations (situations of tension and of harmony) you should invent your own dialogue as well as action. Here, of course, you are integrating left-brain logical and verbal functions with right-brain nonverbal functions.

Situations of Tension

Discovering the United States #2 (Inappropriate Behavior)

You will recall in the last chapter you established environments in the United States in three categories: city, suburban, and country. Use the same three general categories. A volunteer moves into the working space and establishes a specific environment. As soon as a second person knows where the first person is, he or she joins the first person, and they begin a conversation. The third person to recognize the place and relationship also participates in an appropriate way. The fourth person to join the group, however, behaves inappropriately for the relationships established or for the environment, creating a problem for the first three people to deal with. For example, a young couple establishes they are shopping in a jewelry store for a wedding ring. The third person becomes the jewelry salesman. The fourth person joins the group and attempts to shoplift a valuable ring from the display tray.

Don't Get Fresh With Me (Irritation)

A woman sits on a park bench feeding the pigeons. A man enters and tries to pick her up. She has reasons for turning him down and tries to get rid of him. Only the entrance of a police officer rescues the situation.

Robber in the House/Drug Addict Holdup (Fear)

A. A young couple is asleep in bed when a burglar enters the house and attempts to steal valuable items. How do the husband and wife deal with the situation? How does the burglar try to avoid being caught and arrested?

B. Two tourists (male or female) in a big city are accosted by a drug addict, who demands their money and other valuables. How do the tourists handle the drug addict? How does the addict threaten the tourists?

Tug of War/Arm Wrestling/Challenge to a Duel (Rivalry)

A. A real rope is used for a tug of war between members of rival student organizations (clubs or fraternities). The members of the losing team will have to treat the winners to refreshments of the winners' choice.

B. The class divides into pairs of about equal strength. Each pair arm wrestles. The best two out of three rounds wins the first level. In the second level, winners of the first level are matched against each other. The winners continue moving on to successive levels until a final winner is determined. Those who do not win should cheer on a champion of their choice at each level of the competition.

C. This improvisation for a larger group is a period piece. The situation begins with three people, two men and one woman. One man insults the wife of the second man. A challenge is issued to the offender in defense of the lady's reputation. The man challenged chooses weapons. Each man acquires a second, and the wife brings her sister to witness the duel. A physician and a nurse are brought to the scene. A constable enters to attempt to stop the illegal duel, but he is restrained by the seconds. What is the outcome of the duel? What effect does this have on the wife?

Challenging Authority

A. "I want a better grade." A student visits the office of a young teacher and tries to get a grade changed. What are the circumstances behind the weak grade? Why does the student think the grade should be changed? Why does the teacher insist on not changing the grade? What is the outcome?

B. "I don't deserve a ticket." A police officer writes out a ticket for an illegal parking violation. Just as the officer finishes writing the ticket, the car owner returns with an excuse that merits consideration for the violation. What is the reason? The police officer has a quota of tickets to issue (though this need not be brought up by the officer). Who prevails and why?

Situations of Harmony

Remembering When: High School (Nostalgia)

This improvisation idea may be used for the entire class at once. Students have gathered in a typical student hangout—a dormitory lounge, a campus cafeteria, the steps of a student union building. The students bring up things they used to do when they were "kids," activities that they enjoyed when they were in high school. They reenact some of these activities to demonstrate them for the others. After a while one person notices the time, and students have to leave in various directions for different college classes. If taken seriously (as it should be), this can be a very moving and poignant episode.

DISCUSSION
1. How was the behavior in the reenactment different from the rest of the behavior?
2. How was the tempo-rhythm of the past different from the tempo-rhythm of the present?

Getting Married (Commitment)

A young couple decides to marry. Where are they? How long have they known each other? Have they lived together? Who initiates the idea? Do they both have jobs? What kind of jobs? Are they students? Is it financially feasible to get married? Where are they going to live? Did the young man buy an engagement ring? Could he afford it? What about children? Do both of them want children? Immediately? When? What decision is made? Is this a mutual decision to get married or is this an acceptance of a proposal?

Planning a Wedding (Future Plans)

A young bride-to-be, her mother, her sister, and other friends are planning the details of a wedding. How does each person ensure that her particular idea for the wedding becomes part of the final plans? Where is the wedding to be held? How many people are to participate in the wedding? How much money can be spent? How many guests are to be invited? Who makes the final decisions? How does the bride react to the final plans?

Buying a Car (Negotiations)

A young couple goes out to buy their first new car. A car sales manager wants to make a good deal for both the couple and the company. Can they make a satisfactory deal? Which car does the husband want? Which car does the wife want? How does the couple's old car fit into the deal? How much does the sales manager have to cut his or her own commission to close the deal? Does the sales manager have to get approval from another character? The company owner?

Visiting the Family (Celebrations)

The entire class becomes relatives at a family reunion dinner. Two people act as hosts, greeting the others, who arrive as singles, in pairs, and in trios, each person or group bringing a different dish for the meal. (The food brought can establish the ethnic background of the family.) Every person or group establishes its relationship to the hosts on its entrance.

Is the occasion a holiday? What is the season of the year? What is the weather? From what distances did the relatives come? How did they travel? When was the last time they saw each other? Who has new babies? Who is expecting? Who has lost weight? Put on weight? Looking older? Just had a face lift? Growing deaf? Has a hearing aid?

Someone expected cannot come to the reunion. What happened? How does this absence affect the mood of the reunion? Does anyone have to leave as a result?

Radiation: Verbal Activities   The improvisational ideas for radiation in this section use the right-brain radiation technique you developed earlier and add the verbal and logical abilities of the left brain.

Winning Votes

Two people are selected to run for an office. The rest of the class are voters. Local student-government offices or state or national positions may be used. With the voters standing in the middle of the room, each politician claims a different corner of the room and does everything possible to attract voters to that area. The person attracting the most voters to the area wins.

After initial appeals by the politicians, voters may appeal to other voters to follow the candidate of their choice.

DISCUSSION
1. How did the office seekers manage to win approval?
2. How were the appeals of the voters for support for their favorite candidate different from the candidates' appeals?

Accepting the Tony Award

The characters needed are a presenter and five people nominated for "Best New Performer of the Year." When the name of the winner is called out, the other four nominees also come forward to contest the award in as winsome a manner as possible. How can the nominees appeal the decision without losing the backing of their supporters?

Projecting an Image with ESP

Actors are attempting to be psychic all the time. They are transmitting thoughts, experiencing desires, exerting wills, inducing states—and sending out all variety of emanations to an audience who, for their part, are psychically comprehending—or not—depending on the strength or weakness of the actor's signal.

———— *Charles Marowitz,* The Act of Being

The last exercise in this chapter is one that amazes nearly everyone who tries it. It is an experiment with the projection of images through extrasensory perception, the unproven but intriguing possibility that we can communicate in ways other than through the obvious five senses. Though the results may vary with the group, my own classes have had as high as 80 percent success with it. Before you attempt it, you should warm up with a few rounds of "Guiding an Action" given earlier in this chapter.

Using Extrasensory Perception

With the class in a circle, one member of the class volunteers as "it" and leaves the room. The group chooses a specific item from a category, such as "vegetables—cabbage."

Suggested categories include the following:

vegetables
flowers
birds
dogs
household appliances
famous paintings

The volunteer returns to the room and is told only the category. Then all members of the group visualize the item—in this instance, a cabbage—and imagine all its sensuous qualities. The volunteer moves about in the center of the circle and attempts to pick up the image without any visual gestures or cues. (See figure 5.5.) If the volunteer has any difficulty, a designated class member might help by making the following suggestions.

1. Can you pick up the color?
2. Can you pick up the shape?
3. Can you pick up the size?
4. Can you pick up the texture?
5. Can you pick up the flavor?

Frequently if the item cannot be guessed immediately, one or more of the qualities given in the questions will be sensed and the item will be named quickly. Another way to assist the volunteer is for the group to project the image of the first letter of the object alternately with the image of the object. You may find that some members of the class are particularly good senders of images and others are better receivers.

DISCUSSION
1. Can you or other members of your class share experiences that could be explained only by coincidence or by extrasensory perception?
2. Why do you think some people resist the possibility that we have means of communication that go beyond the usual five senses?
3. Even if images are not projected directly from mind to mind, what values do images have for the performer?

Figure 5.5. Image Projecting. When a group develops a strong rapport, the success rate of image projecting increases.

If you find this area of investigation intriguing, you might read some of the references cited at the end of the chapter. The books by Thelma Moss and Russell Targ are particularly interesting contributions to our understanding of psychic phenomena.

Summary

In this chapter you have learned to open yourself to others and work together with others in reciprocal relationships. You have further enhanced your awareness of your habitual behavior and mannerisms and developed additional flexibility in various levels of tension through interpersonal exercises with flying, floating, molding, and radiating modes.

You have explored the use of space as a means of creating meaning between yourself and others. And you have developed further the image-making ability of your right-brain functions and the organizational ability of your left-brain functions through the development of structured improvisations.

In part 3 you will use this basic equipment of communication to develop further those skills that are the foundations of the craft of performance for the theatre.

Notes

1. Desmond Morris, *Manwatching: A Field Guide to Human Behavior* (New York: Harry N. Abrams, 1977), p. 204
2. Edward T. Hall, *The Hidden Dimension* (Garden City, N. Y.: Doubleday, 1966), see Ch. 10.

For Further Reading

Chekhov, Michael. *To the Actor.* New York: Harper & Row, 1953. Ch. 3.
Krippner, Stanley. *Human Possibilities.* Garden City, N. Y.: Doubleday, 1980.
LeShan, Lawrence. *The Medium, the Mystic, and the Physicist.* New York: Viking Press, 1974.
Marowitz, Charles. *The Act of Being.* New York: Taplinger, 1978. Ch. 10.
Moss, Thelma. *The Body Electric.* Los Angeles: J.P. Tarcher, 1979.
Targ, Russell. *The Mind Race: Understanding and Using Psychic Abilities.* New York: Villard Books, 1984.
Targ, Russell, and Harold Puthoff. *Mind-Reach: Scientists Look at Psychic Ability.* New York: Delacorte Press/Eleanor Friede, 1977. Ch. 6.

Part Three

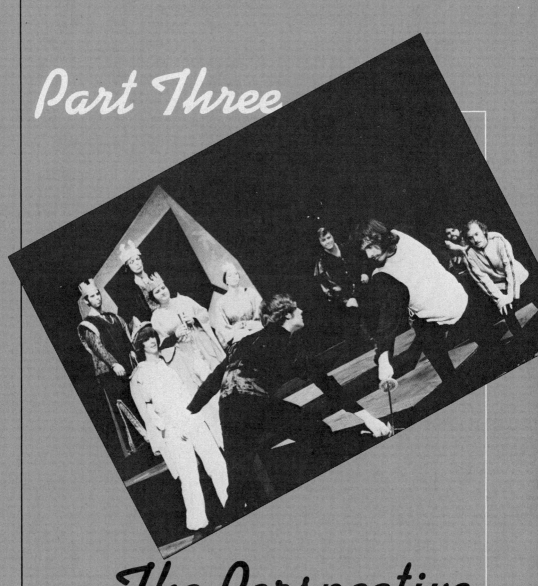

The Perspective
of Craft

Introduction

Explore the Six Levels of Craft

This role has the biggest layers of any role I've played—the biggest jumps from one level to the next in the shortest space of time.

———————*Elizabeth McGovern*

In the six chapters of this section you will find explanations and exercises for the six levels of the craft in the creative processes of acting. These six levels are

1. the level of actions
2. the level of words
3. the level of unconscious role playing
4. the level of conscious role playing
5. the level of emotions
6. the level of aesthetic distance

As you explore this territory, bear in mind that the exercises are to be used for developmental purposes. Some exercises also may be used as rehearsal techniques. But the major exploration and experimentation should be behind you at the time of a public performance so that you can concentrate your attention on the details selected during rehearsals and on your moment-by-moment responses to your acting partners.

While there are many times during development and rehearsals when right-brain intuition can be encouraged to dominate and other times when left-brain evaluation can be valuable, during performance a balance between functions helps to keep your performance on an even keel, neither dependent on elusive inspiration nor stifled by logic and control.

The chapters of this section lead you through a logical course of increasing complexity in developing the craft of acting. In chapter 6 you will begin by examining the action base of a character. Then you will move on in chapter 7 to the verbal level of craft. At the next two levels you will develop believability and variety in characterization, first in chapter 8 through unconscious role playing, then in chapter 9 through conscious role playing. Next you will explore in chapter 10 the emotional nature of yourself and the characters you portray. At the sixth level, in chapter 11, you will consider the various techniques that provide different degrees of aesthetic distance between you and your characterizations.

Parallels to the Visual Arts

You might think of these six artistic elements of the acting craft as parallels to the elements in the visual arts. Playing an action on stage resembles the element of line in painting, for line, like action, defines direction and gives focus to the energies of a painting as action does within a scene. The language level resembles texture; both language and texture appear on the surface with polarities of roughness or smoothness, deepness or shallowness, shininess or dullness, simplicity or complexity. Both unconscious and conscious role playing fill out the outline and detail of characterization as shape or mass defines areas in painting. Emotion dazzles the senses as color dazzles the eyes. Lastly, aesthetic distance is the frame, which gives perspective to the other elements of craft.

The Necessity of Continual Renewal

An interesting and multi-dimensional period of my life now began for me. I can only describe it as a time of living on several levels.

————*Shirley MacLaine*, Out on a Limb

Whatever benefit you may gain from reading about these six levels and from doing the exercises, you should realize that these basic elements of craft are worth frequent review and practice. Acting is a daily art requiring continual exercise, not only of the muscles of the body and voice, but of the imagination and coordination of the senses.

These mental, emotional, and sensuous faculties should be exercised as frequently as muscles if the mental tools of the actor are to be as well honed as the physical tools. Professional performers continue to take classes in movement and voice as well as workshops in scene study to keep their own equipment in top shape. If you wish to master the challenging six levels of the craft of acting, you can expect to do no less. Mastery of the six levels will require the commitment of both sides of your brain to the task.

Chapter 6 _____

The Level
of Actions
_____

At first, a desire arises that becomes the will, then begins to act consciously, aiming
towards its gratification. Only then, altogether spontaneously, and sometimes against
our will, does the feeling come. Thus, feeling is a product of will and the conscious
(and sometimes subconscious) actions directed towards its gratification.

——*Eugene Vakhtangov*, Diary

Character Objectives

The quotation from the Russian director Eugene Vakhtangov at the beginning of
this chapter points to the relationship between playing character actions (or objectives) and emotions. Though we will consider the emotional side of this relationship
in more detail in chapter 10, for the time being it is sufficient to recognize that the
emotional behavior many people associate with acting is not pursued directly. Emotional behavior results from the choices of character actions that arouse emotion in
both performers and audience members. In using a character's actions to stimulate
emotional response, the logical left-brain functions lead, and the intuitive right-brain
functions accompany them as closely as one actor accompanies another in the mirror
exercises you have performed.

When we read a playscript, the words communicate information that we reassemble as actions and characterization in our own minds to create an inner experience for ourselves. The same process functions for the audience, except that the actor
replaces the script. As readers or audience members we recognize the elements of our
experience with words and action as portraits of characterization and as the events of
a plot.

As you divide a play into units to begin work on the action level, you will find it
helpful to determine the goals of the character at three gradations of refinement. The
actions at each gradation are made concrete through the following concepts.

1. the superobjective, which defines the character's overall goal for the entire action
   of the play

2. the scene objective, which defines the character's goal for the smaller unit of a scene
3. the beat objective, which defines the character's goal for a smaller segment within a scene

Closely related to the objectives are even shorter reactive units refered to as "moments." We will look at each of these four terms individually, considering their interrelationships as we proceed. In the appendix the scene from *Ah, Wilderness!* has been divided into units for you and labeled with three gradations of objectives and with moments. You may wish to refer to the scene to see all the terms in use for a single scene as the explanation of each term is given here with other examples.

As important as the actor's delivery of dialogue may appear to be in conveying the content of the play, at best the words in the script alone convey an orderly left-brain impression of plot development and thematic ideas. Subtleties of characterization, emotional depth, and interaction between characters are rarely evident in a library reading of a playscript, for the emotions and behavior of characters are largely actor-endowed. For this reason many people have difficulty appreciating the characterization in reading a playscript. Unless a reader has developed the ability to imagine character behavior in action, much of the potential of the script is lost in the reading. The same problem would exist for a nonmusician who picked up a music score and tried to imagine what the music might sound like in performance. The actor, however, must cultivate those right-brain functions that both sense and convey character impulses, intentions, and actions implied beneath the words. It is at the action level, using elements from both the nonverbal right-brain functions and the verbal left-brain functions, that actors begin to create characterizations that interact with other characterizations and drive forward the events and relationships of the play.

Superobjectives

The driving forces that propel the dramatic action of the play are character objectives, sometimes called character intentions or goals. Konstantin Stanislavsky, the great director-teacher of the Moscow Art Theatre, referred to the major goal of a character throughout the play as the character's "superobjective" and smaller segments of the superobjective simply as objectives. His terms will be used here.[1]

At beginning levels of performance you will be working with characters in scene units more frequently than in full-length roles. For this reason you will find the term "objectives" used here more frequently than "superobjectives," but it is helpful to understand the distinction and to make it when relevant. Through the playing of selected actions to obtain the character's objectives the actor achieves a high level of art. As Stanislavsky observes,

> high art . . . is that in which there exists a superobjective and a through-line-of-action. Bad art is that in which there is neither superobjective nor through-line-of-action.[2]

To clarify the superobjectives and objectives for the characters you play, you should express the superobjectives, the scene objectives, and beat objectives in the infinitive verb form as simply as possible from the viewpoint of the character. For example, supposing you are performing Amanda in *The Glass Menagerie*, you might phrase your superobjective as follows: "I want to insure Laura's future." Or you might word Amanda's superobjective, "I want to guarantee my daughter a better life than I've had." There are no absolute answers in wording the superobjective, but your word choice should reflect the director's interpretation of the entire play (or your own interpretation of the play, if you are working on a characterization without a director).

If the chosen interpretation of *The Glass Menagerie* emphasizes the conflict between the old South and the new, then the first choice for Amanda's superobjective offered above might be made. If the overall interpretation of the play emphasizes the hostility of the world to the sensitive soul, then the second choice might be used. Thus, the choice of superobjectives (and later scene objectives) for each character reflects the selected overall interpretation of the actions and thematic emphasis of a play and helps to communicate that particular interpretation of the playscript to the audience.

Let us look at another example. If the emphasis of the overall interpretation of the play *Hamlet* focused on revenge, then Hamlet's superobjective might be, "I want to avenge my father's murder." If the overall interpretation of the play focused on the need for justice in a corrupt kingdom, Hamlet's superobjective might be phrased, "I want to cleanse Denmark from corruption."

Scene Objectives

Every scene in which a character appears gives that character an opportunity to work toward the achievement of his or her superobjective. In this way the superobjective is separated into smaller segments, the character's scene objectives, which the character pursues on a scene-by-scene basis.

The term scene as used here does not refer to the printed scene number in the script but rather to those major units of interaction between characters that usually extend from the entrance or exit of one character to the entrance or exit of another. These units are traditionally called French scenes, so named from the practice of French publishers starting a new page of print each time a different group of characters is on stage. Except for minor scenes of transitions (hellos or goodbyes), which add little to the dramatic development of most plays, the action of a play grows in momentum with each successive scene, just as a novel develops chapter by chapter.

All the scene objectives of the character should be related to the superobjective as subdivisions or parts of the superobjective. In *The Glass Menagerie* Amanda has a scene with Tom in which she asks him to invite a gentleman caller for Laura. For the first interpretation of the play offered above, in which Amanda's superobjective is "to insure Laura's future," Amanda's scene objective might be expressed, "I want to badger Tom into bringing home a beau who will marry and take care of Laura." For the second interpretation, in which Amanda's superobjective is "I want to guarantee my daughter a better life than I've had," Amanda's scene objective might be expressed, "I want to evoke Tom's sympathy for the tragedy of a helpless, unmarried woman so he'll find a beau for Laura." Though the outcome of either objective may be the same in terms of plot development, the characterization will be different because of the choice of a different scene objective. The first choice of scene objective offered here (to badger Tom) would produce a fussier, bossier Amanda. The second choice (to evoke Tom's sympathy) would suggest a more pathetic, pleading Amanda. Yet each choice can be valid for an appropriate interpretation of the entire play.

The more active the verbs you choose to express the character's superobjective and objectives, the more potential dramatic excitement may be generated in the character's attempts to fulfill objectives. For example, in Hamlet's scene in his mother's bedroom, his scene objective could be expressed, "I want to force Mother to reveal her connection with my father's murder." The choice "I want to coax Mother to reveal her connection with my father's murder," would be weaker dramatically, but it might be more appropriate to the overall focus of a particular interpretation of the play, or it might be a more interesting approach to the characterization.

Negative phrasing such as might be suggested for Laura in *The Glass Menagerie*— "I want to withdraw from reality," leads to weak, undramatic acting. Reword such an objective with a positive action-suggesting verb—"I want to defend my fantasy world," or even more assertively, "I want to overcome my shyness."

The dramatic excitement is also dependent upon the strength of the opposition to the character's superobjective and objectives. This concept will be developed in detail later in this chapter in the discussion on obstacles.

To summarize at this point, objectives at any level—superobjectives, scene objectives, or beat objectives—should be expressed as positive goals in the infinitive verb form with action choices that are consistant with the overall interpretation of the entire play.

Determining Objectives

Selecting any character from a scene in the appendix, use your left-brain functions to choose a specific focus for the interpretation of the play, a superobjective, and the character's main objective in the scene.

DISCUSSION

1. For those plays from the appendix that are familiar to you, how are the characters's objectives within the scenes related to the character superobjectives for the entire play?
2. How do the characters's main objectives for each scene create tension or raise a conflict between them?
3. What actions do characters take within each scene to achieve their objectives? (The action may be physical or psychological.)

Typical Superobjective Patterns

In a full-length play it is through the rising tension produced by the pursuit of the superobjective of one character with the pursuit of superobjectives of other characters that dramatic action builds to a climax (that is, the scene of greatest tension), leading ultimately to one of three possibilities:

1. The character achieves the superobjective and is either satisfied or dissatisfied with the outcome.
2. The character fails to achieve the superobjective and laments or rationalizes the negative outcome.
3. The character's superobjective is stalemated and he or she either rationalizes the outcome, renews the original goals, or establishes new superobjectives.

An example of each pattern from well-known plays (two with scenes in the appendix) will illustrate these three possibilities.

For a character with a superobjective of the first type, the achieved superobjective, consider Richard Miller in *Ah, Wilderness!* Richard's superobjective may be seen as an effort to form a stable intimate relationship with someone equal to his own level of intellect and sensitivity. When he finally overcomes his major internal obstacle (his insecurity) and the major external obstacle (the opposition of Muriel's father), he is able to court Muriel, and he rejoices in the outcome.

To illustrate the second type of character superobjective pattern, the failed superobjective, consider the character goal of Wesley in Sam Shepard's *Curse of the Starving Class*. Wesley wants to renew (or redeem) the family's fortunes. The actions he pursues—whether realistic ones such as mending the front door or symbolic ones such as first treating, then sacrificing the lamb—are actions taken in an attempt to renew or redeem the fallen condition of the family fortunes. Wesley fails and suffers in his awareness of the failure.

The third type of pattern in which the character's superobjective is neither achieved nor fails may be seen in Bertolt Brecht's *The Good Woman of Setzuan*. In this play the good woman, Shen Te, wants to find happiness. But she cannot find the happiness she seeks because she cannot resolve her internal conflict, a conflict between her need for material means and her vulnerability to exploitation. Only "the gods" may be able to resolve this dilemma, and the gods in the world of Brecht's play are petty and powerless.

Objectives and the Through-Line-of-Action

Prior to the discussion on the expression of the superobjectives and objectives you found in the quotation from Stanislavsky the term through-line-of-action. Though the term might seem self-explanatory, it causes a lot of confusion. Many young actors think this concept means they have to express their character's superobjectives and objectives with a lot of physical activity. Frequently, the result is a great deal of unnecessary tension and pointless "busyness" on stage, which does little or nothing to advance the objectives of the character.

Any physical or psychological tactic that you use in the direction of fulfilling the character's superobjectives, scene objectives, or beat objectives—if consistent with the overall interpretation of the play—is a valid means of manifesting a through-line-of-action. For the through-line-of-action simply refers to those actions (either physical or psychological) that the character attempts in the effort to fulfill his or her goals.

Extending an example above from *The Glass Menagerie*, if in order "to badger Tom," Amanda physically confronts him every time he turns away from her, then her through-line-of-action is very physical and obvious. If for alternate choices, Amanda keeps straightening Tom's collar or continually pushes an uneaten plate of food toward him, she may still be badgering him but with less attention to the goal of getting him to bring home a gentleman caller. Amanda might also badger Tom simply by using an insistent tone of voice, which reflects her attention toward her objective.

The exercises that follow the later section "Actions to Enhance Character Objectives" will help you develop your facility with physicalizing the through-line-of-action.

Beat Objectives

The individual scene may be separated into smaller units called beats. If the scenes are like chapters in novels, the beats are like paragraphs. With each new beat, characters may vary the attack on a scene objective. These variations in attack may be called beat objectives. Dividing the scene into beats and identifying beat objectives achieves several purposes.

The first purpose is to provide the character with an opportunity to adjust to the changing circumstances as the scene progresses. As the character's initial efforts are met with resistance or opposition, he or she must adjust plans and counterattack as the circumstances change. This adjustment gives the character the apparent flexibility of lifelike behavior in dealing with obstacles. Later in this chapter the use of such obstacles will be considered in greater detail.

Second, the actor's choices of beat objectives define the emotional nature of the character.

Third, varying the attack on the scene objective with each beat gives variety to the action, which otherwise would be mechanical and colorless. Flat, uninteresting performances are most frequently the result of the actor's failure to choose interesting beat objectives or failure to pursue with vigor the various beat attacks on the character's scene objectives.

While the division of objectives for the scene or beat is primarily a left-brain function, the development of the varieties of attack and the physicalization of the objectives is a right-brain function.

When you examine a scene for beats, you will find natural divisions created by changes in topic or activity. Each new beat shifts attention from issue to issue in such a smooth, orderly way that we frequently are unaware of the progression. Most beats are about half a page long, though some beats may be shorter and some longer.

You have some freedom in deciding where to divide beats, but if you and your classmates independently will divide a couple of scenes and then compare notes, you probably will find agreement on beat divisions within a line or two in most scenes. The scene from *Ah, Wilderness!* in the appendix has been divided into beats for you with a choice given for each character's beat objectives. This example should help you understand the concept and its application.

Refining Objectives

A. The class selects a scene from the appendix to divide into beats. The class then may divide into small groups and go through the scene, segmenting it into beats.

The groups reassemble and compare reasons for different choices in beat division.

B. With a partner select a scene to work on in greater detail. Read the entire play. Independently determine an active superobjective for each of your characters for the entire play. Put your superobjectives in writing with a personal viewpoint: "For the entire play I (my character) want to _____."

Then select an active objective for the scene you have chosen to work on. Write out your scene objective: "In this scene I (my character) want to _____."

DISCUSSION

1. What is the relationship between the character's superobjective for the play and his or her objective for the scene?
2. How specific are your superobjectives and scene objectives? (The more specific, the better.)
3. Are your superobjective and scene objectives phrased as positive (rather than negative) actions?

C. Next examine each beat. Decide on objectives for each beat. Number your beats and write them down: "In beat number _____ I (my character) want to _____."

After you have made these initial decisions, try improvising with your partner in front of class observers, using the individual beats and the character relationships provided by the script but with your own spontaneous dialogue. Do not discuss your own character's beat objectives with your partner at this point. As you improvise the scene, stick to the beat objectives you initially decided on throughout the improvisation.

DISCUSSION

1. What difficulties did you find in performing the improvisation?
2. Compare how you and the class observers feel about the success you and your partner had in achieving the scene and beat objectives.
3. Why did you find difficulty in sticking to the beat objectives you chose initially?

Adapting Objectives

Through the process of testing your objectives you will discover the reason that the predetermined beat objectives you wrote down produce a mechanical or untruthful result if you pursue them without adjustment. The interpersonal relationships that characters have in a play are as dynamic as a similar relationship in life. All characters adapt their objectives to the objectives they perceive in the other characters and to the obstacles in the way of their own objectives.

A. Improvise the same scene you used in the previous exercise a second time. This time you adapt your beat objectives to the manner and objectives of your partner. Do not imitate your partner, but see if you can accomplish your objective by adapting your manner of reaching your scene objective to your partner's objectives and the obstacles they present to your character. Your partner follows the same procedure.

DISCUSSION
1. How did the second improvisation of the same scene differ from the first improvisation (when you did not adapt your objectives to the resistances you found)?
2. Compare how you and the class observers feel about your partner's and your own success in achieving your character's objectives for the scene.

   B. Now return to the beat objectives you recorded on your script. Cross out any beat objectives that no longer fit and redefine them.

DISCUSSION
1. How much flexibility should the performer have in changing beat objectives to adapt to different resistances and obstacles?
2. How could a performer distort the intention of a playwright by overadapting the objectives of characters?

Moments

Within beats there are smaller units called moments, which are shorter units of reaction, realization, decision, or celebration. If scenes are like chapters in a novel and beats are like paragraphs, then moments are like phrases or points of punctuation. Moments are extremely important to fulfill the emotional realization of a character and to increase the impact of a scene on an audience. Often moments are wordless expressions of understanding, sympathy, or love. On the other hand, they may be verbal or nonverbal threats, outbursts of hostility, or revenge. Careful study and use of these small intense moments will bring excitement and depth to your work. In the appendix some possible moments in the scene from *Ah, Wilderness!* have been indicated as examples for your consideration.

Finding Moments

   A. With your class divided into small groups examine a couple of scenes from the appendix to locate potential moments.
   B. Several of the moments may then be improvised in class, first nonverbally, then verbally.

DISCUSSION
1. What insights into a character's inner life do you find revealed through the use of moments?
2. Were there any differences of impact on the class observers between the nonverbal and the verbal moments?

Actions to Enhance Character Objectives

So far in this chapter you have examined the elements of a character's action from the largest unit to the smallest. To review, these elements are 1) the superobjective, 2) the scene objective, 3) the beat objective, 4) the moment.

In the sections that follow, you will explore the means of enhancing a character's objectives for the stage. These means include environmental actions, characterizing actions, and focusing actions in relation to dialogue.

Environmental Actions

One way of enhancing objectives is through development of the reality of an environment and a character's relationship to it. The character's environment consists of all the physical, atmospheric, and social elements stated or suggested by the playscript. Performers utilizing all the elements of the environment help create a sense of reality both for themselves and their audience.

Using the Environment

Examine the environment in the scene you worked on in Exercise A on adapting objectives. Using the furniture arrangement, the atmosphere, and stage props, find at least three things in the environment that your character can use to help achieve the scene objective and the beat objectives. Things you could do might range from using common pocket props to a rearrangement of the furniture to closing a door or window.

Improvise the entire scene a third time with your partner. This time add the use of items from the environment you just developed to assist your character's scene and beat objectives.

DISCUSSION
1. What actions did the class observers perceive as developing the characters' relationships to their environment?
2. How did the environmental actions enhance the characters' objectives for the scene?

Characterizing Actions

There are three major ways in which actions help to enhance characterization:

1. through spatial relationships with other characters
2. through gestures
3. through the use of progressive activities with physical objects (stage properties or "props")

Each of these methods is valuable and may be combined with either or both of the other two. For practice, however, you can work on each technique separately before combining them.

Spatial Relationships   You will recall the exercises with spatial relationships you performed in chapter 4 in which you examined the implications of distances between people and how we interpret them. In character relationships on stage we also interpret the space between characters and the changing distances as having psychological meaning.

Using Space

A. Read over the scene from *Ah, Wilderness!*. Find lines of dialogue in which the characters appear to grow psychologically and emotionally closer to each other. These are lines of advance. Then find lines in which the characters are in disagreement or at a point of tension. These are lines of retreat.

Now, with your partner, use space only to express your characters' changing relationship. Hold your scripts in hand, but instead of the dialogue, use the syllables "la-la" as you weave back and forth, toward and away from each other to express the changing relationship.

Other scenes in the appendix to try with this exercise include: *The Effect of Gamma Rays on Man-in-the-Moon Marigolds*, *The Good Woman of Setzuan*, and *Marat/Sade*.

DISCUSSION
1. How did class observers perceive the changing relationships?
2. Did you find that anyone began to move parts of the body other than those required for advancing and retreating? If so, how did those movements add or detract from the development of the relationship?

B. Add a couple of chairs and a table to the space. Repeat the exercise, using the furniture as obstacles between the characters as they advance and retreat. You may sit or stand on the chairs, tip them over, hide under the table, or do anything that occurs to you with the furniture used as obstacles in the advance and retreat relationship. In figure 6.1 and figure 6.2 note how space and properties relate characters to the environment and to each other.

DISCUSSION
1. How did the addition of the furniture add interest and complication to the spatial relationship of the characters?
2. What did the addition of the furniture as obstacles do to the energy level of the performers?

Gestures   The second method of using characterizing action to physicalize objectives is through gestures. Three major types of gestures are most helpful in this process: occupational gestures, emphatic gestures, and habitual gestures.

Though these categories are not mutually exclusive (that is, a single gesture may be regarded as falling into more than one category), you can add characterization interest by developing gestures of all three types.

1. Occupational gestures include posture, walk, and ways of moving that have been conditioned from the character's occupation or major daily activity. The tensions and tempo-rhythms of librarians, for example, would differ from those of construction workers. The muscles used in different kinds of work adjust to the needs of the

Figure 6.1.   *Gemani* by Albert Innaurato. Compare the uses of space and the environment in this scene from *Gemani* with the scene from *The Birthday Party* in Figure 6.2. (Photograph: Joe Meyer. Courtesy of Montclair State College, Major Theatre Series. Set and lights: John Figola; costumes: Joseph F. Bella.)

worker and affect movement both on and off the job, so when we see characters at home in the evening, there will be some carry-over from their daily occupations into their domestic physical behavior. Occupational gestures may also include the gestures required for a special purpose. A do-it-yourself hobbyist, for example, might have physical habits from working avocationally as a carpenter.

2. Emphatic gestures may be hand, head, or body gestures that are used to strengthen or underline character objectives. Examples include pounding on the table, pointing vigorously, shaking the head, and pulling back the torso. Such gestures are frequently suggestive of intense emotion.

3. Habitual gestures are personal mannerisms that may betray a character's nervousness or hint at inner objectives that differ from the external mask of the character. Fiddling with a collar, running the hands through the hair, straightening one's clothes, and playing with coins in the pocket are all examples of habitual gestures. (See fig. 6.3.)

Figure 6.2.   *The Birthday Party* by Harold Pinter. In this moment from *The Birthday Party*, how does the use of space and environment suggest a different type of relationship from the one in *Gemani* (Figure 6.1)? (Photograph: Joe Meyer. Courtesy Montclair State College, Major Theatre Series. Set and lights: John Figola; costumes: Joseph F. Bella.)

Using Gestures

This exercise combines right- and left-brain functions. With a partner select a scene from the appendix or any scene of your own choice. Determine scene objectives for your characters. Then develop at least one occupational, one emphatic, and one habitual gesture for each character. Show the class a nonverbal presentation of your characters in the scene using the three types of gestures and attempting to achieve their objectives. (You may incorporate the spatial element of relationships you worked on earlier.) Each pair of partners follows this procedure. After every presentation class observers should identify the gestures by category and determine the scene objectives of the characters.

DISCUSSION

1. Which types of gestures and specifically which gestures were most effective in helping to communicate the character objectives?

Figure 6.3.   *"MASTER HAROLD" . . . and the boys* by Athol Fugard. Can you find in this illustration an occupational gesture, a habitual gesture, and an emphatic gesture? (Photo © 1982 by Martha Swope. Used by permission.)

2. Which gestures (if any) were distracting from the objectives or seemed inappropriate for the characters and situations? Why?

Progressive Activities

> Getting the sardines on. Getting the sardines off. That's farce. That's life. That's the theater.
>
> ———*Michael Frayn*, Noises Off

The third method of physicalizing objectives to enhance characterization is through a progressive activity, which is an action or a series of actions which may detail the characterization, establish the environment, highlight objectives, or clarify character relationships. Some directors may call such activities "business," but the term progressive activities implies a more specific use of the concept. Whereas "business" may suggest that the actor is simply given something to fill in time while on stage, a progressive activity reveals something important about the character's individuality or objectives. A progressive activity also helps the actor flesh out the through-line-of-action that the character uses to work toward the achievement of the superobjective. Specific progressive activities may be found in the script, such as the use of the guns and the water in the scene from *Sister Mary Ignatius Explains It All*

For You included in the appendix. Alternately, the progressive activities may be developed by the actor or director.

The progressive activity, like a miniature play, should have a definite beginning, middle, and end. This design gives shape to its purpose. Unfinished progressive activities are confusing. In a recent professional production of Eugene O'Neill's *Anna Christie* a character picked up a broom, swept the floor for a moment or two, then abandoned the activity, never finishing the job by picking up the sweepings. The audience might have interpreted the action as that of an indolent character, but the pointless abandonment of the activity suggested that neither the actor nor the director had used the activity for anything other than a means of occupying the character with an unfinished environmental activity. This activity led nowhere and seemed only to fill in the time when the character was on stage.

In contrast a completed progressive activity enhances character objectives. In a summer stock production of William Inge's *Bus Stop* the alcoholic professor, Dr. Lyman, wanting to charm Elma, the young waitress behind the counter, kept emptying his orange juice glass and moving it closer and closer to the girl for refills. Eventually Dr. Lyman moved from a more distant stool to a closer one in an effort to close the space between himself and the girl. The drinking and refilling of the orange juice (the beginning) began the objective; the movement of the empty glass (the middle) developed the objective; and the completion of the objective—to get closer to Elma—

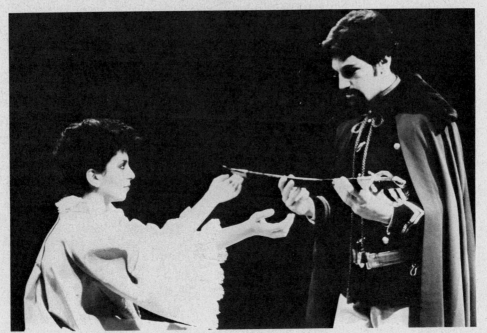

Figure 6.4 *La Ronde* by Arthur Schnitzler. In this turn-of-the-century play, a progressive activity with Freudian overtones was developed with The Count proffering his sword to The Actress. (Montclair State College, Major Theatre Series. Set and lights: John Figola; costumes: Joseph F. Bella.)

was achieved when the character finally moved to the stool closest to the young waitress (the end). This activity had a beginning and a middle directed toward an attainable end. (See fig. 6.4.)

Using Progressive Activities

These exercises require integrated-brain functions.

A. Find scenes in the appendix that contain progressive activities written into the script. What do these activities reveal about characterization, the environment, character relationships, or character objectives?

B. Find scenes in the appendix with no apparent progressive activities written into the script. How many things can you think of that might be used as progressive activities for the characters in these scenes? Perform some of these ideas for the class.

C. Since most progressive activities require the use of hand props (any physical object that can be held in the hand), bring a prop to class that may be called for by the script or that you have decided would be useful in a particular scene. Working individually in your own space, as other class members are doing, find ways in which the prop is normally used.

On an agreed-upon signal leave the prop in the space you worked in, and along with others in the class rotate to a different prop brought by someone else for another character. Find a reason for the new prop appearing in your own scene. How does your character use this unexpected prop?

D. Repeat exercise C, but this time find an unusual way to deal with the prop, an action for which the object was not intended. For example, a deck of cards might be used as a fly swatter or a sock might be used as a handkerchief. First work with the prop that you have brought in, then in rotation, work with props that others have brought in.

DISCUSSION

1. Which progressive activities helped establish the environment?
2. Which progressive activities developed individualization of characters?
3. Which progressive activities developed character relationships?
4. Which progressive activities advanced character objectives?

E. In the next improvisation or scene that you perform for the class, fill the scene with as many props as you can justify your character using. Use one of the props in a fully developed progressive activity.

DISCUSSION

What observations can you make about your concentration and focus when you are using dialogue and dealing with props at the same time?

Focusing Actions: Movement and Dialogue

Objectives can also be physicalized by pointing up actions in relation to speech. Physical actions can exist in three locations relative to a line of dialogue. They may precede a line, they may occur during a line, or they may follow a line. The location of a physical activity may help to stress the physical activity and its implications, or the location may stress the line and its implications.

Pointing Up Movement and Dialogue

Try each of the following lines three times, once each with the suggested physical activity before, during, and after the line given.

A. (Cross from the middle of the room to a door, and pause at the door.) "I have to catch a train right now."
B. (While seated at a desk, slam your fist on the desk.) "I have decided to destroy the competition."
C. (Snap open a fan and flutter it rapidly.) "I will fix you up like a red-hot mama! You can catch a drunken sailor—and 'Man overboard!'"[3]
D. (Fold a newspaper shut.) "If the economy continues like this, my business is ruined."

DISCUSSION
1. Was the difference of emphasis distinct with each placement of movement?
2. How much agreement or disagreement is there among the class observers about the implications of each change in placement of physical activity?
3. In which types of plays do you think the placements of physical activities relative to lines are most crucial?

Obstacles

Character objectives become stronger and more sharply defined when confronted with carefully developed obstacles. Obstacles test a character's will and determination and provide a means of making the pursuit of objectives varied and interesting. Development of obstacles is a challenge to the performer's imagination, for though the playwright may supply a few of the more obvious obstacles in the text of the playscript, most of the development of obstacles will come from the imaginative (right-brain) functions and the logical (left-brain) functions of the performer.

External Obstacles

The most obvious obstacles are those elements in the script itself that stand in the way of the character's achievement of his or her objectives. These obstacles may be of two types. The first type is an environmental obstacle. Anything in the setting, physically (for example, furniture) or imagined (for example, weather), may be used as an environmental obstacle.

A second type of obstacle is that raised by other characters. Character obstacles are the psychological or physical barriers that other characters deliberately or unknowingly put in the way of the first character's objectives.

The more instability the obstacle creates for a character, the greater the effort he or she must make in attempting to restore stability. This is why serious drama, melodrama, and farce are so filled with action. These types of plays contain formidable obstacles that require the characters to exert great effort in attempting to restore stability. Both types of obstacles—environmental and character—will now be examined in more detail.

Environmental Obstacles Anything that occurs in the environment—from an event as large as a fire to an incident as small as dropping a contact lens—creates an imbalance. A character must react and attempt to overcome the obstacle in order to restore stability. Frequently, the script itself will contain specific environmental obstacles. In other scenes where no environmental obstacle is evident, you may enhance and intensify the playing of the scene by creating a suitable environmental obstacle.

Environmental obstacles are most effective when they can be seen as impediments to character objectives. Recently in one of my acting classes, students performed a scene from the second act of Martin Sherman's *Bent*. The characterizations were believable and the objectives clear, but the scene was flat. Inspired by the simple suggestion that the prisoners were using their mental attempts at making love to overcome the cold of the environment, the two performers gave the scene an intensity it had not previously achieved.

Environmental obstacles may be psychological as well. For example, a scene in which characters are fearful of being overheard by others will play more dramatically as the characters intensify their quieter vocal communication.

Determining Environmental Obstacles

A. Examine the scene from *The Good Woman of Setzuan* in the appendix. What environmental obstacle do you find in the script? How many things can you list that the characters might do to deal with the environmental obstacle?

B. Invent environmental obstacles for the characters in the scenes from *Ah, Wilderness!* and *Crimes of the Heart*. How many things can you list that the characters might do to deal with the invented environmental obstacles?

DISCUSSION
1. How would the use of any of the environmental obstacles relate to character objectives?
2. How would the use of the environmental obstacles enhance or intensify the playing of the scenes you have examined?

Obstacles of Opposing Characters Other characters frequently present obstacles to the objectives of a particular character. The obstacles may be physical when characters literally stand in the way of other characters. The obstacles may be psychological when one character intellectually or emotionally undermines the objectives of another character. (See fig. 6.5.) Additionally, the obstacles may be a combination of both the physical and the psychological. For example, a character might both wave a gun and utter a threat.

Figure 6.5. *The Birthday Party* by Harold Pinter. Both physical and psychological obstacles are created in this scene in which Goldberg and McCann badger Stanley. (Photograph: Joe Meyer. Courtesy Montclair State College, Major Theatre Series. Set and lights: John Figola; costumes: Joseph F. Bella.)

Determining Character Obstacles

A. Examine the scene from *Night Must Fall* in the appendix. What is Olivia's objective? What physical and psychological obstacles does Dan present to Olivia? What adjustments must Olivia make to deal with the obstacles?

B. Examine the scene from *Marat/Sade* in the appendix. What is the objective of the inmate playing Duperret in relation to the inmate playing Charlotte? What psychological and physical obstacles does Duperret encounter? How does he attempt to overcome these obstacles?

C. Examine the scene from *Hotel Paradiso*. What is Victoire's objective? What physical and psychological obstacles does Max present? How does she attempt to overcome these obstacles?

D. Improvise any of the scenes in which you have identified objectives and physical or psychological obstacles. Focus on overcoming the obstacles.

DISCUSSION
How does the focus on overcoming obstacles sharpen performances?

Internal Obstacles

Though not as obvious as external obstacles, internal obstacles are just as valuable in intensifying a character's pursuit of objectives. Internal obstacles are any internal character traits, inhibitions, mental reservations, or complexes that complicate or prevent a character from achieving his or her own objectives. An example you are probably familiar with is Laura's shyness in Tennessee Williams' *The Glass Menagerie*. Though Laura would like to make friends (her objective) with Jim O'Connor, her shyness (the internal obstacle) makes her objective extremely difficult to achieve, and creates greater tension both internally and in her relationship with Jim.

Determining Internal Obstacles

A. After you have identified objectives for the characters in the scene from *Ah, Wilderness!*, *Hotel Paradiso*, and *The Effect of Gamma Rays on Man-in-the-Moon Marigolds*, or other scenes of your own choice, find or create internal obstacles for each character.

B. With both actions and words, improvise the scenes from exercise A, first without using an internal obstacle, then using one.

DISCUSSION
What differences do class observers note between the two performances?

Determining Psychophysical Obstacles

Occasionally, the psychological restraint may be the direct or indirect result of a character's physical problem. Cyrano de Bergerac's generous nose, for example, gives him an internal complex about his relationships with women. This complex prevents him from wooing Roxanne for himself, so he woos her vicariously for Christian. Often physical problems create bigger obstacles in the mind of the character than in other characters who relate to them.

Examine the scenes in the appendix from *The Good Woman of Setzuan* and *Crimes of the Heart*.

DISCUSSION

1. Can you find a physical basis for the inhibitions (internal obstacles) of any of these characters?
2. Are psychophysical restraints and inhibitions usable even in characters for whom the playwright has not indicated a physical problem?
3. At what point could psychophysical internal obstacles become distracting?

Tempo-Rhythms of Action

You cannot master the method of physical actions if you do not master rhythm. Each physical action is inseparably linked with the rhythm which characterizes it. If you always act in one and the same rhythm, then how will you be able to embody a variety of characters convincingly?

————*Konstantin Stanislavsky*

The use of tempo-rhythms is one of the most valuable techniques you will learn for creating character actions and repeating them for performance. As a repeatable right-brain function, tempo-rhythm provides a reliable reference point for maintaining consistency in performing character objectives.

Developing Tempo-Rhythms from Life Studies

Observe someone that you know fairly well. Consider age, sex, movement patterns, habitual tempos of moving and speaking, the amount of space typically used for gestures, and whether the person is relatively tense or relaxed, introverted or extroverted. Then consider the person's occupation—its routine or irregularity, whether it is indoors or outdoors, regular or occasional; consider the person's recreational activities—the hobbies, music, books, plays and television he or she enjoys. After you have these things in mind, clap out a tempo-rhythm pattern reflecting as much as you can about the person. Clap this tempo-rhythm for the class. The class should try to describe the personality of each member's life study solely from listening to the tempo-rhythms clapped.

DISCUSSION

1. How many things that you had in mind did the class pick up from the clapped tempo-rhythms?
2. Did the class pick up anything you did not consider about the person but that is, nevertheless, accurate?

Discovering Tempo-Rhythms with Single Objectives

At this point return to the improvisations that you worked on from the section on improvisations with words and movement in chapter 5. Instead of using words, clap your way through the actions of a selected improvisation.

By substituting tempo-rhythms for words you are opening up a direct channel to your right brain, linking the tempo-rhythmic intuition with your external behavior. Focus on trying to influence others in the improvisation with your tempo-rhythm. Do not let the tempo-rhythm of others affect your own tempo-rhythm.

DISCUSSION
1. What discoveries did you make about the tempo-rhythms of differing situations (environments and circumstances)?
2. What discoveries did you make about the tempo-rhythms of differing relationships?
3. What discoveries did you make about the tempo-rhythms of differing objectives?

Creating Complex Internal/External Tempo-Rhythms

Complex characters and objectives require a tension or contrast between internal tempo-rhythms and external tempo-rhythms.

In each of the following improvisations, which require integrated-brain functions, both characters should be portrayed with an external tempo-rhythm that contrasts with the internal tempo-rhythm. Internally, the character is dealing with one objective-obstacle pair, and externally with a contrasting objective-obstacle pair. The first four improvisations are original, and the last three are suggested by scenes (though modified) from contemporary plays. (The play titles appear in the notes at the end of the chapter.) Discussion questions follow the entire group of improvisations.

A. Setting: your room in a dorm or an apartment. You were up late the previous night, studying for a crucial final exam. The alarm clock failed to go off, and you are about to be late for the 9:00 o'clock exam. Your well-meaning roommate, who also overslept, insists while preparing breakfast that you eat something before you leave because you haven't eaten a good meal in a couple of days. The roommate believes you'll never make it through the exam unless you have some nourishment first.

B. Setting: hotel room. You have been attending a convention and you had a blast at the final party last night. In the middle of the night you are jarred from your groggy sleep by the sound of fire alarms. A firefighter appears at the window to get you out of the room safely. The firefighter urges you to come out immediately, but you have valuable papers and clothes that you insist on taking with you.

C. Setting: family living room. You are a college student living at home. You arrive home after a strenuous day of classes to discover that your prized possession, a new stereo speaker, has been broken by a younger sibling. Though seething inside, you try to coax a confession out of your sibling, who initially denies having damaged the speaker. The sibling, nervous with guilt, attempts to hide responsibility, but circumstantial evidence eventually leads to a confession, assumption of responsibility for the loss, an attempt to make restitution and reconciliation.

D. Setting: college instructor's office. A student enters to attempt to have a failing grade changed. The young instructor is up for tenure. During the course of the plea the student informs the instructor that the student's father is chairman of the college board of trustees which will consider tenure for the instructor. Notice how the power situation and the tempo-rhythms shift when this information comes out.

E. Setting: a couple's bedroom, late at night. The husband shambles in upset, but stunned. He has had a minor car accident and therefore returned from an incompleted business trip. This is the third time something like this has happened. His wife, awakened by the noise of his return, is also upset but must help to calm him down. He tries to soothe her by minimizing the incident, but internally he is concerned about his own ability to carry on after this third accident.[4]

F. Setting: the dressing room of a theatre. You stagger into the dressing room, having tried to drown your sorrows over bad reviews for your work in the play you are now supposed to perform. This is not the first time you have come in drunk before a performance. One of the other cast members tries to sober you up and prepare you to go onstage. You want only to enjoy your memories of the good old days before you started getting bad reviews and began to drink heavily.[5]

G. Setting: the bedroom of a physically handicapped, sensitive young painter. A young actress must play a handicapped person in a forthcoming play. She visits the artist to observe his behavior and to understand his attitude toward his handicaps. The artist knows he is on display, but he is attracted to the actress and would like to see her again. Because of his self-consciousness he stammers through the interview.[6]

DISCUSSION
1. For each character discuss the objectives and obstacles used.
2. For each character discuss the inner and outer tempo-rhythms. Were the inner and outer tempos fast or slow? Were the rhythms smooth or erratic (legato or staccato)?
3. What inner feelings were stirred by the contrast between inner and outer behavior?

H. Try improvising a scene from the appendix, giving each character a justification for a different inner and outer tempo-rhythm.

Summary

In this chapter you have examined the action level of the craft of acting. You have worked with the superobjectives of characters, linking them to scene objectives, beat objectives, and moments. You have discovered the usefulness of environmental actions and spatial actions. You have enhanced objectives through characterizing actions—occupational, emphatic, and habitual gestures—and through purposeful progressive activities with a beginning, a middle, and an end. You have deepened the complexity of character actions through the use of internal and external obstacles.

Lastly, you worked with the tempo-rhythms of actions to help make actions consistent and repeatable.

In the next chapter you will examine the word level of the craft of acting and relate the actions of characters to the dialogue that they speak.

Notes

1. Constantin Stanislavski, *Creating a Role*. Translated by Elizabeth Reynolds Hapgood (New York: Theatre Arts Books, 1961). See "Creative Objective," pp. 51-56; "The Superobjective and Through Action," pp. 77-81.
2. Cited by Vasily Osipovich Toporkov, *Stanislavski in Rehearsal*, p. 213 (New York: Theatre Arts Books, 1979).
3. Ramon Delgado, *A Little Holy Water* (Schulenburg, Texas: I.E. Clark, 1983). This is a gag line. At what point was the physical activity most effective in triggering a laugh?
4. This situation is similar to the opening scene in Arthur Miller's *Death of A Salesman*.
5. This situation is suggested by *The Dresser* by Ronald Harwood.
6. This situation is suggested by *The Elephant Man* by Bernard Pomerance.

For Further Reading

Beckerman, Bernard. *Dynamics of Drama*. New York: Drama Book Publishers. 1979. "The Theatrical Segment," pp. 44-56; "The Dramatic Segment," pp. 56-77; "Activity and Action," pp. 120-128.

Chapter 7
The Level of Words

Suit . . . the word to the action.

————*Shakespeare*, Hamlet

Words Follow Action

The words of a play—the lines of dialogue—are second in importance to the actions. Without clear, meaningful delivery of the playwright's language, you could still communicate the dynamic action, but you would lose many of the subtleties of character individualization, the incisiveness of the play's logic, and the beauty of aptly chosen words. That the dramatic intensity may communicate without the words being understand was illustrated in 1984 at New York City's Lincoln Center when Peter Brook's highly acclaimed production of *Carmen* performed in French thrilled a predominantly English-speaking audience. Those who understood French received a double whammy—the action and the words.

The right-brain qualities of words come from the suggestive sensations of their sounds and their image-evoking abilities; the left-brain qualities of words convey their intellectual and logical content. Both types of qualities are necessary for an integration of meaning in creative performances.

First, we will examine the variables of nonverbal sounds. The exercises for nonverbal sounds all use right-brain functions. Then we will consider the image-evoking quality of words, another right-brain approach. Next, we'll look at the left-brain intellectual and logical content of words. Lastly, we'll integrate the right-brain and left-brain approaches by combining them in monologues and scenes.

Sounds

If we dispense at first with words, it is only to make clear that words are the *result* of an inner state, an inner, physical state, related to the senses, which conditions the spoken word.

————*Michael Saint-Denis*, Training for the Theatre

The goal you want to achieve by starting with sound rather than with words is to recapture the inner experience for which the playwright's words are but a pale shadow. The communication theorist Marshall McLuhan recognizes the problem language creates in removing us from the sensations of the original experience when he says:

> Language does for intelligence what the wheel does for the foot and body. It enables them to move from thing to thing with greater ease and speed but ever less involvement.[1]

By first eliminating the left-brain word symbols of language you can gain access to the right-brain, sound-making and tempo-rhythm abilities, which stimulate the senses and increase the vividness of your image-making ability.

Silence as a Canvas for Sound

Returning for a moment to the earlier comparison of acting with the visual arts, you will find it helpful to regard the space of your performance as a canvas now sketched in with the lines of action and waiting for the textures of sound. Silence is the canvas on which this texture clings. The bare surface of silence is made tangible and exciting by the contrasting textures arranged on it.

As you discover the textures of sounds appropriate for a particular character in a specific scene, you will gradually add to the textures on the canvas of silence until you have filled in all but those moments when silence prevails. These patches of uncovered silence are very powerful reminders of the social fabric on which the sounds are placed. The silent patches reveal moments of decision and reaction that are inexpressible in the limited textures of words. At such moments you and your character are suddenly exposed in all your vulnerability to the vicissitudes of fortune. Without the sound textures surrounding these chinks in your social armor, neither you nor your character creation would be recognizable as social creatures.

Words as Sounds

> Jeremy [Irons] uses the instrument of his voice with great variety. He plays all the notes—he's a bit like a jazz clarinetist.
>
> ————*Tom Stoppard*

Vowels As Melody; Consonants As Tempo-Rhythm The melody of the voice comes from the changing pitches of the vowels; the changing resonances give the vowels tonal color. The tempo-rhythms of the voice are produced by the stops and starts of the action of the consonants. Together the vowels and consonants create the music of the spoken or sung voice.

Both the vowels and the consonants have their place in the right-brain/left-brain concept of creative performance. The vowels (with the exception of the neutral, unaccented schwa [ə]) are unconstricted and sustainable sounds, which make them a more effective vessel for carrying the nuance of volitional and emotional right-brain meanings than are the consonants.

The consonants (except for the nasal sounds), are constricted or self-destructing sounds, which make them suitable for shaping intellectual, left-brain meanings. Yet used singly without shaping word symbols, the consonants are just as much a right-brain function as are the vowels.

Voice as the Sound of the Body It is not our purpose here to study the production of sound and articulation with scientific analysis. That you may do in voice production classes. But all the scientific analysis in the world cannot replace the awareness of physical sensations you must cultivate to use your voice creatively as the sound of your body.

As sight is the brain's interpretation of light waves received by the eye, so sound is the brain's interpretation of vibrations picked up by the ear. The major source of body vibrations to extend sound communication to another person are the vocal folds in the larynx.

You can feel these vibrations easily by placing the tips of the fingers of both hands over your throat and under your jaw and humming at a pitch in your own middle range. Note what happens to the vibrations when you move from a hum to an open-throated and sustained "ah." Though the vibrations of your vocal folds do not change, the sensation in your fingertips indicates that vibrations are stronger. This sensation is the result of the reinforcement of vibrations in the throat cavity and oral cavity. The greater the space for the reverberations to bounce from wall to wall as they reinforce one another, the greater the palpable vibrations.

Place your fingertips on your pectoral muscles (upper chest), lower your pitch, hum, then open your mouth to a sustained "ah." Did you feel vibrations in the chest? Though these vibrations may not affect appreciably the actual resonance of the voice, the experience should help you understand the concept that it is the total body producing the sound of the voice, not just the vocal folds. When you are fatigued or ill, your voice reflects the weakness of your body. When you are feeling terrific, your voice is strong and crisp.

Texture of Sounds The texture of sounds comes from resonance. This resonance, or quality of body sound, varies with the placement of the vibrations, the size of the resonating cavities, and the resiliency of the linings of the cavities. You may have studied in a voice class that the three principal resonators are the throat, or pharynx; the mouth, or oral cavity; and the nasal cavity. (See fig. 7.1.) Though there is verifiable left-brain observation in this analysis, such an approach tends to focus vocal resonance work in the head instead of perceiving resonance as the product of the intentions and expression of the whole body. In performing all the vocal exercises throughout this chapter and in your later work, you should cultivate ways to base the voice in a physical context. This context connects the internal impulse of the entire body with the sound so that the voice reflects as much right-brain influence as possible.

There are nine distinguishable resonance textures that are useful to explore: conversational, nasal, denasal, gutteral, oral, aspirate, pectoral, falsetto, and oratund. Though you should practice the nine separately to understand the differences and to develop your range of textures, you should not apply them mechanically while working on a character but rather assimilate them into your own natural expression as your vocal development matures.

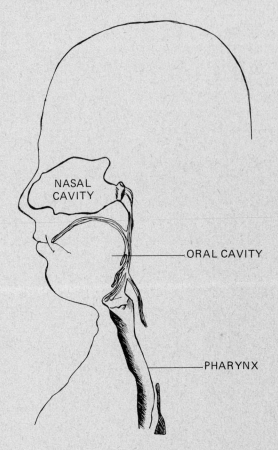

Figure 7.1.   Vocal Resonators. The primary vocal resonators are the pharynx or throat area, the oral cavity or mouth, and the nasal cavity. Control of the placement of resonance creates the nine different vocal textures discussed in the text.

    1. The conversational quality is your normal, everyday, intimate quality. In most people the conversational quality is thinly resonated and does not project clearly beyond a few yards. This is the quality that you hear most of the time from television and film actors. In the media, microphones pick up the conversational quality and amplify it electronically, preserving what you may think of as the lifelike quality of everyday speech. Unfortunately, the conversational texture is usually inadequate in volume for the stage, except in the most intimate theatres. In some regions of the United States the conversational texture may be colored with the nasal or the oral textures, depending on the social level and education of the person speaking.

    2. The nasal quality has an overbalance of resonance in the nasal cavity. It has a reedy, narrow texture with much of the stream of sound flowing out the nose. You can find this quality by humming on an "n," then directing your voice where you feel the buzz of the "n." There are localities such as the Bronx in New York and parts of New Jersey where the nasal quality is so prevalent that it serves as the conversational quality for many people.

    3. The denasal quality has little or no resonance from the nasal cavity. This is a texture you may hear from a person with a nose stuffed up from a cold or allergy. You can force a denasal quality by pinching your nose shut to find the location of the

placement of your resonance. You will find the focal point for this resonance somewhere toward the back of the roof of your mouth (the area of your soft palate).

4. The gutteral quality is a harsh, tension-filled sound, resonated primarily in a
tight throat. If maintained for any length of time, the tensions used to produce the
gutteral texture can irritate the vocal folds and surrounding membranes. We use this
texture naturally when we are angry, and some people who use it habitually gain the
reputation of being grouches. When using this texture on stage in moments of anger
or tension, the least effort that will produce the quality is the most desirable, for
permanent damage can result from the tight throat that produces the quality.

5. The oral quality receives most of its resonance in the mouth (or oral cavity).
This is the quality associated with "pear-shaped tones," the "how now, brown cow"
school of diction. The character of the secretary on the "Beverly Hillbillies" television
series used this quality, which contrasted sharply to Granny's nasality.

6. The aspirate quality has a breathy, sensual texture to it. It is produced by
allowing an excess of breath to pass through the vocal folds. It is a quality useful as
a stage whisper, for it contains enough vibrations to carry the voice and enough
breath to pass for a whisper. The late Marilyn Monroe used this quality well for both
serious and comic effect.

7. The pectoral quality has its source in an extremely open throat, usually accompanied by a lowered pitch. Some older ministers and priests have affected a
habitual use of this quality from the pulpit because it suggests reverence and has a
quality of otherworldliness. Darth Vader (James Earl Jones's voice) in the film *Star
Wars*, and its sequels, uses a pectoral quality.

8. The falsetto quality is a thinly resonated, high-pitched texture that you often
may hear accompanying animated cartoons. This quality may have other texture
colorings such as the nasal or oral. Generally it does not project well in the theatre
because of its thin resonance, but it may be useful for some types of fantasy characters.

9. The oratund quality has a rich, full texture with resonance well distributed
among the throat, oral, and nasal cavities. If it is developed for its own sake, apart
from inner intentions and sensations, it may sound artificial. But a well-grounded
oratund voice is musically alive and full of excitement.

Exploring the Textures of Sounds

A. Take the following series of vowel and diphthong sounds through each of the
nine vocal textures:

ae ah ee ehi ahi o u oi ou

B. Take the following nasal sounds through each of the nine vocal textures:

m n ng ng ng   m n ng ng ng

C. Use the vocal warm-up exercise F from chapter 2 (b-a-d, etc.). Run the entire
series through each of the nine textures.

Pitch of Sounds The more extensive use you can make of your physical
range for pitch, the more possible variety you will have responding in performance for

a range of characters. Variation in pitch animates and energizes vocal sounds, while the pattern of habitual pitches used by a character provides the melody unique to that individual.

Exploring Sound Pitches

A. Step Pitches. 1. Using the letters of the alphabet, start with a pitch as low as you can produce comfortably, and step up to the next highest pitch with each letter. Do not sing the sound, but sustain it on a spoken pitch.

2. Then start the alphabet with the highest pitch you can comfortably produce (without going into falsetto), and with each successive letter step down to the next pitch.

3. Repeat both phases of the exercise, singing the pitches.

B. Slide Pitches. 1. The first time you do this exercise, you should use the spoken voice. Again using the alphabet, start as low as you can, slide smoothly from one pitch to the next on the same letter. Then step up to the next letter and slide up a tone on that letter. Continue until you have covered your entire range.

2. Repeat the alphabet starting at your highest pitch and working down: A-slide, step-B, B-slide, step-C, C-slide, etc.

3. Repeat both phases of the exercise, singing the pitches instead of speaking.

DISCUSSION

1. What differences do you observe between the spoken pitches and the pitches that you sing?
2. Are there any differences between the sensations of stepping and sliding?

Volume of Sounds

Speak loud, or they'll get another little girl.

————*Lillian Gish*

As a child auditioning for the stage, Lillian Gish received the above advice regarding projection. The voice obviously has to carry the words to the audience, yet Charles Laughton used to advise theatre students during his visits to the Dallas Theater Center, "Children, don't shout! You must woo your audience as tenderly as a lover woos his mistress."

The necessity of projection versus the desire for intimacy—how is one to reconcile these opposites? If you project with enough volume for those in the last row to hear you, won't you seem terribly artificial for those near the stage? Yet if you use a natural-sounding conversational texture, will you be heard past the first few rows of the auditorium?

First, you must recognize that performing on a stage in a large auditorium is an artificial condition with accepted conventions necessitated by that artificiality. One of these accepted conventions is the projection of the actor's voice.

Second, you must support the voice from the abdominal muscles and lower rib muscles, not try to achieve projection by tightening the throat in a shout. Tightening the throat constricts sound and strains the vocal folds. Letting the voice rest on the support of the abdominal muscles and lower rib muscles will carry your sound intentions freely through the resonators and to the audience. A voice so supported will have all the flexibility of texture and pitch you are capable of without seeming to audience members in the front of the house that you are straining to be heard in the back row.

Projecting Sounds

A. Talking to the Wall. With your entire class, stand about six feet from the wall. Using nonsense syllables, fill the distance between yourself and the wall with just enough volume to reach the wall. Gradually move backwards, increasing the volume as you move away from the wall. Achieve your projection by focusing the placement of your sounds toward the front of the hard palate (roof of your mouth).

B. Talking to the Deaf Person in the Back Row. The class divides into pairs. The pairs separate as far apart as space allows. If they can do this in an auditorium, all the better. One person at a time gives a line of nonsense syllables to the distant partner, who then responds with nonsense syllables. After everyone has had an opportunity to participate, partners join each other, and, standing about four feet apart, communicate in nonsense syllables again but project the sounds the same distance as when they were separated.

DISCUSSION
1. Did anyone have difficulty in projecting the distance? If so, can changes in vocal placement alleviate the problem?
2. What differences did you find between projecting to a distant partner and projecting with your partner close to you?
3. Have you found the minimum volume level you must maintain to be heard the distance of the space?

Both of the projection exercises above are valuable to work on with partners when you are rehearsing a play in a large auditorium. Use nonsense syllables first, then lines from the play.

Stress of Sounds: Rhythm   The stress pattern of sounds establishes a rhythm. Though the stress patterns of prose are not as evident as the stress patterns for poetry, they are just as important for your actions, characterizations, and delivery of words. In practicing the rhythms in the following exercise, you will sensitize your voice and ear to variations in spoken rhythm patterns.

Using Sound Rhythm Patterns

The following sound rhythm patterns may be used individually or as a group exercise. Repeat each line of sounds, stressing the boldface syllables.

1. Ta-**ta**, Ta-**ta**, Ta-**ta**, Ta-**ta**
   Ta-**ta**, Ta-**ta**, Ta-**ta**, Ta-**ta**

2. **Ta**-ta, **Ta**-ta, **Ta**-ta, **Ta**-ta
   Ta-ta, **Ta**-ta, **Ta**-ta, **Ta**-ta
3. **Ta**-ta-ta, **Ta**-ta-ta, **Ta**-ta-ta, **Ta**-ta-ta,
   Ta-ta-ta, **Ta**-ta-ta, **Ta**-ta-ta, **Ta**-ta-ta,
4. Ta-ta-**ta**, Ta-ta-**ta**, Ta-ta-**ta**, Ta-ta-**ta**
   Ta-ta-**ta**, Ta-ta-**ta**, Ta-ta-**ta**, Ta-ta-**ta**
5. Ta-**ta**-ta, Ta-**ta**-ta, Ta-**ta**-ta, Ta-**ta**-ta
   Ta-**ta**-ta, Ta-**ta**-ta, Ta-**ta**-ta, Ta-**ta**-ta
6. **Ta**-ta-ta-ta, **Ta**-ta-ta-ta, **Ta**-ta-ta-ta
   Ta-ta-ta-ta, **Ta**-ta-ta-ta, **Ta**-ta-ta-ta
7. Ta-ta-ta-**ta**, Ta-ta-ta-**ta**, Ta-ta-ta-**ta**
   Ta-ta-ta-**ta**, Ta-ta-ta-**ta**, Ta-ta-ta-**ta**
8. Ta-**ta**-ta-ta, Ta-**ta**-ta-ta, Ta-**ta**-ta-ta
   Ta-**ta**-ta-ta, Ta-**ta**-ta-ta, Ta-**ta**-ta-ta
9. Ta-ta-**ta**-ta, Ta-ta-**ta**-ta, Ta-ta-**ta**-ta
   Ta-ta-**ta**-ta, Ta-ta-**ta**-ta, Ta-ta-**ta**-ta

Try the same rhythm patterns with different consonant and vowel pairs (for example, Bo-bo, De-de).

DISCUSSION

1. Do any of the rhythm patterns suggest particular moods or atmospheres?
2. Do different consonant and vowel combinations change your response to the sounds or the rhythms?

Tempo of Sounds The length of all vowel sounds (except the neutral schwa [ə]) and some consonants may be sustained without interruption, limited only by the capacity of your breath support. Quickly paced dialogue comes from the short duration of vowels and variable consonants, while slowly paced dialogue comes from the elongation of vowels and variable consonants.

Using Sound Tempos

To practice the differences in sustained and unsustained sounds repeat the previous exercise on sound rhythm patterns at three different speeds, sustaining the vowels on the slower tempos:

1. very slowly
2. moderately
3. very fast

DISCUSSION

1. Do you find different internal reactions to different tempos of sound?
2. Do any of the rhythm patterns seem to suggest different things when set at different tempos?

Words

The Transfer to Words

All the qualities you have worked on with sounds—texture, pitch, volume, rhythms, and tempos—may be applied to words. You should go back to the previous exercises substituting words for sounds but treating the words as if they are sounds rather than symbols of concepts. The important point is that you develop a kinesthetic sensitivity to the sounds of words and minimize your intellectual distancing from them. As the vocal coach Kristin Linklater suggests:

> The aim is to get the words out of the head and into the body where they are experienced emotionally and viscerally. The usual approach to the text is to worry out the sense in your head first.[2]

The exercises in the first half of this chapter have been relatively easy for the right brain to perform, for using sounds alone is so foreign to the left brain that it ignored your experiences in what it regards as nonsense. But when we move into the use of words, the left brain perks up and begins to encroach on right-brain efforts to connect the body's intentions with symbols that the left brain thinks it should be controlling. In the next exercise we shall sneak past the left-brain monitor and connect right-brain body intentions with words.

Producing Words from the Body

This exercise builds on the tempo-rhythms and the body exercise you worked on earlier in chapter 3.

Select two lines from a scene in the appendix or from a scene of your own choice. In turn with every other person in the class, stand and deliver the lines as meaningfully as possible to the class. Then follow the eight steps below.

1. Still standing, place a large, resonant hum in the mouth. Let it swell upwards, vibrating into the nasal cavities and cheekbones, *dans le masque* as the French say. Lower the head slowly, letting the vibrations travel down the neck and spine. Take a breath as you need it to keep the vibrations of the hum going. Drop the arms and chest forward, encouraging the vibrations of the hum to travel down the spine, through the rib cage and lower back. Go all the way over until your dangling fingers touch the floor. If you have any difficulty encouraging the vibrations down the spine as you lean forward, then actively vibrate the muscles of your body as you go down.

2. Keep the sensation of the vibrations of the hum centered in the lower back and stomach as you slowly elevate the body from the base of the spine upwards. Vibrate the muscles of the body if necessary to maintain the sensation of the low center of the hum.

3. Repeat steps 1 and 2, first with the sound "A-a-ah," then with the sound "O-o-oh."

4. Repeat steps 1 and 2 alternating the words "no" and "go."

5. Repeat steps 1 and 2 using the exclamation "No, I won't go!"

6. Take the first line from the two you have selected and delivered earlier. Use only the vowel sounds from the line, repeating the vowels as you move them on a round trip through step 1 and step 2.

7. Add the consonants to the vowels of your line from the scene. Take the words through the round trip of step 1 and step 2.

8. Maintaining the physical connection with the body that you have established in the exercise so far, but standing erect, repeat your first line and move on to the next line, first with vowels only, then with consonants and vowels.

For practice you may continue the process throughout an entire scene.

DISCUSSION

1. At what points in your body did you find tensions that inhibited the transfer of vibrations? The jaw? The neck? The shoulders? The middle of the rib cage? The lower rib cage? The middle of the back? The lower back? (There will be a variety of locations in different people.)
2. Did the physical vibrations help to loosen the points of tension so that the vibrations could travel more easily?
3. What differences in delivery of the lines did you experience after doing the exercise?
4. What differences in delivery did the class observe in each person after the exercise?

Words as Image Makers

An actor is creative only when he uses sound to paint an image he visualizes.
——*Konstantin Stanislavsky*

Creating Images from Words

Class members sit in a circle. With a specific visual image in mind for each word spoken, one person at a time delivers the single word. After each word is said, other class members tell the impression they received from the delivery of the one word. (See fig. 7.2.)

A. Concrete Words (Visualize a specific image):
dog   car   room   food   tool
B. Abstract Words (Visualize a specific situation):
justice   honor   love   truth

DISCUSSION

1. When class members came close to naming the visual image or the situation visualized by the speaker, what characteristics in voice or body language suggested the image?
2. When class members did not come close to the visual image or situation visualized by the speaker, can any reasons be identified to explain why the images did not come through?

Figure 7.2.   Image Projection with Words. The projection of images stirs a response. Even if a different image from the one projected is received, the imagination of both sender and receiver has been activated.

The Literal Word: Denotations

HENRY: Words . . . [a]re innocent, neutral, precise, standing for this, describing that, meaning the other, so if you look after them you can build bridges across incomprehension and chaos. But when they get their corners knocked off, they're no good any more. . . . If you get the right ones in the right order, you can nudge the world a little or make a poem which children will speak for you when you're dead.

————*Tom Stoppard*, The Real Thing

Words, of course have literal meanings, as Henry declares in the speech above from Tom Stoppard's play, *The Real Thing*.[3] Words stand for objects present and not present, for abstract ideas and fantastic dreams. They are symbols we use to communicate political differences and exchange gossip. Dictionaries give us the generally accepted, literal meanings of words: these are the denotative meanings. For clarity and intellectual meanings the actor must understand all the literal, or denotative, meanings of the words in a script.

Using Word Denotations

Using the scenes in the appendix, and your left-brain functions, find five words whose literal meanings you are unsure of or do not know. Look them up in a dictionary. Find the correct meaning for the words in the contexts of the lines.

Share your five words, their meanings, and the lines they came from with the rest of the class. Deliver the lines as free from interpretation as possible, sticking to the dictionary meanings of the words.

DISCUSSION
1. Were any of the meanings brought into class not suitable for the lines they came from? If so, how could this create confusion for an audience?
2. Why were the deliveries of the lines using only denotative meanings unexciting?

The Suggestive Word: Connotations

The eccentricities in her delivery reduced some of the play's least controversial passages to a special kind of meaninglessness. Often it had merely to do with where she put the emphasis in a sentence; almost invariably an unsuitable action indicated that she had entirely missed the point of the words.

———*Mimi Kramer*

Words change in meanings from their dictionary definitions as they are used or misused by characters. The literal dictionary meanings may be modified by usage so that the words imply other interpretations. Words also may be used ironically to mean exactly the opposite of their literal meanings. Such usages are connotative.

Using Word Connotations

From the scenes in the appendix or scenes from a play of your own choice, find five words whose meaning in the context of the lines probably would not be found in the dictionary. Read the lines and give your understanding of the meaning of the word in this context. The word may be used ironically, or in a figure of speech that changes the usual dictionary meaning.

DISCUSSION
1. What differences do class members have with the meaning you attribute to the connotative words in context?
2. Why are there fewer agreements on the connotations of words than on the denotations?

To Illustrate or Not to Illustrate

Sometimes words may be illustrated or emphasized with gestures. At other times the same illustration or emphasis may be redundant or distracting. Usually the style of the play and the nature of the character will help you decide whether an illustrating gesture is useful or necessary. In more realistic plays, for example, we can frequently distinguish appropriateness by the social level and education of the character. The more refined and sophisticated the character, the fewer illustrative gestures; the more uneducated and unmannered, the greater likelihood of using more illustrative and emphatic gestures to accompany words.

The Subtext of Words

Treasure the words of a text for two important reasons: first, not to wear the sheen off them, and second, not to introduce a lot of mechanical patter, learned by rote and bereft of soul, into the subtext of the play.

———*Konstantin Stanislavsky*, Creating a Role

Discover the Subtext

The message underlying the words is called the subtext. The subtexts of words may include the character's objectives (that is, what the character wants from other characters) and the character's awareness of circumstances surrounding the relationships with other characters. The subtext may also include internal images and impressions stirred by the language of the dialogue. Actors uncover the subtext so that they can reveal the character's thoughts and intentions to the audience.

Finding Subtexts

A. Subtext in Individual Words. Mark Twain once reported that he made his way around Germany with only four words: please, beer, kiss, and thanks. Saying one word at a time, see if you can convey the following subtexts:

Please
1. May I have a taste of your ice cream?
2. Leave me alone.
3. Don't leave me all alone.
4. I want to make love to you.
5. What did you say?
Beer
1. This is very good.
2. You call this good beer?
3. I'm drunk, but I want to get drunker.
4. You spilled your beer on me.
5. May I buy you a drink?

Kiss
1. You contemptible swine!
2. Do me a little favor.
3. Deep and sensuous.
4. Goodbye, my dearest one.
5. A candy sweet for Valentine's Day.
Thanks
1. No one's made me feel like that in ages.
2. He didn't even give me the time of day.
3. For directions to the rest room.
4. For directions to the next town.
5. I won't forget the little favor you did.

B. Subtext in Dialogue. Take a few lines of dialogue from any of the scenes reprinted in the appendix or from a play of your own choice. Write out a subtext for the lines. Next, read the lines to the class conveying only their denotative meanings. Then interpret the lines with the subtext that you have written. Members of the class then offer their interpretation of what they think your subtext might be. Lastly, read the subtext that you have written.

DISCUSSION

1. Can class observers distinguish the difference between the lines spoken as denotative words and spoken with subtext?
2. How close did class observers come to understanding your subtext?

Covering the Subtext

I'm thinking one thing but trying to mask it by saying another. You have to find the thought line of the character and inform every moment onstage with it. You know what you're thinking, and the lines sit on top.

————*Jeremy Irons*

In his observation on playing the role of Henry in *The Real Thing*, the British actor Jeremy Irons suggests a technique that instead of illuminating the subtext attempts to mask it. (See fig. 7.3.) We will work with this technique again later from the viewpoint of characterization. But for the present, we will focus on the word level of the problem.

Masking Subtexts

Use a few lines from a scene in the appendix or from a play of your own choice. First read the lines to the class for the denotative word level meaning. Next present the lines attempting to reveal the subtext. Lastly, present the lines with the subtext in mind, but attempt to conceal the subtext with a different intention.

Figure 7.3. *The Real Thing* by Tom Stoppard. Jeremy Irons as Henry sometimes deceives Glenn Close as Annie by playing against the literal meaning of the text. (Photo © 1983 by Martha Swope. Used by permission.)

DISCUSSION
1. What are the internal differences between revealing and concealing subtext?
2. What differences do class observers perceive between presentations of revealing and concealing?

The Monologue

The techniques suggested here are useful for monologues, long speeches, and audition pieces. In addition, many of these principles may be easily applied to the development of scenes of interaction with other characters.

The characters in effective monologues must have objectives just as they do in improvisations or scenes with other characters. They must also struggle to overcome obstacles, either external ones such as environmental obstacles or the use of props, or internal ones such as an inhibition or counter-objectives to the primary desire of the characters. One of the most effective means of playing a monologue is to find the two sides or objectives within the character that oppose each other. Think of the monologue as an internal debate between these opposing sides. If one of these sides is right-brain oriented and the other left-brain oriented, all the better. For example, in Diane's lengthy narrative speech from *Sister Mary Ignatius Explains It All For You* (see the appendix) Diane's right-brain pleasure in revenge could be in conflict with her left-brain demand for understanding.

The questions below will help you focus on the important elements of a monologue. Answering the questions will help you develop the monologue with meaningful variety and excitement.

Developing a Monologue

A. Use one of the longer speeches from a scene in the appendix or a monologue or long speech from a play of your own choice.

Analyzing the speech with your left brain, ask

1. What does the character want?
2. Whom does the character want it from?
3. What tactics does the character use to obtain it?
4. Where is the conflict? External? Internal?
5. What is the surprise? To the character? To others?

Analyzing the speech with your right brain, ask

6. What images in the language involve the senses?
7. Where are the high points and low points (peaks and valleys) of intensity?
8. Where is the humor? Towards yourself? Towards others?
9. Where is the love? For people? Things? Ideas?
10. What is left unsaid? Why?

B. Decide on two sides of the character that are in contention as suggested above. Develop a progressive activity that helps to manifest the character's objectives. Then perform the monologue.

DISCUSSION

1. Which of the points raised above were clearly evident in the monologue?
2. Which of the points raised above were not clearly evident? What could be done to make them more clear?
3. How did the performer create a sense of truthfulness at the action and word levels that made the class observers believe the character?
4. What could the performer do to achieve a greater sense of truthfulness at the action and word levels?

The Scene

Apply the principles of performing monologues to scenes on the action and word levels. Select a scene from the appendix of this text or from a play of your own choosing. First, examine the scene from the viewpoints of the action level and the word level. Then perform the scene for the class. Try one or more of the following listening exercises before presenting the scene a second time to the class.

Listening for Subtext

Half of acting is reacting to the other actor in character. One reason for weak reactions is a lack of effective listening to the words and intentions of the other characters. Each of the three exercises below is a way of sharpening your listening skills so you will listen intently to the words and voice of the other character and be able to respond with greater sensitivity.

A. Sit or stand back-to-back with your partner and listen carefully to each other's words and voice before responding with each successive line.

B. First, clear the rehearsal space of sharp or dangerous objects. Then turn off the lights and move about at random in the dark room. (You can accomplish the same thing in the light by putting on blindfolds.) Play the objectives and subtexts of your lines with as much vigor as possible, aiming your response towards the location of your partner when you heard your partner's last line.

C. Play the scene using only physical movements (spatial relationships and progressive activities), vowels, and diphthongs to communicate your intentions and subtexts. Do not indicate anything that you cannot communicate through natural gestures and voice.

After you have tried one or more of the three approaches to sharpening your listening and reacting, play the scene for the class again with the dialogue from the play script.

DISCUSSION
1. What differences did either you or your partner perceive in your performances of the same scene after doing the exercises?
2. What differences did the class observers perceive in your second performances?

Summary

In this chapter you have examined the second level of the actor's craft, the level of words. You have experimented with those right-brain variables of body sound that give texture, rhythm, tempo, melody, and projection to words. You have looked at both the left-brain surface meanings and the right-brain underlying meanings of words, the images they evoke, and the intentions they convey.

You have put your new awareness of the action and word level of the craft of acting into practice with monologues and scenes from plays, developing reactive responses to your partner with techniques for more sensitive listening. These techniques serve as a sound foundation for your next level of development, the level of unconscious role playing.

Notes

1. Marshall McLuhan, *Understanding Media* (New York: McGraw-Hill, 1964), p. 79.
2. Cited by Helen Dunbar, "Plumb the Heart of the Bard's Words," *New York Times*, 28 August 1983, p. H 5.
3. Tom Stoppard, *The Real Thing* (London: Faber and Faber Limited, 1982), p. 54. Courtesy of the publisher.

For Further Reading

Balk, H. Wesley. *The Complete Singer-Actor*. Minneapolis: University of Minnesota Press, 1977. Chs. 10, 11, 12.

Berry, Cicely. *Voice and the Actor*. New York: Macmillan, 1973.

Fincher, Jack. *Human Intelligence*. New York: G.P. Putnam's Sons, 1976. Ch. 3.

Grotowski, Jerzy. *Towards a Poor Theatre*. New York: Simon & Schuster, 1968. "Actor's Training," pp. 175-204.

Lessac, Arthur. *The Use and Training of the Human Voice*. New York: Drama Book Publishers, 1967.

Linklater, Kristin. *Freeing the Natural Voice*. New York: Drama Book Publishers, 1976.

Machlin, Evangeline. *Speech for the Stage*. New York: Theatre Arts Books, 1970.

Shurtleff, Michael. *Audition*. New York: Walker, 1978. Ch. 2.

Chapter 8
The Level of Unconscious Role Playing

HENRY: It's to do with knowing and being known. . . . Knowledge of each other, not of the flesh but through the flesh, knowledge of self, the real him, the real her, *in extremis*, the mask slipped from the face. Every other version of oneself is on offer to the public. We share our vivacity, grief, sulks, anger, joy. . . . [I]n pairs we insist that we give ourselves to each to other. . . . Personal, final, uncompromised.

———*Tom Stoppard*, The Real Thing

As suggested in the above speech from Tom Stoppard's play, *The Real Thing*, people reveal themselves on different levels.[1] Characters in plays are also revealed in different levels of behavior. In this chapter and the two that follow you will develop three important levels of characterization—the level of unconscious role playing, the level of conscious role playing, and the level of emotions. As suggested earlier, unconscious role playing and conscious role playing shape the overall impression of characterization as mass and shape form the image on the painter's canvas, while emotion provides the coloration of the image.

Unconscious Role Playing vs. Conscious Role Playing

The first level of characterization, unconscious role playing refers to the way in which characters in plays, like people in daily life, relate to one another in recognizable, unself-conscious social relationships. The unconscious role-playing relationships are those without any manipulation or self-awareness about the nature of the relationship as a role being played. Such roles are performed effortlessly in life. Unconscious role playing includes mother-child relationships, lover-lover relationships, friend-friend relationships, student-teacher relationships—all relationships that are naturally assumed and performed in life without the participants being consciously aware that a relationship is being enacted by social beings. As the philosophy professor Arthur C. Danto observes in his book review of *Personal Being* by Rom Harre, "To be a person is to be a set of roles, where each role has its place in a different structure of social life. . . . [T]he reality of the self is exactly the set of roles one plays."[2]

On the other hand, conscious role-playing individuals (or characters) are aware of the nature of the roles they are playing and may even consciously plan their behavior to accomplish clearly defined goals for themselves. For example, a car salesperson and a customer clearly understand the purpose of their roles—the salesperson to make the most money, the customer to get the best bargain. Each may be very aware of the gamesmanship involved in the purchase of a new car—the offers and counteroffers. With the salesperson eager for the highest price and the customer eager for the best bargain, each conscious role player uses whatever tactics he or she may possess to maneuver into the most advantageous position.

Any time a person or a character becomes aware of the social roles he or she is performing—even those roles that are more frequently played unconsciously (such as those of mother and child)—then the relationship becomes a conscious role-playing relationship. Hamlet is an excellent example of a character who plays the conscious role of a "madman." With Polonius and with Rosencrantz and Guildenstern, Hamlet as madman puzzles and confuses those who seek to know what he is really trying to do. At other times Hamlet unconsciously plays the role of "friend" to Horatio, "hale-fellow-well-met" with the gravediggers, and "dutiful son" to his father's ghost. In each role Hamlet unconsciously plays there is no level of pretense, as there is with those he consciously plays. The actor playing Hamlet must be skillful enough in portraying Hamlet in the conscious madman role to convince Polonius and the others that he is indeed mad.

In the creative processes of acting, these two levels of role playing—unconscious and conscious—frequently will merge with each other and blend with the other levels as well. However, these two levels of characterization have features that are so distinctive that you can identify and develop them separately before assimilating them into the craft of unified creative performances. In this chapter you will work on the seemingly more natural process of unconscious role playing for characterization, and in the next chapter you will develop the more manipulative, layered craft of conscious role playing. Also in the next chapter you will work on an additional refinement, the semiconscious role-playing technique, which blends the unconscious level with the conscious level.

Unconscious Role Playing in Daily Life

Unconscious role-playing relationships are not always the obvious family, friendship, boss-employee, or husband-wife relationships that are self-evident in daily life. Nor are the roles played unconsciously limited to those nominally supplied by a playscript. Rather, they consist of the complex, changing roles of dynamic relationships that develop in mature social exchanges.

Let us look first at an obvious example from life. At present you are playing the role of "scholar" on an unconscious level while dutifully reading your assignment. You may find a statement in your reading that you do not understand. You then become a "puzzled student," but you don't have to examine your puzzlement consciously to play this role. The role results unconsciously from your reaction to the text. You read a statement that you disagree with, and you become an "aesthetic critic." You read an exercise that you think might be exciting to try, and you become an "eager, budding performer."

You go to class, playing "chum" with your fellow students. You disagree over a point with your teacher, playing "star debater." You chat with the teacher after class as "student" with "adviser," or possibly as "friend" and "confidante." Your teacher conducts rehearsals that evening and the two of you are "actor" and "director."

At each moment of the experiences mentioned you were yourself, yet the attitudes that you had at any given moment defined a different unconscious role (or relationship) that you were playing. The role you were playing unconsciously shaped your physical and vocal responses. Notice that you are playing different roles even when reading this text, for the social relationship is with the personality created by your impression of the person behind the words of the text or even with the words themselves. So a character on stage alone can unconsciously play roles with whatever objects are present, just as he or she can unconsciously play roles with other characters.

Although you are able to make observations about yourself relating to others and to objects through different unconscious roles in daily life, you are not necessarily conscious of playing the roles at the time you play them. When you perform a characterization on stage, however, one that is varied by many unconscious relationships, you, the performer, consciously select the roles the character plays unconsciously.

Unconscious Role Playing on Stage

Portraying the unconscious roles of a character on stage, the actor uses art to conceal craft. It takes a great deal of conscious effort on your part to make the performance seem spontaneous for the audience. In rehearsals you set up the boundaries or framework for this apparent spontaneity. This is a marvelous paradox of acting. In an effective performance there is the freedom and honesty of truthful response framed by the illusion of a real event, fostered by the character's actions within the given circumstances of the playscript. The actions and given circumstances firmly set in your left brain supply the boundaries beyond which your behavior cannot stray, but your right brain is free to improvise, even during performance, within those boundaries.

Advantages and Limitations

To achieve both the left-brain control of unconscious role playing and the right-brain freedom of expression within those roles requires deep personal honesty, openness of expression, and a strong personal identification with the relationships that your character has with other characters. (See fig. 8.1.) Some actors and directors believe this is the only level at which an actor should work. For many performers, however, the unconscious role-playing level of characterization severely limits creative growth, for confinement to this level tends to encourage work on a personality basis. Acting only within the bounds of personality keeps actors from stretching their own self-images and thus limits the range of character roles they can convincingly portray and the scope of styles they can perform.

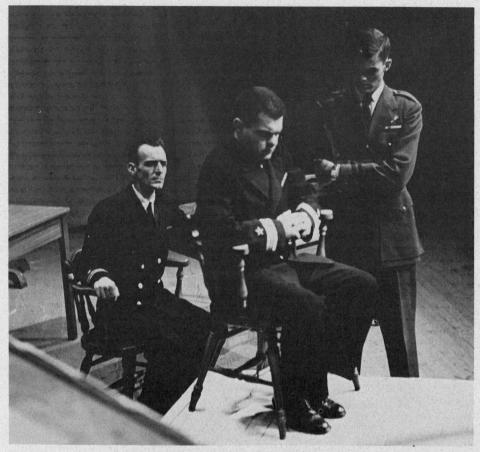

Figure 8.1.   *Caine Mutiny Court Martial* by Herman Wouk. The characters in this intense courtroom drama are made believable by close association of the actor's unconscious roles with those of the character. (Photograph by Kent. Courtesy of Stover Theatre, Stetson University. Director: Charles C. Ritter; set: Bruce Griffiths; costumes: Lisa Hammond.)

Limiting yourself to a personality approach to characterization also keeps you from taking those exciting risks that result in artistic growth. Nevertheless, your personality is an excellent level of characterization with which to begin, for it demands honesty and truthfulness from yourself at your present level of self-awareness. Additionally, the intelligent application of your present self-image can carry you deeper into a characterization unlike yourself than you might initially suspect.

Growth through Role Playing

You will discover that the more social roles you attempt to characterize for the stage, the more social roles you may become comfortable with in daily life. This development will show you that your personal growth is just as much a product of the growth of your imagination as it is a result of broadening your experiences in daily life. Developing social roles is somewhat like the unfolding of a lotus blossom. For every petal that unfolds to catch the sun, another petal begins to peel off from the undifferentiated clump in the center.

Playing Campus Types: Students and Instructors

A. With your right brain, identify specific types of students on campus. You might find types such as "the jock," "the nerd," "the grind," "the campus queen." Do these types have characteristic ways of dressing, walking, gesturing, and talking? Though there may be a degree of conscious role playing in some individuals, most of these student types will not think of themselves as consciously playing a role.

Individually in your own working space, explore the walk, posture, gestures, facial expressions, energy levels, and tempo-rhythms of a particular student type you have observed.

B. With both sides of your brain, develop a group improvisation with a variety of different student types meeting in a student hangout and present it to your class.

DISCUSSION
1. What made the student types recognizable to the class observers?
2. Though the types were recognizable, were there also details in the presentations which individualized the unconscious role playing of the characters?

C. With your right brain, identify specific types of instructors such as "busy committee member," "burned out has-been," "pompous scholar," "horny lecher," "social activist," and "sentimental romantic."

D. With both sides of your brain and with your class paired off as partners, improvise scenes between an unconscious role-playing student type and an unconscious role-playing instructor type.

Suggested situations include the following:

1. Student appeals a poor grade.
2. Instructor propositions a student.
3. Student propositions an instructor.
4. Instructor and student want the same book in the library.
5. Student spills coffee on instructor in dining room.

DISCUSSION
Use the same discussion points as those suggested under exercise B.

The Character's Unconscious Roles vs. The Actor's Unconscious Roles

MERRICK. You must display yourself for your living then. Like I did.

MRS. KENDAL. That is not myself, Mr. Merrick. That is an illusion. This is myself.

MERRICK. This is myself too.

————*Bernard Pomerance*, The Elephant Man

In this passage from *The Elephant Man* we have an observation on stage performance that extends the paradox of performing.[3] While the characters of Mrs. Kendal and Merrick are saying "This is myself," the audience knows that the performers playing Mrs. Kendal and Merrick are creating on stage the character illusion that Mrs. Kendal says she creates when she acts on stage. (See fig. 8.2.)

The characterization illusion created for the audience and the unconscious roles the characters appear to play in this illusion rest on the ability of the performer to analyze with the left brain the roles that the character plays in relationship to other

Figure 8.2.   *The Elephant Man* by Bernard Pomerance. In theme and presentation this moving play examines the parallels between the illusions and realities of beauty, life, and performance. (Photograph: Jonathan Stealey. Courtesy of Findlay College, Ohio. Director: Barry Alexander; set: Charles Ackerman; costumes: Teresa Clark; performers: Brien Hagerman, Pam Fiser.)

characters. But the illusion and roles also are dependent on the right-brain ability of the actor to bring to his or her own consciousness the unconscious roles he or she plays in life. It is your own unconscious roles then, that are the basis for developing the unconsciously played social roles of the characterization. As the British director Peter Brook observes:

> For theatre to be seen at its most alive, there has to be a very, very exact balance between the living personality of the performer and the second personality, which is that of the character. . . . It is a flash of insight that comes from the confrontation of the performer's hidden world and the hidden world of character. . . . It's not a question of the actor saying, "What would *I* do in these circumstances?" But, "given these circumstances, how can I understand what *he*, the character, is doing?"[4]

The right-brain functions and left-brain skills are brought together in putting the characterization on stage. The actor consciously blends the knowledge of the character's unconscious roles with his or her own awareness of unconscious roles in daily life. As Jean Benedetti writes in his survey of the Stanislavsky system of acting:

> By creating organic links between the actor's own personality and the character he was playing, the damaging rift between the actor as human being and as performer could be healed.[5]

Exploration of Your Own Unconscious Roles

The first step, then, in developing the character's social roles is to explore the roles that you yourself unconsciously play in everyday life.

Getting to Know Yourself through Others

We will tackle this problem first through a right-brain exercise, then through a left-brain exercise.

A. Role-playing Mirrors. Scene: a student apartment or dorm room. This right-brain exercise is improvised first without dialogue.

1. The class divides into pairs of the same sex (men paired with men, women with women). One person in the first pair begins the exercise by engaging in activities typical in his or her own dorm room or dwelling. Activities might be eating, studying, or cleaning the room. The second person in the first pair immediately mirrors the activities of the originator. This exercise may be performed by pantomiming the use of props, but everyone should be explicit in the details of using any imaginary objects. After the activity is established in the room by the first pair, a second pair interrupts the first. The originals in each pair greet each other and are mirrored as closely as possible by the "mirrors" to each person. The original in the room then engages the guest in a new activity, such as dancing, helping with the cleaning, eating, or making love. Again the "mirrors" follow suit.

2. The exercise is performed a second time without words but reversing roles (that is, the originators become the mirrors and vice versa). The originators should choose their own different activities for the second round.

3. After the exercise has been performed the second time without words with roles reversed, it is performed a third time, improvising words.

4. Lastly, the exercise is performed a fourth time (also with improvised words), swapping originals and mirrors.

After everyone has completed these four steps, then the class should engage in discussion of the exercise. (If space permits, several quartets may be working on the exercise simultaneously. If not, everyone in the class should have an opportunity to work through the entire exercise before discussion.)

DISCUSSION

1. What social roles can be identified either by individuals themselves or by others in their quartet?
2. What social roles can be identified by class observers (if the exercises were performed for class viewing)?
3. In what respects did classmates find the observations of their own social roles by others to surprise them?
4. Why do you think your social roles were played even more unconsciously after the arrival of the second pair? (If they weren't, why not?)

B. Comparing Roles. The object of this left-brain exercise is to discover through comparison with a series of partners the kinds of roles you unconsciously play with others. By searching for likenesses and differences in four major areas you can put together a mosaic of the way you impress others, and you can use this profile as a basis for formulating a list of the roles you might be playing unconsciously with your classmates in your own daily life.

1. The group is divided into pairs, and each person in turn explores two questions: a) How are we alike? and b) How are we different?

To make these comparisons, use the following Personality Profile form to gather your information in four categories: physically, socially, psychologically, and spiritually. The form may also be used as a device for creating information for the biography of a character from a play. It may help your comparisons to jot down the answers to the questions.

Personality Profile

1. PHYSICALLY?

    a. race _____

    b. sex _____

    c. age _____

    d. birthmarks _____

    e. scars _____

    f. operations _____

    g. childhood diseases _____

    h. muscular development _____

    i. coordination _____

    j. health _____

    k. physical activities enjoyed _____

    l. sleep habits _____

   m. eating habits _____

    n. physically dominant or submissive _____

2. SOCIALLY?

    a. family life _____ (single, married, divorced, children)

    b. introverted or extroverted _____

    c. organizations active in _____(number and importance)

    d. recreational activities _____ (number and importance)

    e. cultural activities _____ (number and importance)

    f. friends and/or lovers _____ (number and importance)

    g. business activities _____ (number and importance)

    h. political activities _____ (number and importance)

3. PSYCHOLOGICALLY?

    a. ambitions _____

    b. phobias _____

    c. feelings of guilt _____

    d. confidence or insecurity _____

    e. attitudes toward sex _____

    f. greatest sense of satisfaction _____

    g. greatest frustrations _____

4. SPIRITUALLY?

    a. importance of spiritual beliefs _____

    b. believer or skeptic _____

    c. member of organized religion _____

    d. beliefs about spiritual being _____

    e. beliefs about an after life _____

    f. beliefs about ethical values _____

    g. relationship of spirit and body _____

_____

    2. Compare the likeness and differences between yourself and your partner.
    3. With the entire class participating, identify and discuss the variety of roles you can now identify that you have played or may play in daily life.

DISCUSSION
1. As the class discussion proceeds, how many roles mentioned apply to you personally as well?
2. Which (if any) of the social roles mentioned also might be played consciously (that is, with deliberate intention for specific results)?
3. If there are roles that you play unconsciously that make you uncomfortable, can you find reasons why they do so?
4. If there are roles that you play unconsciously that you enjoy a great deal, can you find reasons why they do so?

Exploration of the Character's Unconsciously Played Roles

You're no emperor; you're an onion.
And I'm going to skin you, Peer, old top!
. . .
(Starts peeling an onion layer by layer.)
This outer layer, like a torn coat—
It's the shipwrecked man on the drifting boat.
. . .
The prospector life was a run for the money;
. . .
And now this rough-skinned layer—why,
That's the fur trader up at Hudson's Bay.
. . .
Here's the archaeologist, brief and brassy.
And here's the prophet, green and juicy.
. . .
(Pulls off several layers at once.)
These layers just go endlessly on!
Shouldn't it give up its kernel soon?
(Pulls the whole onion apart.)
Damned if it does! To the innermost filler,
It's nothing but layers—smaller and smaller—

                        ————*Henrik Ibsen*, Peer Gynt

    It is unusual to find a character who lists the roles he has unconsciously played after playing them, as Henrik Ibsen's Peer Gynt does in the quotation above.[6] Therefore, for most plays you will have to study the script and experiment with several different social roles until you find those unconsciously played roles that best suit the character's superobjective and the objectives for a given scene.

Identifying Unconsciously Played Roles

For this integrated-brain exercise use any of the scenes from the appendix (except the scene from *Marat/Sade*, which has a double role-playing problem for later work) or a scene from a play of your own choice.

1. Read the entire play.
2. Determine the major unconsciously played roles (relationships) the character plays in the entire play.
3. Determine beats in the selected scene as you learned in chapter 6 on the level of actions.
4. For each beat create a change of unconsciously played social roles. (See the examples in the appendix provided for *The Effect of Gamma Rays on Man-in-the-Moon Marigolds*.) In a production the same unconsciously played social role may be repeated within a scene, but until you learn to develop the social roles as a matter of craft, try a different role for each beat.
5. Practice the scene, and either with scripts in hand or as a major memorized project, present the scene to the class.
6. How close do class observers come to identifying the unconsciously played roles you attempted to portray?

Psychophysical Techniques for Unconscious Role Playing

Linda is not the usual thing I do . . . There is not a whole lot of screaming and yelling and carrying on. She is very contained. In a way, that is more tiring. You can't get rid of any of the feelings.

———*Kate Reid*

The roles the characters play unconsciously usually are not extravagantly theatrical. Theatricality and flair will be found at times when the characters dramatize themselves in conscious role playing, which you will work on in the next level of craft. Your unconscious role-playing characters in the theatre should appear as natural on the stage as your own unconscious playing of roles appears in life. This is not to suggest that such portrayals should be inaudible or life-size, but rather that unconscious role-playing characters should flow easily and naturally from the inner connections you have made with your own unconsciously played roles from daily life. In the next five exercises you will work on naturalness, ease, and spontaneous, unconscious role playing through situations and improvisations.

You are not limited to your own unconsciously played roles in those portrayed for characters, but in order to give the characters' unconsciously played roles validity, you will want to find similarities or parallels to your own. The last exercise under this section will address the technique of using parallels.

Entrances With Unconsciously Played Roles

Entrances are extremely important in establishing social roles. The three integrated-brain exercises that follow will help you create the credibility for the character's offstage life as well as provide you with the opportunity to develop social roles on stage.

Entering to a Surprise

A. Scene: a student's apartment. This is an exercise for an entire class of 8 to 15 students. If the class is larger, it may divide into two groups, each performing the exercise simultaneously in its own space. One person goes out of the room. The rest of the group plans a surprise party for a special occasion for the departed classmate. When the group is ready, the person outside is summoned to reenter. When the entering person returns, however, he or she has received news of an emergency and must pack immediately to return to the parent's home. The person should invent a reason for the emergency that leaves the outcome of events uncertain.

B. Scene: an apartment shared by a couple. One member of a couple returns at the end of a day with champagne to celebrate an anniversary (the anniversary should be appropriate to age and probability, as, for example, wedding anniversary, living together, or going steady for a certain amount of time). The person waiting has the unhappy news that the relationship is over. He or she has a new lover. A third person, the new lover, enters from another room in the apartment in the middle of the scene between the first couple.

Make the relationships believable and life-size. Do not anticipate or plan reactions or relationships, but adjust to new obstacles as they arise.

DISCUSSION (for both A and B)
1. What differences did you perceive between the expected events and the events that occurred? How does this spontaneous adjustment relate to playing an unconscious role when the actor knows what events will occur in the script?
2. How real did your own reactions and the reactions to others in the improvisations seem to be?
3. How was the concept of unconscious roles aided by the surprise elements in the improvisations?
4. What is the value for performance preparation in a scene in which a character expects one situation but on entering finds a different one?

Entering the Shell of Social Roles

You will recall that while working on getting in touch with yourself in chapter 3, you did an exercise in which you stepped outside of your shell. This exercise reverses the process, except that here you will use unconscious role-playing shells of characters instead of your own habitual ones.

1. Select one of the scenes from the appendix or a scene from a play of your own choice. Working with a partner, you can take turns guiding each other through the narrative suggested in steps 3 and 4, pausing where appropriate for action.

2. Decide on three social roles that the character plays unconsciously in the selected scene.

3. Narrative: "Close your eyes. Visualize a dark forest ahead of you. From separate points in the forest come three similar, yet different, human forms. They are somewhat like yourself in height and weight, but the posture and walk are slightly different. As the forms come closer, you can see that they are wearing identical clothing and their faces are almost the same, but there is something slightly different in the gestures and facial expressions. When they are close enough, you realize that they are the three unconsciously played social roles of your character. Visualize the character in the three social roles directly in front of you."

4. Narrative: "Open your eyes, cross behind the first imaginary role-playing character. Unzip the shell from the back and step into the shell. Then zip it up. Move around in the 'shell'. Perform a progressive activity appropriate to the character's social role. When you have finished with the first shell, unzip it, and go on to each of the other two shells in turn, performing an appropriate progressive activity while inside each shell."

When everyone in the class has finished performing in all three social role shells, gather for discussion.

DISCUSSION

1. What differences did you perceive among the behavior patterns, tensions, or tempo-rhythms of the three shells?
2. What differences did you perceive between your own habitual behavior patterns, tensions, or tempo-rhythms and those of each of the shells?

Entering in Character

Using the given circumstances of the scene from which you chose your character in the previous exercise, you will now enter the room or location in the scene with the initial unconsciously played social role of the character. Use one of the shells from the previous exercise as your entering social role. You may use a flat or a two-fold screen as an entrance marker or a free-standing door frame, or you may use the door of your classroom or rehearsal hall. When you enter your scene, keep in mind the following:

1. Where is your character coming from? Why?
2. What social role does your character unconsciously engage in upon entrance?
3. What objective does your character have upon entering the scene?
4. What obstacles confront your character immediately upon entrance?
5. What adjustment(s) does your character have to make in achieving the initial objective?

DISCUSSION

1. What difficulties (if any) did anyone have in maintaining the illusions asked for in the five questions above?
2. What were some of the most interesting adjustments made?
3. How did the adjustments made affect the unconsciously played social roles of the characters?

Unconsciously Played Roles Through Improvisation

I feel like there are territories within us that are totally unknown. Huge, mysterious and dangerous territories. We think we know ourselves, when we really know only this little bitty part. We have this social person that we present to each other. We have all these galaxies inside of us.

————*Sam Shepard*

Exploring Unconscious Role Playing with Line Delivery

The purpose of this right-brain exercise is to tap your intuitive unconscious role-playing ability by experimenting with different ways of delivering lines. (The exercise may be done simultaneously by your entire class, with everyone saying their own lines in their own space at the same time.) Use the dialogue, one line at a time, from a scene you have presented for unconscious role playing only once to the class. Throughout the exercise you must keep moving randomly about the room. As you move, you may follow the instructions below for delivering each line aloud. After trying the same line in each of the five ways suggested, move on to the next line and deliver it in each of the five ways also.

1. Try the line as inflammatory political harangue.
2. Deliver the line as if you are worshiping at a religious shrine.
3. Whisper the line as if you are afraid of being overheard.
4. Give the line cynically, sarcastically, as if you didn't believe a word of it.
5. Proclaim the line as a declaration of love.

Move on to the next line and repeat steps one through five until you have gone through the entire scene. After you have completed the process for the entire scene, present the scene for the class, incorporating whatever discoveries you may have made.

DISCUSSION

1. What differences in complexity and variety of unconscious role playing do the class observers find in your postexperiment presentation?
2. Even though you are using words in this exercise, you are overriding the censorship of left-brain logic. What are the factors that help you override logic and tap into intuition?

Parallels to Unconsciously Played Roles

When you find that the roles the character plays unconsciously are foreign to your own experiences, you can bridge the gap by finding parallels in your experience. For example, if you were to play characters like those in the scene from *Night Must Fall* in the appendix, and you have never seriously threatened anyone or been seriously threatened by anyone, find within your experiences the closest applicable parallel. This might be an experience in which you were in physical danger.

If you were working on Olivia, you might examine a time when you were in a dangerous situation such as a traffic accident or even a near miss. Recall the experience as vividly as possible. What physical reactions did you have? Where were the tensions? What did you do or say? Who else was involved? What explanation can you find for Olivia's fascination with Dan despite his threat toward her?

If you were to work on the portrayal of Dan, you could consider the last time you were under such great pressure that you blamed someone else for your own failures— doing poorly on an exam, perhaps, or being late for an important appointment. Bring the details of the experience to mind. Who was involved? How did you behave? How did the other person react? Why does Dan break down?

Playing Parallels in a Scene

For a scene of your own choice, with your own parallels in mind, use both sides of your brain to perform two improvisations, one for your partner's parallel, and one for yours. Then rehearse your scene as it appears in the play.

DISCUSSION
1. Were you able to bring back the reality of the parallel experience through the improvisation?
2. Were you able to use the reality of the parallel experience in developing the actions and unconsciously played roles of the characters in your scene from a play?

Centering

Through our years of developing our own self-image, we tend to concentrate our energies in physical areas that reinforce our ideas about ourselves. As a result some areas of the body have greater focus, greater tension, or greater importance, than others. As these areas become part of our self-image, the way we hold our bodies suggests psychological attitudes to other people and so affects the roles we play with them. You were introduced to this concept of centering energy in chapter 3 as a technique for self-awareness. Here you will apply centering as a means of suggesting dominant unconsciously played roles for characters. You will recall from your earlier work that seven centers of focused energy are most useful: the head center, the oral center, the chest center, the stomach center, the gravity center, the genital center, and the anal center. In exaggerated forms focusing on these centers is an excellent way to begin the physicalization of roles for farce, but in subtle forms this technique is just as useful in developing unconscious role playing.

Developing Centers for Unconsciously Played Roles

A. As the members of the class walk around the room, they use the right brain to focus on one of the seven centers. Then they perform simple activities such as sitting, standing, or opening and closing a door, while maintaining their focus on a specific center.

B. In this right-brain exercise the class stands in a circle and divides into pairs. Each partner chooses a different center and then adapts his or her body to the selected centers. The first pair moves to the middle of the circle where the partners initially greet each other pleasantly. Then they threaten each other. Each pair repeats the process until all have participated.

C. With your left brain, observe your classmates and instructors. Which centers can you find among them? Can you identify from your acquaintances at least one person for each center?

D. With both sides of your brain, use one of the scenes you have been working on for unconscious role playing from the appendix, or from a play of your own choice. Rehearse the scene using a dominant center for the characters.

DISCUSSION
1. How does the use of the center change your interpretation of the character's unconsciously played roles?
2. How does the use of the center unify the other unconsciously played roles you have been working on?

Movement Types

From his study of movement (a left-brain analysis of a right-brain function) Rudolf von Laban, the choreographer for the Allied State Theatres of Berlin in the 1930s, observed eight distinct movement types based on the way in which people use tempo, intensity, and direction in moving. (See fig. 8.3.) These movement types, found in a simplified chart below, are valuable in developing unconscious social roles for the characters that you may portray.[7]

By using the extremes of each variable: weak or strong intensity, fast or slow tempo, peripheral or central origin of movement, Laban observed the eight basic movement types listed at each side of the chart. Thus, for example, a person whose movement flows from the periphery (or appendages) toward the trunk with weak intensity and fast tempo is a flutterer. A person with weak intensity and fast tempo whose movement originates in the trunk and flows out toward the periphery is a shaker.

Movements of Peripheral Origin (In-coming Movements)	Intensity	Tempo	Movements of Central Origin (Out-going Movements)
1. flutterer	weak	fast	5. shaker
2. striker	strong	fast	6. thruster
3. floater	weak	slow	7. slider
4. drawer	strong	slow	8. presser

Figure 8.3.   Movement Types

You should regard the eight movement types as starting points for character unconscious role playing rather than as finished physical movement patterns. Though most people tend to move with a single dominant pattern, changing emotions, situations, and relationships modify external behavior.

Combining each one of the eight movement types with each one of the seven centering types gives you a possibility of 56 different patterns of moving. You will find, however, that some of the centers will not work as well for some of the movement types as others. The large variety of movement patterns are a lot of fun to experiment with and can open up many more ways of responding physically than were previously in your movement role-playing vocabulary.

Developing Movement Types

A. In this right-brain exercise, as with the development of centers, you should first familiarize yourself with walking, gesturing, and performing simple activities such as sitting in a chair and getting up, or setting the table, consistently using each of the eight movement types in turn. Practice until you can move as a flutterer, shaker, striker, thruster, floater, slider, drawer, and presser with the least effort required to execute the activities.

B. With your left brain, observe your classmates and instructors for the intensity, tempo, and origin (direction) of their movements. Can you identify at least one person for each of the eight movement types?

C. With both sides of your brain, develop one of the eight movement types approoate to your character for a scene with unconsciously played roles. Rehearse the scene with your character moving according to the principles of that movement type. Then select a movement type you feel is inappropriate to your character. Rehearse the scene with your character moving according to the principles of that movement type. Play the scene both ways for your class. Which movement type does the class find most appropriate? Which movement type do they find most interesting?

DISCUSSION
1. For what jobs or occupations might each of the eight movement types be appropriate?
2. What are some unconscious roles each of the eight movement types suggest to you?

Contrasts for Variety

How do you know the shade of gray without a black and white?

Whichever techniques of developing unconscious roles you may find most helpful, the unconsciously played roles themselves should contain as much variety as possible within the range of the character's superobjective. As a painter uses a variety of shapes and forms to create more interesting pictures on canvas, so should you use contrasting unconsciously played roles to increase the variety of your characterization on stage.

Developing Contrasts for Unconsciously Played Roles

Using both sides of your brain and one of the scenes for which you have previously developed unconsciously played roles, develop one unconscious role with a weaker relationship to the other character and a different unconscious role with a deeper relationship. Perform the scene again with the new unconsciously played roles.

DISCUSSION
1. What differences did the class observers perceive in the performances?
2. How does the deliberate selection of contrasting unconsciously played roles enhance or detract from the characterization?
3. How does the deliberate selection of contrasting unconsciously played roles enhance or detract from the playing of objectives?

Summary

In this chapter you have examined the nature of the roles that characters unconsciously play in social relationships with other characters. You have observed similar unconscious role playing in your own life and developed your conscious use of this ability to portray characters as they play unconscious roles in scenes. The techniques of observation, self-analysis, using parallels, centering, and movement types suggested here for development of your unconscious role-playing ability integrated both right-brain and left-brain functions.

The principles used for developing the unconscious role playing of characters in scenes are applicable, of course, to full-length roles for which variety and development of unconsciously played roles enhance the interest of a characterization. In the next chapter you will add conscious role playing to the techniques you have learned so far in the creative craft of acting.

Notes

1. Tom Stoppard, *The Real Thing* (London: Faber and Faber, 1982, 1983), p. 63. Courtesy of the publisher.
2. Arthur C. Danto, "You Are What You Say," *New York Times Book Review*, 29 July 1984, p. 14.
3. Bernard Pomerance, *The Elephant Man* (New York: Grove Press, 1979), p. 28. Used by permission of the publisher.
4. Cited by Richard Eder, "The World According to Brook," *American Theatre* 1, no. 2 (May, 1984): 38.
5. Jean Benedetti, *Stanislavski: An Introduction* (New York: Theatre Arts Books, 1982), pp. 30–31.
6. Henrik Ibsen, *Peer Gynt* Translated by Rolf Fjelde. (Minneapolis: University of Minnesota Press, 1980). Used by permission of the publisher.
7. For another approach, see "Eukinetics," by Angiola Sartorio in *The Dance Encyclopaedia*, ed. Anatole Chujoy and P.W. Manchester, rev. ed. (New York: Simon and Schuster, 1967).

For Further Reading

Chekhov, Michael. *To the Director and Playwright.* New York: Harper & Row, 1963. Ch. 8.

Gregory, W.A. *The Director.* New York: Funk & Wagnalls, 1968. "Rite-Role Analysis," pp. 54–76.

Harre, Rom. *Personal Being: A Theory for Individual Psychology.* Cambridge, Mass.: Harvard University Press, 1984.

Laban, Rudolf von. *The Mastery of Movement.* 3d ed., rev. by Lisa Ullman. Boston: Plays, 1974. Ch. 5.

Stanislavski, Constantin. *Creating a Role.* Translated by Elizabeth Reynolds Hapgood. New York: Theatre Arts Books, 1961. pp. 44–50.

Wilshire, Bruce. *Role Playing and Identity.* Bloomington, Ind.: Indiana University Press, 1982. Chs. 11 and 12.

Chapter 9
The Level of Conscious Role Playing

Why, I can smile and murder whiles I smile,
And cry 'Content' to that which grieves my heart,
And wet my cheeks with artificial tears,
And frame my face to all occasions.

———*Shakespeare*, Henry VI, Part III

Relation of Conscious Role Playing to Unconscious Role Playing

In the above lines the future Richard III lays claim to being a conscious role-playing character, for the role that he presents to the world hides his true intentions as a mask hides the face of the wearer.

The technique of conscious role playing is the layer of frosting on the cake of the character's unconscious role playing. When we use the term *conscious role playing*, we refer to the self-aware use of social roles by the character in his or her relationship to other characters. This concept should not be confused with the actor's awareness of self when he or she plays a role. Conscious role playing is not a substitute for unconscious role playing; it is an embellishment that gives color and variety to the substance of the character's unconscious roles.

As with Richard III, conscious role playing sometimes is written directly into the script. (See fig. 9.1.) At other times conscious role playing may be a performing choice that you might make to enliven your characterization. In either situation you can use the technique to bring variety and excitement to a role. Professional actors such as Ron Moody use the technique, recognizing the need for contrast within a role. While creating the role of Fagin in a recent revival of the musical *Oliver!*, Moody referred to three consciously played roles, "I made him [Fagin] basically a clown or a tragic comedian. I also brought in a bit of the Pied Piper."[1]

At the end of the chapter you will consider a third identifiable mode of role

Figure 9.1. *A Little Holy Water* by Ramon Delgado. In this Cuban-American romantic comedy, the fortune teller Consuelo (Gretchen Pickeral) is consciously role-playing with her neighbor Mercedez (Carmen Zapata) to divert suspicion from her own affair with Mercedez's husband. (Photograph: Cass Mackert. St. Cloud State University Theatre. Set: Richard Baschky; costumes: Harvey Paul Jurik.)

playing—semiconscious role playing. Semiconscious role playing shares characteristics of both unconscious role playing and conscious role playing.

There are five major applications for the technique of conscious role playing in the development of characterization.

1. as a psychologically manipulative device
2. as a deliberate physical disguise
3. in jest
4. in animated narration of previous or imagined events
5. as a "characterization facade" for characters who are actor-characters in the playscript

We will examine each of the five types of conscious role playing separately, and you can develop your conscious role-playing skills with exercises for each type.

Conscious Role Playing as Manipulative Device

I love playing characters who seem to be one thing and are revealed to be something else. . . . It's wonderful for an actor to play deception onstage, because in effect it's the essence of the actor's art.

———*Jerome Kilty*

Frequently, characters have ulterior motives for their actions. Similarly, a character may distract other characters from their ultimate goal by means of an action that placates or deceives, as was illustrated with Hamlet's conscious role-playing madness in the previous chapter.

Characters thought of as villains are constantly deceiving other characters. But when you create the characterization for a villain, you should not let the character's ulterior motives become apparent to the other characters, for the other characters will appear naive not to see through the villain's chicanery. Indeed, the most interesting portrayals of villains are those that make them seem reasonably to be righting wrongs (as for example, Richard III) or repenting of past mistakes as does Moliere's Tartuffe when he grovels in repentance before Orgon, knowing full well that Orgon will praise his "piety" and trust him all the more.

Separating the Mask and Intentions

The following is a three phase exercise, requiring integrated-brain functions, that separates the mask of the character from concealed intentions in order to demonstrate the layering technique required for concealment.

1. In the first phase characters deceive one another through conscious role playing. Improvise the following situations:

A. An insecure employee has been persuaded by the employee's spouse to ask the boss for a raise with the threat to quit if the boss refuses. The boss is fearful of losing the valued employee but has been warned by the board of trustees to keep down expenses.

B. An aggressive car salesperson knows that the new models have a defect, but he or she needs the commission. The prospective customer tries to gain a higher trade-in value for an old car, but he or she has set the odometer back from 50,000 to 30,000 miles.

C. A man accuses his woman friend of going out with another fellow behind his back. The woman has done so, although she denies it, while the accusing man has been seeing another woman behind the first one's back.

2. In the second phase, separate the internal intentions from the concealing mask. After the first run-through of the improvisations, set up four chairs in a row, each chair a few feet from the next. The chairs on the two ends are for the inner thoughts of the character, the chairs in the center for the external behavior of the characters. (See fig. 9.2.) Improvise the same three situations a second time, but this time before each response, each character must sit in the end chair and reveal his or her inner thoughts to the audience before moving to a center chair to relate to the other character.

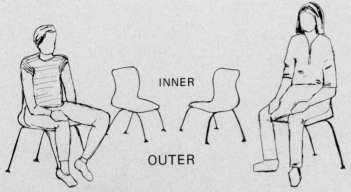

Figure 9.2.   Four Chair Exercise. Separating the inner thoughts from the outer response helps in understanding the conscious role-playing process.

3. In the third phase the mask and the concealed intentions are reintegrated. Repeat the improvisation in each situation without the extra chairs but internalizing each character's inner thoughts.

DISCUSSION
1. What differences in performance did the class observers perceive between the first and third presentation of the improvisation?
2. To what insights can the performers attribute any differences between the first and third presentations?

Working on Scenes

In the appendix you will find scenes from *Hotel Paradiso* and *The Effect of Gamma Rays on Man-in-the-Moon Marigolds* which contain opportunities for practicing psychological deception in conscious role playing. Examine these scenes or others of your own choice in which characters deceive or conceal their ulterior objectives.

Perform a scene for the class in which you portray a deceptive, consciously role-playing character. Consider the following points as you work on the scene, and discuss class reaction to the points after your presentation.

DISCUSSION
1. What are the true objectives of the deceiving character?
2. What objective does the deceiving character wish to suggest to the other character(s)?
3. What conscious social roles does the deceiving character play to mislead the other character(s)?
4. How do the other characters react to the deception?

You may also try the previous four chair exercise on a memorized scene in which characters are deceiving one another or otherwise have complex inner reactions that are not shared with the other characters. You will find this technique valuable for making the inner reality of the character come to life.

Conscious Role Playing with Physical Disguise

Physical disguise is not often used as a plot device in contemporary plays, though a few recent examples will be cited. This device is, however, a staple of classical comedy, and you may have enough occasions to use the technique to make it worth your attention.

Disguise is most frequently achieved by cross-dressing one character in a costume of the opposite sex. The script may take three major approaches that will affect the way in which the actor attempts this type of conscious role-playing disguise. First, we will examine the situation in which only the audience is let in on the disguise, then we will consider the situation in which some of the characters are aware of the deception, but others are deceived. Lastly, we will review examples of those plays in which both the audience and all the other characters in the play are deceived.

When Only The Audience Knows

Rosalind in Shakespeare's *As You Like It*, Viola in *Twelfth Night*, Pentheus in Euripides' *The Bacchae*, and the two male musicians in the musical *Sugar* are examples of characters whose disguise is intended to deceive other characters but not the audience. In these instances the actors are dressing and behaving like members of the opposite sex.

Since the disguise should convincingly deceive the other characters, the conscious role-playing behavior should be carefully detailed. If the imitations are too authentic, however, the audience may be uncomfortable with the androgyny of the characters. For this reason, it may be helpful to leave an element of costume or a mannerism from the undisguised character's original sex role in the disguise of the conscious role portrayal.

Men who are disguised as women may raise the pitch and lighten the resonance of the voice without attempting a total imitation of female inflection. For women disguised as men, the problem of lowering the pitch and deepening the resonance may be a bit more difficult, but this task is somewhat easier in Shakespeare's disguised women, for they costume themselves as young boys whose voices would have higher pitches and thinner resonance than those of men anyway. (In Shakespeare's day, when the women's roles were played by boys, his performers had the reverse problem of portraying the female characters from the beginning without calling attention to the fact that they were male actors.)

Role Playing with Cross-Dressing

In this right-brain exercise, make a life study of a person of the opposite sex. Focus on the posture, the walk, the gestures, the energy level. Obtain a wig or rearrange your hair in a style appropriate to the historical period for a character who cross-dresses for disguise. Find garments appropriate to the disguise of the character, either historical period costumes or contemporary dress.

For an improvised performance of the character in class make an entrance as the undisguised character. Perform a simple progressive activity appropriate to the undisguised character. Then while the class watches, put on your disguise—costume and makeup, but continue to move as the undisguised character until you finish your transformation. After you have finished disguising yourself, change your posture, walk, and gestures to that of the disguised character. Then in disguise perform the same activity the character performed before he or she was disguised. Next perform another progressive activity typical for the disguised character. Then go back to the dress of the original character, but retain your disguised character's physical behavior until you have completed the costume and makeup change; then resume the physical behavior of the original character.

DISCUSSION

1. What differences do class observers perceive between the character with and without the disguise?
2. In what ways were disguises and behavior not total transformations to the opposite sex?
3. In what ways were members of the class uncomfortable while performing this exercise?
4. Did the level of discomfort (if any) change from the beginning of the exercise to its conclusion?

This exercise may also be performed with one half of the class at a time disguising themselves while the other half watches, or it may be performed simultaneously with each class member working in his or her own space and the discussion points adapted appropriately.

When Only Some Characters Don't Know

In comedies or farces in which some characters are aware of the deception and others are not, the scale of the conscious role-playing elements tends to be enlarged and exaggerated. In such plays strong contrasts are desirable between the behavior of the original character and the consciously played role of the character in disguise. Examples of this use may be found in Brandon Thomas's *Charley's Aunt* and Shakespeare's *A Midsummer Night's Dream*. In these plays both the original characterizations of Charley and Flute should be in marked contrast to the awkward adaptations made for Charley's aunt and Thisbe, roles which the respective characters play consciously.

In a script such as *La Cage aux Folles*, on the other hand, where the cross-dressing character is a professional performer with a high degree of finesse, the consciously played roles must be sensitively portrayed. (See fig. 9.3.) George Hearn recognized this in preparing for the roles of two females (Zaza and Georges's wife) in *La Cage aux Folles*:

Figure 9.3.   George Hearn in *La Cage aux Folles*. Characters who consciously role-play characters of the opposite sex should be portrayed with a sensitivity to the reality of the differences in behavior between men and women in the social context of the play. (Photo © 1983 by Martha Swope. Used by permission.)

> It's an empathetic feeling . . . to perfect a feminine gesture—a certain walk, or pose, or something small as making a fist without tucking in my fingertips. Each time I did this in rehearsal, I'd think, "That's how my mother or sister or wife must have felt when she made that gesture."[2]

When Both the Audience and Other Characters Don't Know

In plays such as *Sleuth* and *Witness for the Prosecution*, in which both the audience and the other characters are not supposed to know that a character is disguised, the consciously played roles should be as convincingly performed as the character's unconsciously performed roles. Since you have already worked on unconscious role playing in chapter 8, we will not repeat those exercises at this point.

Conscious Role Playing in Jest

Particularly in comedies, characters may briefly inject consciously played roles when teasing or toying with other characters. In the appendix the scenes from *Hotel*

Figure 9.4. *Hotel Paradiso* by Georges Feydeau. The maid Victoire consciously plays the role of "flirt" to seduce the "bookworm" Max. (St. Cloud State University Theatre. Set: Stephen R. Meyer; costumes: Harvey Paul Jurik.)

Paradiso and *Crimes of the Heart* contain such passages. Victoire's line, "Are you sure I can't help with your work?" can be played as if she were fully conscious of herself as a "bold flirt," as can the later line, "Has anyone ever told you you're quite a good looker?" (See fig. 9.4.)

In the scene from *Crimes of the Heart*, Meg's line, "Well, I was looking for the ones with nuts," might be delivered as a regression to the consciously played role of "innocent child."

Such small touches capture the spontaneity and game-playing quality that enliven daily human relationships and add variety and interest to the unconscious character roles.

Pulling the Leg

1. In this integrated-brain exercise, present a scene with a partner in which one or both characters tease each other. You might use *Hotel Paradiso* or *Crimes of the Heart* or a play of your own choice. First present the scene to the class without using any conscious role-playing techniques.

2. Using your right brain, repeat the scene, but each time a character teases the other, you literally pull the person's leg or pinch their cheek. You play a consciously developed role appropriate to the relationship, making physical and vocal adjustments as necessary.

3. Using both sides of your brain, perform the scene with the vocal and physical adjustments of the conscious role-playing moments in the appropriate spots but without the leg-pulling.

DISCUSSION

1. How do the performers deal with the concentration problem when they must switch quickly from unconscious to conscious role playing and back again?
2. Do the performers genuinely give more awareness to what they are doing while consciously playing roles, or is the conscious role playing only more theatricalized than the unconscious role playing by its difference in size and directness?
3. Can the performers or the class observers perceive what effect the physicalization of the tease (the leg-pulling or cheek pinching) had on the development of the final presentation?

Conscious Role Playing in Animated Narration

In any dialogue of extended narration of past events or imaginary ones, whether totally expository or including conversation, there is usually an opportunity to enliven the stage action and the animation of your character by developing some degree of conscious role playing. Your performance may go so far as to imitate completely characters in the story, or you may only suggest with slight physical demonstration or vocal imitation the various characters in the narrative or your character's own different behavior under different circumstances.

In the scene from *Sister Mary Ignatius Explains It All For You* Diane's lengthy speech about the tragedies of her life is a good example of narration in which a character indirectly characterizes other characters. As Diane describes the tragic events, she may consciously suggest, without fully or deeply characterizing, the vocal and physical traits of her mother, the doctor, and her psychiatrist.

A less obvious example may be found in the scene from *The Effect of Gamma Rays on Man-in-the-Moon Marigolds* in the appendix. When Ruth is reflecting on the expected reactions of Miss Hanley to Mama's feathers, it might be effective for Ruth consciously to imitate Miss Hanley as she is paraphrased ("She said Mama blabs as though she was the Queen of England . . ,") through the rest of the speech, and later when Miss Hanley will be "just splitting her sides."

In the scene from *The Good Woman of Setzuan*, Yang Sun's narrative about the pilots contains direct quotations that can be similarly characterized with the conscious role-playing technique. Here the various voices and even the "voice" of the textbook may each have a different placement and tempo-rhythm.

The amount of detail effective in the conscious role playing of another character in a narrative passage will depend on several things, including the seriousness of the scene, the degree to which the character is animated and would imitate other people, and whether the narrative is clearer with or without the illustrations.

Using Role Playing in Narration

1. With your left brain, select a speech from one of the narrative passages in a scene from the appendix or from a play of your own choice. First develop the unconscious role-playing qualities of the characterization. Then deliver the speech sitting in

a chair in front of the class without using any conscious role-playing techniques in dramatizing the characters in the narrative.

2. Using your right brain, deliver the speech a second time, beginning the speech in the unconscious role-playing mode but facing left. Then when you come to conscious role sections, turn your face and torso to the right as you adapt your voice and body to the consciously played roles of the narrative. Revert to the left for your character's unconsciously played role(s).

3. Using both sides of your brain, deliver the same passage using audience focus—that is, speaking to the audience as if they were the other character on stage—but continue to make vocal and physical adjustments for the consciously played roles in the narrative.

DISCUSSION
1. How did the different deliveries feel to the performers?
2. Which type of delivery did the class observers think was most interesting or effective? Why?

Conscious Role Playing with Characters as Actors

In plays such as *Marat/Sade* and *Noises Off* in which the characters function as actors playing other characters, the clearest approach to the role-playing problem is to develop the characterization for the underlying "actor" role first, then to superimpose the consciously played role over the original character. For example, in *Marat/Sade* you would develop the role of the asylum inmate first, then superimpose the conscious role-playing "character" the inmate portrays in the play-within-the-play.

The completeness and expertise of the consciously played role should reflect the supposed skill of the "actor-character." If the original character is an amateur actor, then the consciously played role should be presented awkwardly or ineptly, as with the performance of "Pyramus and Thisbe" by the amateur rustics in *A Midsummer Night's Dream*. On the other hand, the actor-characters in *The Real Thing* are supposed to be accomplished professionals, so the "characters" that they portray while in their play-within-the-play should appear more accomplished without losing the delicate edge of awareness that they are supposed to be performing a play for an audience. This is a difficult acting task to perform with finesse, but after you have mastered conscious role playing, you will find the skill easier.

Conscious Role Playing and the Mask

At your feet, Ancestors still present, who rule in pride the great hall of your masks defying time.

———*Leopold Senghor*

One exotic right-brain approach to developing conscious role-playing skills for any of the situations discussed earlier is through using a mask as a stimulus to the imagination. A primitive tribal mask similar to the illustrations here (figs. 9.5 and

9.6) may be used, or you might try the range of Oriental masks from placid damsels to fiery demons.

Masks from other cultures can evoke deep—sometimes primitive, sometimes sophisticated—universal responses. They suggest social roles that you might not otherwise consider, expanding not only your role-playing ability but your understanding of the range of human behavior as well.

You may use actual masks if available or pictures of masks in books from the library.[3]

Figure 9.5, Figure 9.6.   African Masks. Masks may be used as a stimulus for the role-playing level of characterization. (Photograph: C. Spaccavento. Masks courtesy of Montclair Public Library: Michael Connell, Director.)

Transforming Yourself with a Mask

For this right-brain exercise, obtain a real mask or the picture of a mask. You also need a paper bag big enough to cover your head, a pair of scissors, and several crayons, felt markers, or sticks of pastel chalk in assorted colors. With a mask or the picture of a mask in front of you, proceed through the following steps. Steps 1 through 8 may be done either outside of class or in class. The rest of the procedure you should do with classmates in a large working space, outdoors if possible.

1. What is your initial reaction to the expression on the mask? Is it comic or serious? Is it imitative of a person, an animal, or a mythic creature? Does its impact seem social, psychological, or religious?

2. Imitate as much as possible the expression on the mask with your own face. The expression of the forehead? The eyes? The shape and fullness of the lips? The flare and size of the nose? The wrinkles? The tension of the cheek muscles? Examine your face imitating the mask in a mirror. Does your imitation confirm or change your initial reaction?

3. What might cause a person to have the reaction the mask gives you? Is this reaction related to one of the following? A relationship to a member of the family? A friend? An enemy? A frustration or fulfillment of a deeply-held goal? A relationship to nature? A spiritual relationship? An aspect of one's occupation? The condition of one's health? The effects of one's age?

4. What sounds might the appearance of the mask suggest? Non-verbal sounds? Sounds made with parts of the body? Slaps? Stomps? Sounds made with the vocal cords or mouth and lips? Vocal qualities? Pitch? Textures? Tempo? Rhythm? Volume?

5. What colors are suggested by the mask? Pastels? Rich colors? Cools? Warms? Solid colors? Shades and tints?

6. What textures do you find in the mask? Smooth? Rough? Shiny? Dull?

7. What types of lines predominate in the mask? Curves? Straight lines? Horizontals? Verticals? Broken lines? Continuous lines? Thick or thin lines? Geometric figures?

8. Use colors to create your own mask on a paper bag. Cut out holes for the eyes, and shape the mask any other way you feel appropriate for the nose, mouth, and ears. Your mask should capture the same qualities you found in the original mask, but it should be your own design.

9. Put your paper bag mask over your head, and for 10 or 12 minutes work in your own space. Find a role appropriate to the experience you have had with the mask. Perform activities you might find in a village of primitive people—gathering food, hunting animals, preparing food, cleaning a hut, making clothes, or building a fire. Consider your relationship to the environment as you work, consider the weather, the climate, the living conditions.

10. After adjusting to your new world, gather with your masked classmates in small groups of five to eight to engage in group activities appropriate to a primitive society. You may use single, isolated nouns and verbs in a simplified type of communication, but do not use complete sentences.

Suggested tribal activities include

a. building a canoe
b. building a hut
c. hunting and skinning an animal
d. washing clothes
e. making weapons
f. making pots and utensils

g. preparing for a wedding
h. preparing for a fertility dance

Engage in these small group activities for 15 or 20 minutes; then remove the masks for discussion.

DISCUSSION

1. As a result of using your mask to stimulate the development of your character, what type of role did you find yourself playing in the primitive society? Leader? Follower? Facilitator? Obstacle maker? Jester? Priest?
2. To what extent did each paper bag mask shape the reactions of the primitive villagers toward one another?
3. Did classmates find that they wanted to be treated differently, but that the paper bag mask gave an impression they did not wish to create?
4. To what extent are your ideas of the social roles that people play shaped by the visual mask (or facial expression) they send and perceive?

Exploring the Jungle

This exercise for both sides of the brain has proven popular with both beginning and advanced students. In addition to its value for conscious role playing, it has provided an opportunity for the development of self-awareness and establishing genuine relationships with environmental elements.

1. The class should divide into two equal groups. Members may use the same paper bag masks as in the previous exercise, or they may try a different mask with the same process to create a new character.

2. The working space is divided in half, so that each group can work independently of the other group. Each group belongs to a different tribe and is in the jungle on an expedition. Each determines a reason for being out on expedition—hunting, searching for water, looking for a new village site, preparing for warfare, for example. One by one, the following complications are added to the situation.

a. It is late afternoon. The group is running out of food and water.
b. The sun begins to set, and the group discovers that it is lost. The group attempts to return to the village, but it cannot find the way.
c. The group hears unfamiliar animal sounds.
d. It begins to rain.

3. The groups remove their paper bag masks. The members of each group retain their same approach to the character they played as members of the native tribe, but now each group is a team of anthropologists in the jungle searching for a primitive tribe they hope to study. The same complications confront them.

a. The team is running out of food and water.
b. As the sun sets, the anthropologists become lost.
c. They hear unfamiliar animal sounds.
d. It begins to rain.

4. One group puts on the paper bag masks and reverts to being primitive tribe members; the other group without masks remains anthropologists.

Morning arrives, and the two groups encounter each other. Their problem now is to deal with the common situation of being lost and to decide what happens if either group discovers the way out of the jungle.

5. The groups reverse roles, so that the tribal members become anthropologists and the anthropologists become tribal members. They repeat the improvisation with the reversed roles. They may change the ending if they wish.

DISCUSSION

1. How did individuals define their roles within the groups? Leader? Follower? Expediter? Obstacle?
2. Did individuals perceive their own roles the same way as others perceived them?
3. What reactions came out of your characters that surprised you or were new ways of role playing?
4. What were individual reactions when one group encountered the other?
5. What happened between the two groups when both groups understood their mutual condition of being lost?
6. What differences did you perceive in relationships when everyone wore masks? When no one wore masks? When the encounter took place between the masked tribal members and the unmasked anthropologists?

Masking Your Intentions

This integrated-brain exercise is an advanced, but highly effective one, which uses two masks for developing character deception. As in the earlier exercise on transforming yourself with a mask, develop a character role from the mask you choose. Decide upon an intention to be communicated to another character. Then use a second mask as the stimulus for the cover-up of the first. The covering facade of the second mask will become your character's conscious role-playing approach.

With a partner develop two situations, one for your own two-faced character and one for your partner's two-faced character. Present your improvisations to the class.

Masking in a Large Group

A. Scene: apartment with a student cast party under way. The cast has received poor reviews of a new production from the school paper. The critique was written by a classmate whose opinion had previously been favorable and respected. Though the cast members are hostile toward the student critic, who arrives at the party late, they attempt to cover their hurt feelings with politeness toward the critic.

B. Scene: living room of one of the members of a high school class which is celebrating the tenth anniversary of its graduation. Two expected members of the class are late. In their senior year, the couple now married to each other, were elected

"Most Popular" and "Most Likely to Succeed." For the past few years they have been serving a sentence in prison for a criminal offense (your option). They have just been released from prison, and no one has seen them since their release. All members of the class define for themselves an uncomfortable attitude toward the couple. However, each person attempts to greet the couple with the same attitude they had toward them when they were in high school together.

Masking for Another Person

1. You want to declare your love to someone you are infatuated with, but fearful of rejection, you hurl insults at the object of your affections.
2. You are frightened of your boss, but with bravado you boldly demand a raise.
3. You are a confirmed agnostic, but you proclaim publicly your religious piety.
4. You are jealous of the honor another person has received, but you extend congratulations.

DISCUSSION
1. How did the difference between your internal intention and the covering mask affect your role playing with the other person?
2. Can class observers perceive the discrepancy between your internal intention and your external role playing? Should they be able to?
3. What perceptions did partners have of each other's character objectives?

Semiconscious Role Playing

"I can't explain myself, I'm afraid, sir," said Alice, "because I'm not myself, you see."
———*Lewis Carroll*, Alice in Wonderland

Characters who are confused, insane, drugged, excessively fatigued, or in other ways out of control, strangely seem to be consciously role playing even when they are not, simply because their moments of irrational role playing are radically different from their normal unconscious role playing. (See fig. 9.7.) These conditions might be regarded as semiconscious role-playing situations.

King Lear, Ophelia, Willy Loman in *Death of a Salesman*, perhaps even Amanda in *The Glass Menagerie*, all have moments of semiconscious role playing, when they almost cross the line from their normal unconscious role-playing status into a fully conscious role-playing situation.

Behaving Semiconsciously

A. Scene: student apartment at breakfast time. You and a roommate have been up more than half the night finishing term papers. You had very little sleep before the alarm clock went off at eight o'clock. You have to get ready to go to your nine o'clock class. You and your roommate decide you'd better eat breakfast because you'll have no

Figure 9.7.   *Angel Street* by Patrick Hamilton. In this melodrama set in the Victorian era Mrs. Manningham (played here by Betsy Keller) has many semi-conscious role-playing beats as a result of the attempts of her husband to drive her mad. In the scene pictured here Inspector Rough (John Chervak) helps return her to sanity. (Courtesy of Wilkes College. Director and photographer: Jay D. Siegfried; set: Klaus Holm.)

break in your schedule until mid-afternoon. Weary but determined, you prepare and eat breakfast before you leave.

   B. Scene: an abandoned old house. You and a friend have had many adventures together at the old abandoned house through junior high and high school. You have just finished the summer after your senior year in high school. This night is the last time that you will have together. You are going off to college, and your friend is moving away to another city to get a job. Though you pledge to write and visit each other, you both understand that this is probably your last goodbye. You have celebrated the evening with your favorite alcoholic beverage, which you are in the process of finishing.[4]

DISCUSSION

1. How did your experience in working on the semiconscious role-playing character differ from your experience with the unconscious role-playing character and conscious role-playing character?
2. What differences do class observers note among performances of unconscious role playing, conscious role playing, and semiconscious role playing?

Role Combinations

In many recent plays, characters switch quickly from one type of role playing to another. Some of the plays of Sam Shepard, Megan Terry, and Tom Stoppard contain many examples of such characters. For experience in these quick changes, you can use unconscious, conscious, and semiconscious role playing in performing the scene from *Sister Mary Ignatius Explains It All For You* in the appendix or from another contemporary play that suggests these three modes.

Shifting Modes of Role Playing

A. Perform the scene with smooth transitions from one mode of role playing to the other.

B. Perform the scene with abrupt changes from one mode to the other.

DISCUSSION

1. How did class observers react to smooth transitions as opposed to abrupt ones?
2. Where are the moments within the same scene when smooth transitions are more believable?
3. Where are the moments within the same scene when abrupt transitions are more interesting?
4. Did anyone in your class experience more difficulty with one type of transitions than with the other? If so, which type? Why do you think such difficulty might occur?

Summary

In this chapter you have examined the fourth level of craft, the level of conscious role playing. You have observed a variety of ways in which conscious role playing may be part of the character in the script: 1) as a psychologically manipulative device, 2) as a deliberate physical disguise, 3) in jest, 4) in animated narration of previous or imagined events, and 5) as an actor-character's facade. You have seen the various ways in which a character may use role playing to disguise true intentions from other characters, from the audience, or from both.

Through several approaches, including the cross-dressing and mask exercises, you developed your ability to use the conscious role-playing technique. You also found in semiconscious role playing a middle ground between unconscious role playing and conscious role playing. Lastly, in scenes performed in class you have experienced both as performer and observer the interesting variety and theatricality that all three modes of role playing can add to characterization.

Notes

1. Cited by Michael Kuchwara, "Actor returns to 'Oliver!' after a 24-year absence," *Newark Star-Ledger*, 21 April 1984.
2. Cited by Robin Reif, *PLAYBILL: The National Theatre Magazine* 2, no. 6 (March 1984): 19.
3. Two excellent sources are *Masks of Black Africa* by Ladislas Segy (New York: Dover, 1976) and *Masks: Their Meaning and Function* by Andreas Lommel (New York: McGraw-Hill, 1972).
4. This situation was suggested by the one in *Minnesota Moon* by John Olive in *The Best Short Plays 1982*, ed. Ramon Delgado (Radnor, Pa.: Chilton, 1982).

For Further Reading

Alkema, Chester J. *Mask Making*. New York: Sterling, 1981.
Levi-Strauss, Claude. *The Way of the Masks*. Translated by Sylvia Modelski. Seattle: University of Washington, 1982.
Lommel, Andreas. *Masks: Their Meaning and Function*. New York: McGraw-Hill, 1972.
Saint-Denis, Michael. *Training for the Theatre*. New York: Theatre Arts Books, 1982. "The Mask," pp. 169–176.
Segy, Ladislas. *Masks of Black Africa*. New York: Dover, 1976.
Wilshire, Bruce. *Role Playing and Identity*. Bloomington, Ind.: Indiana University Press, 1982. Ch. 14.

Chapter 10 _____
_____ *The Level of Emotions*

An action directed towards the gratification of will is continuously accompanied by a series of spontaneous feelings, the content of which is the anticipation of the coming gratification or the fear of failure. Thus every feeling represents a gratified or non-gratified will.

———*Yevgeny Vakhtangov*, Diary

The Use of Emotions in the Creative Process

The level of emotions in the creative process of acting refers to character behavior that arouses emotional awareness in both performers and spectators. The behavior may be as simple as the character's smile or as exciting as an embrace and kiss. It may be as subtle as a veiled threat or as obvious as confronting another character with a gun. Emotional awareness for both the spectator and the performer arises internally at the end of an action process, not at the beginning of one. Performers do not "act" emotions; they perform actions that arouse emotions.

Pattern of Emotional Awareness

Do not speak to me about feeling. We cannot set feeling; we can only set physical action. . . . First of all, you must establish the logical sequence of your physical actions.

———*Konstantin Stanislavsky*

In the normal pattern of emotional awareness the procedure follows the four steps in the order given in figure 10.1.

1. stimulus →   2. external →   3. neurological and →   4. conscious
                 action   glandular activity   awareness

Figure 10.1.

Although the four steps leading to awareness may occur almost simultaneously, we can identify separately each of the steps in the creative process for the performer.

In step 1 the performer perceives a stimulus, which evokes a response. The stimulus may be an internal desire or need or an external demand from another character or from the environment.

In step 2 the performer makes physical adjustments, which may include actions as subtle as changes in muscular tension or as large as dueling.

As the second step begins, step 3 overlaps it. Neurological and glandular activity change the internal electrical and chemical mix of the body.

Lastly, in step 4, which may overlap step 3, the performer becomes aware of the physical and mental changes associated with a recognizable emotional state.

Exploring Emotional Awareness

A. Let us look at the scene from *The Effect of Gamma Rays On Man-In-The-Moon Marigolds* in the appendix to illustrate the process of emotional awareness in practice. After everyone has read over the scene, two girls in the class should improvise the section of the scene in which Ruth brushes Tillie's hair.

DISCUSSION
1. What stimulus (motivation) does Ruth have for this action?
2. What physical responses did the observers see when Ruth brushes Tillie's hair hard?
3. What physical responses were the performers aware of?
4. What inner responses were the performers aware of?
5. What emotional responses did the observers have while watching?

B. Improvise active moments from other scenes.

DISCUSSION
1. Are there differences between what the observers attribute to the significance of the activities and what the performers experienced themselves?
2. Can you draw any conclusions regarding the relationship between physical activities and emotional awareness for the performer and for the audience?

Emotion and Control

Through examining the questions above, you will gain some background for understanding the connections between the actor's physical actions, the emotions aroused in the actor, and the emotions aroused in the audience. As you have discovered, actors do not "act" emotions—they arouse them for both the audience and themselves through the appropriate action.

There has been more disagreement on the emotional expression of the actor than on any other aspect of the creative process. The reasons for the disagreement are matters of cultural conditioning in the expression of emotion and personal taste regarding the appropriate manner to express emotions on stage. A major part of the disagreement comes down to the differences between those who prefer primitive uninhibited emotional flow on stage (right-brain spontaneity) and those who prefer a firm intellectual coolness (left-brain channeling) in performances.

As an advocate of the use of both sides of the brain, I find either approach limited if the opposite approach is excluded. Allowing for appropriateness of style, my general view expressed here is that during training and rehearsal the creative performer will get in touch with spontaneous emotions through action-producing exercises. During performance the performer will release emotions primarily through carefully chosen actions and activities that are likely to stimulate the desired response from the members of the audience.

An actor who is uncontrolled during performances is likely to jar both himself or herself and other performers out of the artistic decisions made during rehearsal. Such a performer can also affect the audience in unexpected and undesirable ways.

Emotion and Inspiration

Inspiration is encouraged during training and rehearsals, but an actor inspired to try radically new things during performance risks losing control of himself or herself and the audience, as well as losing the confidence of fellow players. This view does not in any way minimize the need for honest, emotional behavior, but rather it emphasizes the necessity of shaping the design of the emotional life of the character as well as those other aspects of characterization you already have learned to develop (actions and role playing).

Since aroused emotions and emotional awareness are the end product of a chain of events, they are biologically based on changes in the signals of the nervous system and in differences in the chemical output of the glands. Neither the nerves nor the glands can be controlled directly outside of laboratory experiments, so they must be influenced by those things that change the messages of the nerves and the chemical output of the glands. There are two devices that can make such changes:

1. internal images
2. muscular tensions and movement

Both processes are primarily right-brain functions.

Variations in Emotional Interpretation

Because the external expression of emotion is shaped by cultural factors as well as by biological adjustments, a great amount of variable interpretation may be attributed to any one display of emotional behavior. The following anecdote from Mark Twain's *Innocents Abroad* illustrates the range of disagreement in interpreting emotional signals.

> There is an old story that Matthews, the actor, was once lauding the ability of the human face to express the passions and emotions hidden in the breast. He said the countenance could disclose what was passing in the heart plainer than the tongue could.

"Now," he said, "observe my face—what does it express?"

"Rage?"

"Stuff, it means horror! This!"

"Imbecility!"

"Fool, it is smothered ferocity! Now this!"

"Joy."

"Oh, perdition! *Any* ass can see it means insanity!"

Expression! People coolly pretend to read it who would think themselves presumptuous if they pretended to interpret the hieroglyphics on the obelisks of Luxor—yet they are fully as competent to do the one thing as the other.

This divergence of intention and interpretation helps to explain why a single performance can elicit totally opposing views by critics and audience members. Not only does each member of the audience understand emotional signals differently, but the perception of each person is different because perception itself is shaped by an individual's innate intelligence and cultural conditioning. Individuals are what they are able to perceive, and since we perceive through cultural filters, our understanding is partial and incomplete. That any message is ever understood, especially an emotional message, is a near miracle! Nevertheless, we shall forge forward, attempting to spread more light than heat.

The Actor's Goal in Using Emotions

Though emotional awareness in the actor during the moment of performance may help create emotional behavior that the audience believes to be more honest, recent experiments suggest that the performer's body may respond internally in ways that indicate emotional activity, such as nervous and glandular adjustments, without the individual's awareness of the nature of the internal emotional changes.[1]

The important thing for the audience member during performance is not that the actor feels an emotion, but that the audience member does. Therefore, the excuse "I couldn't do it because I didn't feel it" sometimes offered by inexperienced actors at rehearsals ignores the importance of executing an action to elicit an emotional response and suggests that the actor is trying to make the cart of emotions pull the horse of action.

Communication of Emotions

Feeling is the same in theatre and life, but the means and methods of presenting them are different. The grouse is the same, whether served in the restaurant or at home. But in the restaurant it is served and prepared in such a manner as to have a theatrical ring to it, while at home it is just a homemade piece of meat.

———*Yevgeny Vakhtangov*, Zapiski

Audience Empathy

An audience participates in the emotional experiences of creative performances through the process of empathy. Members of an audience allow themselves to participate in the illusion created by the performers in this process. The audience members imitate the muscular tensions and internal reactions of the images the performers suggest to them through action and activity. This imitation by the audience recreates the emotional experience within their own bodies. In addition to this imitative response in reaction to a single actor, the members of an audience will react to the stimuli in the play that the characters are reacting to as well.

In this way individuals in the audience become participants in the actions of the play and measure the truthfulness of the emotional portrayal of each actor by their own reaction to the situation and circumstances in the play. Therefore, it is just as important for each stimulus of the character's emotional reactions to be clear as it is for the reaction itself to be clear. The actor and playwright Sam Shepard agrees:

> Well, hopefully in writing a play, you can snare emotions that aren't just personal emotions, not just catharsis, not just psychological emotions that you're getting off your chest, but emotions and feelings that are connected with everybody.[2]

Emotional Freedom

The chances for sharing emotions with an audience are greater if the performer is capable of spontaneous, easy expression of emotional behavior. This freedom to exhibit honest emotional behavior comes in part from the removal of internal and external obstacles that inhibit free expression.

Let's examine this problem more closely. Internal inhibitions of emotional expression are common in human society, for as each child grows up, the child is socialized into getting along with other people. This process requires giving up a degree of spontaneity and personal desire for the smoother flow of social interactions, first within the home, later in the school.

Remember how the class clowns in school were punished for their "misbehavior"? The comedian David Brenner reveals that he was expelled from school 200 times for disrupting classes with his spontaneous humor until a sympathetic science teacher intervened. The teacher offered David a five-minute spot at the beginning of class to entertain his classmates in exchange for a pledge of restraint for the rest of the class period.[3]

Usually, however, students are punished for such intrusion into the classroom routine. If the punishment is effective, the class clowns learn to inhibit expression, and eventually even their desire to vent their feelings may be suppressed. This process not only kills the external expression, but to an extent it also kills the internal impulse behind that expression. The same repressive process effectively squelches the class troublemakers.

In opening up emotional channels for performance, both the class clown and the class troublemaker must be revived in each performer and given an opportunity to escape both the physical armoring (the tensions that have become habit from constant suppression of impulse) and the mental inhibitions caused by the need for social approval. This freeing from restraints should be done in an atmosphere of controlled permissiveness so that individuals can practice even the "unacceptable" social behavior so necessary for depicting the complexities of character behavior in the theatre.

Playing Clowns and Troublemakers

In this integrated-brain exercise two people at a time are designated class clown and class troublemaker respectively. Another student plays the role of teacher. On a prearranged signal (such as a hand clap or desk bell) the class will regress to junior high (ninth-grade) level of interest and behavior. The clown and troublemaker are to do as many things as possible to disrupt the class. The clown tries to make the class laugh. The troublemaker tries to disrupt the lesson through a more serious distraction. On a second prearranged signal the clown and troublemaker tap two other individuals to play their roles. After everyone has had a turn to play either clown or troublemaker, class members resume their own college behavior. (I hope there is a difference!)

DISCUSSION
1. What actions were taken by the clowns to amuse the class?
2. What actions were taken by the troublemakers to disrupt the class?
3. Compare internal reactions of individuals when they were clown or troublemaker to their reactions when they were conforming junior high students.
    a. Was there any sense of satisfaction or release in being clown or troublemaker?
    b. How did people feel when they had to stop being clown or troublemaker?
    c. Was there any annoyance or irritation with the clowns and troublemakers when you were a well-socialized junior high student?
4. What motivations (if any) did individuals find to explain their disruptive behavior?

Displacement

Another interesting aspect of repressed emotional behavior is the process of displacement. When a person or character is unable to give direct expression to a stimulus, he or she may channel the resulting action into unexpected or irrelevant behavior. Such inhibitions may be the result of social conditioning or of personal internal obstacles. For example, an angry person in a formal meeting who may not be able to let the anger out in a gesture or shout, may grind the teeth, adjust a tie, or smash a cigarette into an ash tray. A person or character too shy to display affection with a hug or kiss, may simply smile weakly, drop the eyes, and nervously straighten a collar or hem.

Letting It Hang Out—Holding It Back!

In these integrated-brain exercises you will use improvisations (actions and words) to explore four basic emotional areas—fear, anger, love and awe. The first time you improvise the situation you may express the emotion freely. Do not hesitate to behave irrationally. The same situation is then improvised a second time using displacement activities. Be as inventive as possible to find alternative ways to express the inhibited reactions. These improvisations can be an excellent help in developing your emotional expressiveness with both direct and indirect actions.

1. Expressing Fear
A. Fear for one's life. A young couple is held up by a drug-crazed sidewalk bandit who points a gun at them. The couple has no idea whether the bandit will use the gun or not. They cannot run away for they are caught in a dead-end alley.

B. Fear of hunger. A young, jobless couple, living in a low-rent apartment, has run out of food. Their infant is ill and undernourished. They are concerned for the life of the child and for their own health. They have sold everything of value, and appeals to welfare organizations have fallen on deaf ears because of bureaucratic red tape. A blizzard begins, and they are cut off from any emergency relief.

C. Fear about job security. At a business meeting of heads of various departments (for example, sales, production, promotion, etc.) of a corporation the chairman of the board sets extremely high goals for the next year. If anyone fails to meet the expectations, he or she will be fired. The department heads do not believe the goals are achievable and are concerned about their jobs.

2. Expressing Anger
A. Anger in desperation. A student believes he or she has been treated unfairly on the grading of a paper. The student approaches the teacher to challenge the grade, which must be passing if the student is to complete the required course. The student must maintain the goodwill of the teacher. If the student flunks this course, he or she will not graduate at the end of the semester.

B. Anger at injustice. The same relationship between student and teacher is varied by the student's not having to get a passing grade in the course. He or she focuses only on the unfairness of the grade and does not care whether the goodwill of the teacher is maintained or not.

3. Expressing Love
A. Loving mutually. Improvise the final scene from the O. Henry short story "The Gift of the Magi." It is Christmas morning. The young wife has cut her beautiful long hair to purchase a watch fob for her husband. He has pawned his watch to buy a set of tortoise shell combs for her hair.

B. Loving tentatively. A young man and young woman meet in a singles bar. Each has just had an unfortunate relationship with someone else. They are lonely, but are attracted to each other and want to establish more than a surface relationship, but because of their recent experiences they hesitate to become vulnerable.

C. Loving fearfully. Another couple has a similar relationship, but it is complicated by a character's feelings of guilt. The man has just been released from prison for a murder, which he did, in fact, commit. The woman, a lawyer, suffers from inferiority feelings as the result of losing her plaintiff's case to a male defense lawyer in a rape trial.

4. Expressing Awe

A. Religious awe. A sister takes her crippled brother to a religious shrine. They have high expectations of a miracle occuring to heal the brother. The waters of the holy fountain flow, and upon drinking the water, the brother is healed. The two honor the saint for whom the fountain is named. What can the two do to pay homage to the saint?

B. Awe in defiance of the state. A young couple lives in a country where they are forbidden to wear religious symbols in public. Religious leaders have proclaimed this day a time of defiance against civil authorities and urged all citizens to wear the symbol of their faith. What does the couple do? A policeman enters with orders to arrest those who display the religious symbol.

DISCUSSION (for all four emotions)

1. In which improvisations did you see emotions aroused by the pursuit of character objectives?
2. In which improvisations did you see the repression of emotions and displacement activities?
3. In which improvisations did characters seem to be consciously role playing with other characters? Did there seem to be more than one layer of emotional behavior in this type of relationship?

Mechanism of Emotions: The James-Lange Theory

Around the turn of the century, the American psychologist William James and the Danish physician Carl George Lange developed a concept about the production of emotions, a concept later known as the James-Lange theory. This theory expresses the opinion that emotions are either the same as physiological changes or the perceptive results of physiological changes.

The classic example used to illustrate this view is the situation of a mountain climber who rounds a corner on a mountain where he or she bumps unexpectedly into a bear. Upon seeing the bear, the climber runs away to safety. It is only during and after the run that he or she becomes aware of the body changes recognizable as fear.

If, however, someone else (an audience) were watching the situation but could not warn the mountain climber (performer) of impending danger, the spectator would have similar emotional fears before the mountain climber experienced them. Because the spectator sees the conditions that will produce fear in the climber before the climber does, the spectator undergoes the tensions and glandular changes preparing for flight. These tensions are released with the safe retreat of the mountain climber, and both the climber and the spectator will take deep breaths of relief, supplying additional oxygen to replace that depleted either in tension while the spectator observed the run or in the performer's actual running.

Breath as the Path to Emotions

Since breathing may be controlled consciously, it is one of the major right-brain physical routes the performer can use to reach an emotional condition.

Using the Breath to Tap Emotions

A. Tag. The class pairs off. One person in each pair chases the other until the other is tagged. Then the roles are reversed.

B. Tightrope and Time Bomb. One person is designated to carry a "time bomb" across the room on a "tightrope." A wastebasket is placed at the receiving end of the line designated as the "tightrope." A book or volleyball serves as the bomb. A timekeeper regulates the amount of time left before the bomb goes off, counting backwards from a selected number to zero. If the count reaches zero before the bomb is disposed of safely in the wastebasket, the tightrope walker is blown up.

To complicate the situation half of the class moves around in the space between the tightrope walker and the wastebasket to heckle and physically distract (but not touch) the tightrope walker. If the timekeeper's count reaches zero before the bomb is disposed of, the hecklers supply the sound of the explosion. (See fig. 10.2.)

The other half of the class observes, focusing on the emotional behavior displayed by those participating. Everyone in the class should have a turn at removing the bomb, heckling, and observing.

C. Haunted House. The class forms a circle. A person volunteers to be "it" and steps out of the room while identities are assigned to the rest of the class. One person is selected to be the good ghost, who is the only character able to help "it" get out of the haunted house. One-third of the class become enchanted princesses or princes, who are helpless to aid "it." The rest of the class become witches (female) or warlocks (male) capable of turning "it" into a toad by their touch, but people in the circle cannnot move their feet from their position. "It" is called back to the center of the circle. To get out of the circle of the haunted house, "it" must find the good ghost, who will let him out. But "it" must be within arms's reach of the good ghost, who tags him out with the exclamation, "Boo!" The witches and warlocks may turn "it" into a toad by tagging him and exclaiming, "Toad!" The princesses and princes can only exclaim, "Help!"

To begin the exercise "it" crosses to within arms's distance of a person and asks, "Can you help me out of here?" If "it" has appealed to a witch or warlock and is successfully tagged, "it" becomes a frog (or any other animal wished upon him or her)—physicalizing appropriately—and then continues to seek assistance out of the haunted house, asking the question in a voice appropriate to the animal inflicted upon "it." When "it" is finally successful in getting out, a new "it" is selected and new role assignments made.

Figure 10.2.   Time Bomb and Hecklers. The breath plays an important part in preparing the body for a release of emotional response and in building suspense for an audience.

DISCUSSION (for all the breath exercises)

1. In each exercise how and when was your breath pattern altered?
2. When you altered your breath pattern, what changes could you detect elsewhere in your body?
3. When you altered your breath pattern, where did you experience tensions and releases in your body?

Physical Inducement of Emotions

Since the James-Lange theory was first set forth, it has endured its share of criticism, but recent experiments by Paul Ekman and others at the University of California School of Medicine in San Francisco offer laboratory results that appear to confirm the basic assumptions of the theory.

In Ekman's experiments he tried two approaches to create measurable emotion-specific activity in the autonomic nervous system. In one approach the subjects of the experiment created mental images of remembered emotional moments to produce emotional effects. (We will look at the memory approach to emotion in the later section in this chapter on emotional recall.) In the second approach the subjects of the experiment followed detailed instructions for facial expressions, which then induced the emotions. One of Ekman's conclusions is of special interest to us:

> Particularly intriguing is our discovery that producing the emotion-prototypic patterns of facial muscle action resulted in autonomic changes of large magnitude that were more clear-cut than those produced by reliving emotions (a more naturalistic process).[4]

Producing Emotions Physically

Bring a hand mirror to class to use the second time you go through this right-brain exercise.

1. Without using the mirror try the four different facial expressions given below one at a time. Make a mental note of your inner response before you move on to the next expression.

2. Go through the series a second time, checking your expressions with the mirror.

3. Check the identification of each emotion in the notes at the end of the chapter. Then try the expressions a third time, using the mirror.

Emotion A:
1. Elevate your eyebrows and pull them toward each other.
2. Raise your upper eyelids.
3. Stretch your lips toward your ears and narrowly part them.

Emotion B:
1. Force your eyebrows down and toward each other.
2. Narrow your eyelids to slits.
3. Part your lips and tense them, tightening your jaw and pushing it forward.

Emotion C:
1. Elevate your eyebrows.
2. Open your eyes wide.
3. Open your mouth slightly and round the lips.

Emotion D:
1. Relax the eyebrows.
2. Narrow the eyes, slightly tensing the lower lids.
3. Keep the lips together, pulling the corners slightly back and up toward the ears.[5]

DISCUSSION (for all four emotions)
1. What physical changes did you experience other than in your face?
2. Did the use of the mirror change your experiences in any way?
3. How could you distinguish among the four different effects produced?
4. Could you distinguish the point at which you became aware of any emotional changes?

Development of Emotional Responsiveness

"Consider anything, only don't cry!"

———*Lewis Carroll*, Through the Looking Glass

The development of the actor's own emotional response as character will come automatically, if the actor deals with the stimulus and is physically and psychologically free to respond. (See fig. 10.3.) These are important qualifications, which need further examination.

Figure 10.3.   *Earnest in Love*, book and lyrics, Anne Croswell; music, Lee Pockriss. In this musical based on Oscar Wilde's *The Importance of Being Earnest* relaxed and open performers freely express the emotion of the moment. (Photograph: Joe Meyer. Courtesy of Montclair State College, Major Theatre Series. Set and lights: W. Scott MacConnell; costumes: Joseph F. Bella.)

Emotional freedom comes from

1) relaxed, supple muscles
2) an atmosphere of uninhibited permissiveness to express feelings

The performer can work on these two things to enhance responsiveness to the stimulus that triggers emotional expression. You have already worked on the first element, relaxation, in part 2. The later exercises in this chapter will explore the second element, the atmosphere of uninhibited permissiveness to express feelings.

The rest of the exercises in this chapter should be performed only in the context of a class, a workshop, or a rehearsal where a controlled situation exists. Outside of a controlled situation these exercises can result in nonproductive self-indulgence or in disturbing emotional experiences. As some of these exercises may open channels to powerful and repressed experiences, please follow all precautions given on individual exercises.

Honest Expression, Indulgence, and Indication

It is not possible to judge a work or the experiences it contains, if you have not recognized some part of yourself in the author's writing. If the actor is in a prepared state to learn alien ideas and feelings armed with his internal forces and his external apparatus, which makes physical characterization possible . . . he will learn what he needs.

———*Konstantin Stanislavsky*

The performer's external action response to a stimulus, which the audience interprets as emotional response, should come from an honest use of the performer's inner life as adapted to the given circumstances of the play and the nature of the character being portrayed.

If the performer's response appears disproportionate to the stimulus, the audience will either 1) not believe the response, 2) fail to understand the response, or worse still, 3) laugh inappropriately at the response. (Indeed, two techniques of comedy are making a response too little or a response too large for the stimulus.) In a realistic performance if the response is too big for the stimulus, the performer is "indulging" in the emotion. If the response is too small or appears too perfunctory, the performer is "indicating." Both disproportionate responses may have their place in comedy, conscious role playing, or period styles, but in the style of realism that is emphasized at this point in your development, they should be avoided.

Responding in Different Proportions

For these exercises using both sides of the brain, classmates should work first independently, then show their work to the class, and lastly share their experiences together. In your own working space, you are to improvise with actions and words the same emotion-arousing activity in three different ways.

1. The first time you perform the activity overdo it, indulging, exaggerating, emotionalizing.

2. The second time, indicate the emotion by demonstrating how you feel. This second performance should be approached as if you are showing someone how to portray the emotional attitude, but without your making a total physical commitment to the objective.

3. The third time, picture an internal image of the stimulus for the activity or a parallel in your own experience while you perform the activity.

You may select activities from the following list.

a. You have just been given a present that you have wanted for a long time. Jump and holler to celebrate.
b. You have just heard the news that your dearest pet met an untimely end. You must discard items that remind you of it.
c. A younger brother or sister has scratched a favorite record and is not around for you to vent your frustrations.
d. You are alone in your room studying late at night, and you hear someone breaking in the front door.

DISCUSSION
1. What internal differences did you detect among the three ways of performing the same activity?
2. In those exercises viewed by the class, compare the internal experiences of the performers with the internal feelings aroused in the viewers. Is there general agreement on which presentations were the most honest? The most emotionally indulged? The most indicated?

Emotional Recall or Spontaneous Expression?

"'Emotional states' What is that? I never heard of it."

———*Konstantin Stanislavsky*

In his early work Stanislavsky led actors to revive memories of earlier emotional experiences to help them have access to associated feelings for use on stage. Later, however, he preferred to direct the actor's attention to the psychophysical actions that might induce truthful internal feelings.

Acting teachers today are divided over the value of using the technique of emotional recall in rehearsal or performance, but you should know what the technique is and how it may be used by those who find it beneficial. The reason some acting instructors dismiss the value of emotional recall is that some performers, particularly inexperienced ones, will become too introspective, playing an action of recapturing the past, rather than using the reality of the past as the basis for developing the character's present actions.

It is desirable to respond spontaneously to the given circumstances of the play and the actions of the other actors, but there are times when the use of emotional recall may be the only way for you to make connections between the character's behavior and your own.

In the process of emotional recall, the performer finds an incident from past events in his or her own life that parallels or raises emotions similar to those raised at a particular moment for the character in a play. The performer does not attempt to summon up the emotion directly but rather visualizes in imagination the events of the real life scene from the past similar to the situation in the play. An example of application follows in the next exercise.

Using Emotional Recall

With a partner select a scene from the appendix or from your own choice for this integrated-brain exercise. Read over the scene together with as much depth as you can give it on an unrehearsed reading. Find from your own life an experience parallel or similar to that of the character. Your partner will do the same. Improvise both of the true life experiences, yours and your partner's. Then improvise the scene from the play using actions and words.

DISCUSSION
1. What new insights did you bring to the scene after performing both your parallel experience and your partner's?
2. What physical activities did you discover in either your personal improvisation or the scene improvisation that might be used in the scene itself?
3. How did the goals you had in the improvisation from life differ from the character goals in the scene improvisation or in the scene itself?

Private Moments or Public Fantasies?

As beginning performer you may find that sometimes the behavior of characters is foreign to your own values. You are either unable to understand why a character reacts as he or she does, or you are unable to allow yourself to perform the actions required by the script. This experience is more common with contemporary scripts, which often call for extremely uninhibited behavior or for the use of language that was not used on the stage even a few years ago. If you have such a problem and want to expand your emotional possibilities, the two integrated-brain exercises that follow will help you without offending either you or your classmates, some of whom may have different values from your own or the character's.

Expanding Emotional Expression

A. Silent Embarrassment (Fear). Working on your own in your own space, reenact silently an incident in which you were embarrassed. Maybe someone overheard you gossiping about him or her, or you did something not acceptable in a certain social situation. First visualize yourself and the others who were present at the time before you improvise this scene.

B. Phony Cursing (Anger). Imagine a situation in which you are very angry with the actions of another person. See how many ways you can degrade that person with the phrase: "You mother-hugging, son-of-a-witch!" Class members can practice aloud in their own working space. Then volunteers can perform this exercise for the rest of the class with partners using the volunteer's situation.

C. Bear Hugs and French Kisses (Love). Along with everyone else in the class, move at random in the room. Every time you encounter a person, give him or her a big bear hug or a formal French kiss (on both cheeks).

D. Celebrity Worship (Awe). Take a pencil and paper with you. You and everyone else in the class are celebrities. Each person chooses the name of a real celebrity and tries to suggest that person's posture, walk, gestures, and voice. At the same time each of you is also an autograph hound desiring the signatures of all the other celebrities. Move at random in the room. See who can be the first to obtain legible celebrity signatures from the entire class.

DISCUSSION
1. Which (if any) of the emotional areas did you feel uncomfortable with? Do you understand why?
2. After the members of the class have shared their apprehensions about what they feel free to express honestly on stage, have attitudes of the class changed?

Emotional Circles

If you have form'd a circle to go into,
Go into it yourself, and see how you would do.

———*William Blake*

The following exercise is one of the most powerful psychophysical right-brain approaches for helping you learn to have access to your inner emotional nature. Be careful to take all the precautions given.

Using Emotional Circles

Study the diagram of concentric circles in figure 10.4. These circles may be chalked on the floor, or imaginary boundaries may be set for each circle with the size of the circles depending on the amount of space available and the number of students in your class. The inner circle (fear) should be at least six feet in diameter, and each of the other concentric rings should be at least four feet across the band. Please note the four neutral corners outside the circles. **NEVER PERFORM THIS EXERCISE WITHOUT THESE NEUTRAL CORNERS!** These corners are recovery areas for anyone who finds the emotional buildup within any circle too great to control. This is a powerful exercise, and can open many emotional gates and remove inhibitions. The class members should pause after each phase of the exercise to re-orient themselves before continuing.

1. Absorbing the Mood. With fellow members of the class, move at random among the four emotional circles. Work for yourself only, and ignore everyone else.

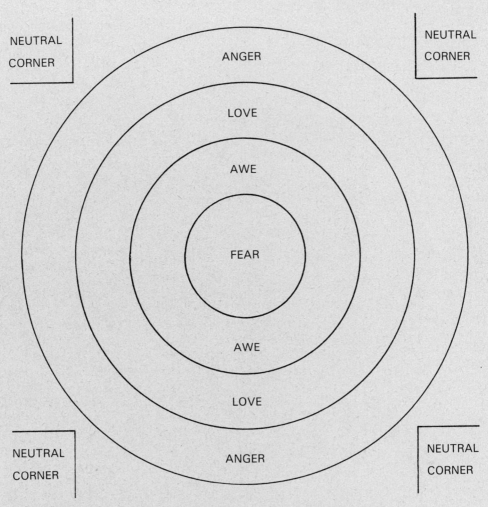

Figure 10.4.

Breathe in the atmosphere of the circle—fear, awe, love, or anger. Bathe in the pervasive hostility of anger, the warm glow of love, the grave wonder of awe, the austere chill of fear. Let the atmosphere penetrate your pores; see, smell, touch, taste, hear the atmosphere of each circle as you encounter it. At some point in your wandering, move from the center circle of fear through the progression outward to anger and back again. You may make any nonverbal sounds you wish and use any movements you wish, but do not use words, and do not invent a situation for this phase. Concentrate on experiencing the atmosphere. Then pause.

2. Relating to an Animal. This time go through the circles, and create a relationship with an imaginary animal in each circle. The animal may be a real one from your memory or an animal created by your imagination. In this phase you may use improvised words to relate to the animal, but ignore any other people who might be in the same circle. Pause.

3. People of Like Nature. This time as you wander through the circles you must relate to anyone you encounter within the same circle. You should behave in a manner appropriate to the nature of the circle, and you may use words, but you must not touch anyone except in the love circle where touching is permitted. Remember the neutral corners. They may be necessary for some people at this point. After you have been through all four circles several times, pause.

4. People of Different Natures. This time as you wander through the circles, relate only to people in adjacent circles—fear to awe, awe to either fear or love, love to either awe or anger, and anger to love.

Take time with this exercise. It will deepen your experience if you repeat the exercise in later sessions. It is also helpful to end a session of emotional circles with all circles merging into one large wheel of love, in which touching is encouraged. This ending will counter any downbeat feelings you might have if you should be in the fear circle or anger circle at the end of the exercise.

DISCUSSION

1. What differences in intensity of emotion did you experience among the four phases of the exercise? To what do you attribute the differences?
2. Can you find similarities between the tensions in each emotional circle and those you experienced in the four modes of dealing with space (flying, floating, molding, and radiating) in part 2 of this text?[6]
3. What happened to body movements and gestures as you moved from the center circle (fear) outward into the larger circles (awe, love, anger)?[7]
4. In which phase of the exercise did you find the greatest amount of tension? Why?

Tempo-Rhythms of Emotions

You will recall your work on tempo-rhythms with actions in chapter 6. An excellent way to help maintain a consistent interpretation of the emotional level for a character is to find an appropriate tempo-rhythm. Since a tempo-rhythm is a repeatable right-brain function, it may provide a reliable reference for the emotional level of performance.

Finding Tempo-Rhythms for Character Emotions

For this right-brain exercise, study one of the characters in a scene from the appendix or from a scene of your own choice. Develop a tempo-rhythm for the chosen character. Clap the tempo-rhythm for the class. Follow the same discussion procedure as for the life study tempo-rhythm exercise in chapter 6.

Now work on a scene with a partner using the tempo-rhythm pattern as a basis for the character's emotional nature and level. Perform the scene for the class.

DISCUSSION

1. What value do performers find in this approach for increasing the reliability of the emotional level of performance?
2. What reactions do viewers have toward performances in which tempo-rhythms were developed?

Dominant Temperament and Emotional Contrasts

Characters usually have a dominant temperament, which is determined by their

1. emotional capacity (ability to express emotions)
2. volatility (excitability)
3. strength of will (determination)
4. vulnerability (sensitivity to the emotions of others)
5. emotional honesty (openness)

After determining the dominant temperament of a character, you should find an element or two of emotional contrast that help to color the character with individuality and variety.

Finding Dominant and Contrasting Emotions

For this integrated-brain exercise, select a character from one of the scenes in the appendix or one of your own choice. Determine the dominant temperament using the above guide. Then find one or more contrasting emotional elements. Perform the scene for the class with a partner.

DISCUSSION

1. What perceptions did the viewers have of the characters's temperament? Openness? Volatility? Determination? Vulnerability? Honesty?
2. What contrasting emotional elements did the viewers perceive in the performances?
3. What differences (if any) were there between your intentions and the perceptions of viewers?

Mythic Emotions

If emotions that come up during a play call up questions, or seem to remind you of something that you can't quite put your finger on, then it starts to get interesting. . . . It starts to hook up in a certain way. Those, to me, are mythic emotions.

———*Sam Shepard*

In a number of contemporary plays, particularly those of Harold Pinter and Sam Shepard, a degree of ambiguity shrouds the nature of emotional relationships between characters. Frequently this ambiguity suggests primitive, undefined fears, anxieties, or aspirations that go to the heart of our relationship as human beings to a universe that seems indifferent or hostile. To placate the demonic forces, characters suffer for unknown offenses, and redemption comes for the tribe—if at all—through sacrifice, as the innocent suffer along with the guilty.

Persecuting a Scapegoat

For this integrated-brain exercise one member of the class is sent out of the room. The class then invents a wrong that the person (the scapegoat) has done against some member of the class. Members of the group devise various psychological means of punishing the person, such as verbal abuse, shunning the person, or closely surrounding him or her without touching. When the person returns, he or she is persecuted by the group until the victim discovers the alleged wrong. The group should not give hints, but it cannot deceive as the scapegoat seeks to discover the alleged wrong from other members of the group. When the alleged wrong is discovered, the scapegoat proclaims his or her innocence but is driven out of the group.

The exercise is repeated with several different scapegoats; some are driven out, but others are forgiven and accepted.

DISCUSSION
1. How did individual members of the group feel as the group banded together to punish the scapegoat? What actions brought about the feelings?
2. How did scapegoats feel about the unjust accusations? What actions did the scapegoats take to try to refute the accusations?
3. How did both the group and scapegoats feel about the rejection (or forgiveness) of the scapegoats after the guilt was discovered? What actions were taken to communicate rejection (or forgiveness)?

Summary

In this chapter you have explored the emotional level of the creative process of performing. You have found that emotions in both performers and audiences are aroused by actions and images. You performed right-brain exercises to overcome your inhibitions and to develop your emotional responsiveness. You examined your reactions to the experiences with left-brain discussion. Lastly, you worked on exercises that integrate right- and left-brain functions to widen the scope of your emotional expression and on tempo-rhythm exercises to help make the emotional expression consistently repeatable.

Notes

1. Paul Ekman, Robert W. Levenson, and Wallace V. Friesen, "Autonomic Nervous System Activity Distinguishes Among Emotions," *Science* 22 (September 1983): pp. 1208–1210.
2. Cited by Amy Lippman, "Rhythm & Truths," *American Theatre* 1, No. 1 (April 1984): 9.
3. From an interview on the "Donahue Show," WNBC-TV, 11 July 1984.
4. Ekman, p. 1210.
5. The emotions are: A. Fear, B. Anger, C. Awe, D. Love.
6. Suggested parallels: fear = flying, awe = radiating, love = floating, anger = molding.
7. In general, body movements progress from closed and protective in the fear circle to more open and larger movements and gestures with each successive circle.

For Further Reading

Ekman, Paul, Robert W. Levenson, and Wallace V. Friesen. "Autonomic Nervous System Activity Distinguishes Among Emotions," *Science* 22 (September 1983): 1208–1210.

Morris, Desmond. *Manwatching: A Field Guide to Human Behavior.* New York: Harry N. Abrams, 1977. "Introduction," "Actions," "Gestures," "Displacement Activities," "Re-Motivating Actions," "Metasignals."

Restak, Richard M. *The Brain: The Last Frontier.* New York: Warner, 1979. Ch. 14.

Chapter 11 _____

The Level of
Aesthetic Distance

Theatre is a mode of discovery that explores the threads of what is implicit and buried in the world, and pulls them into a compressed and acknowledgeable pattern before us in its "world." Theatre discovers meaning, and its peculiar detachment reveals our involvement.

———*Bruce Wilshire*, Role Playing and Identity

Welcome to the awesome "Sixth Level." Up to this point you have discovered the following:

1. the power of action
2. the subtlety of language
3. the psychological complexity of unconscious role playing
4. the gamelike quality of conscious role playing
5. the honesty and depth of emotions

And now you are ready to explore the framing of aesthetic distance, which establishes the viewpoint of the character for both performer and audience.

Aesthetic Distance

Aesthetic distance is the separation between a work of art and the experience it captures or represents, which enables both the creator and the spectator to experience the creation at both an emotional, empathetic level and at a comprehensive, intellectual level simultaneously. Does this concept sound familiar? It should. It is the artistic sensibility of both logical, left-brain analysis and intuitive, right-brain comprehension. For the actor this double awareness permits himself or herself to identify so closely with a character that the performer and character appear to be inseparable. On the other hand, it also permits the actor to place the character at some distance from his or her own personality, showing the character in a sort of quotation marks, similar to the way a director might demonstrate character behavior for an actor during rehearsals. Through aesthetic distance the sensitive audience member also can experience simultaneously both the illusion of a character in a story and the excellence of an actor's performance on the stage.

The Experience of Doubleness

Those who succeed in giving a mystic sense to the simple form of a robe and who, not content with placing a man's Double next to him, confer upon each man in his robes a double made of clothes—those who pierce these illusory or secondary clothes with a saber, giving them the look of huge butterflies pinned in the air, such men have an innate sense of the absolute and magical symbolism of nature much superior to ours, and set us an example which it is only too certain our own theater technicians will be powerless to profit from.

———*Antonin Artaud*, The Theatre and Its Double

The achievement of doubleness is a bit closer to our reach than the French theoretician Antonin Artaud wrote in his important treatise.[1] This experience of aesthetic distancing may be shared by both audience and performer without using an actual double or second actor.

The Effect of the Audience

The audience assists in the process of creating the effect of doubleness, for the level and composition of the audience may have a subtle influence on the performance of the actor as the actor responds to the audience's reactions. The Soviet actor and director Michael Chekhov notes while playing Hamlet that at different performances his audiences were comprised of identifiable groups of people, such as workers, soldiers, teachers, or doctors. Although Chekhov's basic interpretation of the melancholy Dane remained the same from performance to performance, subtle changes adapted his interpretation to the understanding and special interests of the specific audience. He reports that

on one night I was Hamlet and a medical doctor at the same time; the next, I was Hamlet and a farmer, or a writer, but always remaining Hamlet on the upper level. This experience taught me that there must and can be deeper, stronger links between the characters and the audience, and only by appeals to multileveled performances can we forge them.[2]

In a similar vein the ages of audience members may create differences of reception and affect the nuances of performance. Recently my college theatre department presented a production of *Arsenic and Old Lace* to one audience composed of high school students, and another of senior citizens. (See fig. 11.1.) For the high school audience, the love scenes and thrilling moments brought giggles; whereas, the older audience smiled nostalgically at the romance, squirmed noticeably at moments of increasing tension, and gasped in concern when the central characters were threatened. The performers, aware of the feedback from the audiences, adjusted their performances both consciously and unconsciously to please the different groups, making the romance and grotesquerie just a little more exaggerated for the high school students, and deepening their emotions for the more mature crowd.

Figure 11.1. *Arsenic and Old Lace* by Joseph Kesselring. Sensitive performers make both conscious and unconscious adjustments to the response of the audience, generally emphasizing those aspects which evoke overt audience response. (Photograph: Joe Meyer. Courtesy of Montclair State College, Major Theatre Series. Set and lights: W. Scott MacConnell; costumes: Joseph F. Bella.)

The ability to control these subtle and necessary adjustments is dependent largely on the actor's mastery of the design of the role at the level of aesthetic distance. The adjustment must be subtle because the basic presentation of the role does not change. The adjustment is necessary because the collective response of one audience differs from the collective response of another audience.

You may well wonder if such an adjustment to the audience isn't playing down to a lower, more unsophisticated level of taste. I think rather that this adjustment is the honest recognition that in any flow of communication, understanding begins where viewpoints meet. The actor brings to the performance an interpretation and weeks of rehearsal and work; the individual members of the audience combine their collective viewpoints and previous experiences from life and as theatregoers. As social beings of various ages and maturities, the members of the audience collectively comprise a brook of potential response upon which the actors will toss the impressions of action and characterization.

Like stones thrown into a brook, the actor's behavior initiates ripples of understanding, delight, empathy, and laughter at the point of impact. But in almost an instant, the ripples from individuals and groups of individuals in the audience are united into a unified wave of response. This phenomenon occurs continuously on a moment-by-moment basis throughout the performance. (See fig. 11.2.) Because the

Figure 11.2.   Ripple Effect. The responses of individual audience members unite into a response that embraces the total audience and provides a feedback to the performers, completing the circle of communication.

process is on-going, the actor's adjustments to the audience continue throughout the performance.

When the communication from the performer blends harmoniously with the communication from the audience, great moments in theatre are possible. As Frederick Frank has put it,

> WHO IS MAN, THE ARTIST? . . . HE IS THE UNSPOILED CORE OF EVERYMAN, BEFORE HE IS CHOKED BY SCHOOLING, TRAINING, CONDITIONING UNTIL THE ARTIST-WITHIN SHRIVELS UP AND IS FORGOTTEN. . . . At times it [the artistic sensibility] responds to Nature, to beauty, to Life, suddenly aware again of being in the presence of a Mystery that baffles understanding and which only has to be glimpsed to renew our Spirit and to make us feel that life is a Supreme gift.[3]

It is through the achievement of right-brain/left-brain aesthetic distance that such moments in theatre exist.

Actor as Observer

An actor lives, weeps, laughs on the stage, but as he weeps and laughs he observes his own tears and mirth. It is this double existence, this balance between life and acting that makes for art.

———*Tommaso Salvini*

In chapter 8 we considered ways in which observation in everyday life aids the actor in developing characterization. At this point we will consider exercises to develop the actor's observation of the self, both in everyday life and in rehearsal and performance. For in teaching the right brain to become more aware, we increase the ability of the left brain to monitor performance.

Seeing Yourself

With the class divided into pairs for this right-brain exercise, each partner should take turns reading aloud the next paragraph and the questions that follow. The people being read to should visualize their responses with eyes closed.

"Close your eyes for a moment, and with the visualization abilities that you have been developing, see how many details you can recreate from the time you got up from bed this morning. Picture this experience with your right brain in as vivid and minute detail as possible.

1. What were you wearing?
2. What color were the sheets, and what did the texture feel like?
3. What woke you? Alarm clock? Radio? Music? Noise? A person?
4. Did you dress first, or wash your face and brush your teeth first?
5. What color was the toothbrush? What flavor was the toothpaste? What color?
6. What did you eat for breakfast? Did you prepare the food yourself or watch someone else prepare it? What beverages did you drink? At what intervals did you drink the beverages? How rapid or leisurely was your eating?
7. What items did you gather before you left your residence? Books? Projects? Sweater? Jacket? Keys? Purse or wallet? Did you find everything easily, or did you have to look for anything? Where did you have to look?
8. Can you see yourself leaving your residence, opening and closing the door? Which hand did you use to open and close the door?
9. How did you get to class? Walk? Car? Bus?
10. What was the most unusual thing you saw on the way to class?
11. Who was the first person you saw when you arrived at class? What is that person wearing? How did you greet that person?"

After each partner has visualized a response, you may gather for discussion.

DISCUSSION
1. How did the vividness of the recalled events vary from moment to moment?
2. Which type of details did you have the most difficulty visualizing? Why?
3. Which details were the easiest to recall? Why?

Observing Your Acting

Try this right-brain exercise before you perform your next scene. Close your eyes and visualize your scene from the perspective of your partner as you say your lines aloud. Picture the movements that you make, the use of props; hear the nuances of your own voice responding as you give your own image (which you are visualizing) your character's lines. Then imagine the image of the character you play repeating the lines you have just spoken aloud. After you have gone through this process, perform your scene for your class.

DISCUSSION
1. What effect did you think the image-making exercise had on your performance?
2. What effect did your classmates think the exercise had on their own performances and on yours?

Observing Yourself with a Partner: Lights Out!

In this integrated-brain exercise, after you are well rehearsed on a scene, practice the scene in the dark with your partner, each of you visualizing in as much detail as possible what both of you are doing. Listen to the rhythm, tempo, and nuance of your partner's voice. Listen to the rhythm, tempo, and nuance in your own voice.

DISCUSSION
1. How does the air in your rehearsal space feel? How does it smell?
2. How should the atmosphere in your scene be different from the atmosphere of the rehearsal space?
3. How does this exercise change your interaction and handling of props?

Presentational vs. Representational Modes

"It's as large as life, and twice as natural."
———*Lewis Carroll*, Through the Looking Glass

The clearest and quickest approach to developing the ability to place some distance between the character and the actor is to place the character in a presentational rather than a representational style. Since naturalism and realism have been the prevailing theatrical styles of the last hundred years and most young performers see more performances on film and television than in the theatre, the concept of the presentational performance of character may be somewhat foreign to your experience. Yet historically it has been more often the rule than the exception.

Today we encounter presentational performing in the professional theatre far more frequently than we did 30 years ago, but even when used in the commercial theatre, it is frequently combined with representational presentation. If these terms are unfamiliar to you, you can remember them by associating them with certain types of plays.

Plays written for fourth-wall realism or naturalism attempt to "represent life as it is" with a fourth wall removed or, if the scene takes place outdoors, as the scene might be observed by a hidden or unseen observer. These plays use representational performance. The actors appear to ignore the audience and interact only among themselves. Writers who use this approach to character portrayal in their best-known plays are Henrik Ibsen, Anton Chekhov, and more recently Lillian Hellman, Arthur Miller, William Inge, Lanford Wilson, and Marsha Norman. Scenes usually presented representationally that are printed in the appendix of this book include those from *Ah, Wilderness!*, *Night Must Fall*, and *Crimes of the Heart*.

On the other hand, in the presentational mode the actor stays in character but speaks directly to the audience and appears to interact more actively with the audience than with the other characters on stage. There are various degrees of involvement with audience and other characters. In the extreme use of the presentational style the actor might focus delivery entirely in the audience and react to other characters as if they were located in or behind the audience. This technique may initially demand a different focus of concentration in order to overcome any distractions created by peering into the sea of audience faces, reflecting a variety of expressions from empathetic smiles to boredom, with a few closed eyes of those who have fallen asleep!

Performers who prefer the relative safety of the representational style may find their initial experiments in the presentational style hazardous to their security. But the adjustment does not take long, and the prevalence of plays today that shift quickly from the representational to the presentational mode demand that the performer develop facility with both approaches to playing and with the transition from one mode to the other.

The following list summarizes the major distinctions between representational and presentational approaches to performance:

representational	*presentational*
1. illusionary theatre—attempts to make audience forget the artifice	nonillusionary theatre—reminds audience of the artifice
2. does not address audience	may address audience directly
3. attempts to create lifelike characters	may only indicate or suggest characterization
4. theatre as a mirror	theatre as a mask
5. theatre of "being"	theatre of "seeming"

Despite the general differences, you will find many shadings between the polarities just listed, and the choices you make for performing a particular play may vary with the individual style of the play, the period of the play, and the interpretation of a director.

Scenes in this text that use both presentational and representational approaches are selected from *Sister Mary Ignatius Explains It All For You*, *Hotel Paradiso*, and *Marat/Sade*. There are also asides (isolated lines spoken to the audience) in *Hotel Paradiso* and *The Good Woman of Setzuan* that provide a token experience in presentational performing.

The next three exercises will help you develop your ability to perform presentationally.

Interacting with a Group: Playing Ball

To improve reflexes in responding to a group's reaction, try the following right-brain exercise. In groups of six to nine, one person stands in front of the rest, separated by 10 to 15 feet. An imaginary ball is thrown from the individual to some member of the group. The receiver transforms the size and weight of the ball. The individual catches the new ball, again transforms it, and throws it back.

Periodically, the tempo of the game should vary, with a designated coach calling out tempo and spatial changes from time to time: "Moderately fast." "Very slow." "Extremely fast." "Slow motion." "Underwater." "In outer space." "In hot lead." Individuals rotate until all have had the experience of being in front of the group. The exercise ends with a brisk tempo and a pleasant atmosphere.

DISCUSSION
1. What physical and mental skills did you have to use to keep the ball moving by the rules?
2. What difficulties did you experience with the tempo and spatial changes?

Presenting Zero-Line Delivery

A. For this left-brain exercise, take a speech from a scene you are working on. Stand in front of the group. Deliver the lines flatly, devoid of interpretation and characterization. Make your pitch a monotone, and use a steady, moderate rate of delivery.

DISCUSSION
1. What new understanding of the actor-audience relationship did you perceive?
2. What new perceptions did the rest of the group have?
3. Did you experience the sensation of delivering the author's words in an objective, presentational manner?

B. Deliver the same speech as if you were an uninvolved third party reading a telegram to the recipient.

DISCUSSION
1. Are you now able to separate the intellectual content from the character and emotional content of the material?
2. Do you feel that you are not "acting" when you make this separation?
3. Are you "acting" when you tie up your emotions in knots and hide behind personality masks?

Presenting Character Delivery

For this integrated-brain exercise, take a speech from one of the presentational scenes in the appendix or of your own choice elsewhere. Develop your interpretation of the character, using all the levels of craft you have developed so far. First place your focus on stage, and perform in the representational mode.

After you have performed representationally, then perform the same material presentationally, directly to your class.

DISCUSSION
1. What were the internal and external adjustments you had to make (other the obvious one of changing your focus) in the shift from representational to presentational style?
2. What adjustments were class members aware of when you gave your presentational performance?

Alienation and Distance

One of the most misunderstood and misused techniques to create aesthetic distance is the alienation approach suggested by the German playwright Bertolt Brecht. In his first theoretical statement, "A Short Organum for the Theatre," Brecht states:

> 42. . . . A representation that alienates is one which allows us to recognize its subject, but at the same time makes it seem unfamiliar. . . . 48. At no moment must he [the actor] go so far as to be wholly transformed into the character played. . . . He has just to show the character.[4]

Realizing that his first statement had created more heat than light, Brecht attempted to clarify his concept:

> The contradiction between acting (demonstration) and experience (empathy) often leads the uninstructed to suppose that only one or the other can be manifest in the work of the actor. . . . In reality it is a matter of two mutually hostile processes which fuse in the actor's work. . . . His particular effectiveness comes from the tussle and tension of the two opposites, and also from their depth.[5]

If Brecht's explanation doesn't enlighten you sufficiently about his meaning of alienation, maybe John Gassner's account of the origin of Brecht's approach will. Gassner reports that Brecht attended readings of plays presided over by Erwin Piscator during the early days of the Weimar Republic. The actors sat at a table on a bare stage, reading their lines without entering into the embellishments of performance. Gassner explains:

> But, although the actors made no pretense of being "in character," as we say, the audience were more completely held than by the plays which attempted full theatrical illusion. Suddenly Brecht saw that what held them was not character, not illusion, but the moral relationship between the characters, the moral argument of the play. The actor was quoting the words, imitating the actions; he was estranged from the character. The moral conflict was seen isolated, at a distance, as history. This is the effect of "estrangement," of "alienation," which is Brecht's particular contribution to the theatre. He calls it the *Verfremdungseffekt*.[6]

Brecht's analogy for "alienation" or "estrangement" was that of a watch (not the microchip digital type but the old-fashioned, jewel-driven watch, which operates by intricate interactions of gears and springs). On its face a watch is an ordinary, familiar object, but take it apart and the pieces and their interrelation become fascinating. This viewpoint causes one to study the relation of the parts to the whole and to the final function more carefully.

The biggest mistake we may make in attempting an alienation approach is to misunderstand the object of the alienation. Some performers or directors have mistakenly thought the audience was to be alienated from any empathy with the characters, so that misguided actors have presented their work with a hostility that has driven audience members from the theatre. Others have thought that the presentation of character should be so devoid of humanity that actors appear only as cardboard mouthpieces for the words of the play.

In actual practice Brecht used all the sound approaches to the development of character and reality that we have explored in this text, but he interrupted the realistic, presentational illusion that the actors created in one of two ways. In one approach his actors moved in character directly from the representational mode to the presentational mode, as we have just examined. His second approach went one step further, moving the actor from the representational mode in character to an ultranaturalistic mode in which the actor as person, rather than actor as character, addressed the audience directly. The next three exercises will help you to develop both modes.

Reexamining the Stage Environment

A. In an exercise in chapter 4 you narrated aloud the details of your stage environment in order to feel at home in it. Then you transformed that environment into an imaginary environment. Let us now create aesthetic distance within a scene by adapting the earlier exercise to a new use. Using both sides of your brain, perform in a representational style a two-character scene that you have prepared with your partner. A third person calls out the instructions "stop" and "go" at arbitrary moments in the scene. On the instruction "stop" you and your partner suspend performance of the scene, and one of you reports what is being experienced in the stage environment. On the instruction "go" the scene resumes. At the next "stop" the other one reports on the stage environment and on "go" resumes the scene. Alternate responses throughout the exercise.

DISCUSSION
1. Were you able to move in and out of the scene quickly and thoroughly?
2. How did you feel about the sudden, unexpected interruptions, even though you knew they might be coming?

B. Try the same exercise in front of a group of classmates.

DISCUSSION
What are the reactions of your classmates to the interruptions and to the impact of the scene when you return to it?

Inserting a Character Biography

Using both sides of your brain, perform a two-character scene for which you and your partner have each prepared your character's biography. As in the previous exercise, another person outside the scene will call "stop" and "go" at arbitrary points. This time at the interruptions you will give biographical information about your character while you remain in character. Alternate with your partner in giving additional information about your character each time you are stopped. Discuss the same points raised with the previous exercise.

Reexamining Subtext

A. Using both sides of your brain, perform the same scene you used in the previous exercise with the same signals for interruptions. This time when "stop" is called out, report the narrative of your character's inner thoughts and observations, speaking in a nonemotional manner but remaining in character. Alternate your narrative with your partner's.

B. Perform the scene again, and on the "stop" command, try the extreme of this exercise by alternately narrating the character's inner life from your own viewpoints as performers.

DISCUSSION

1. Does the shift in process suggest anything to you about left-brain/right-brain functions?
2. How do you feel the shift in process aids or hinders the emotional honesty of the character?
3. How do you perceive the differences between "being" in character and "seeming" to be the character?

Gestus and Distance

Gestus, another of Bertolt Brecht's concepts, can be helpful in placing the characterization at an aesthetic distance for the actor and the audience. Used in various ways at different times by Brecht, the word *gestus* was coined from the German word *Geste* which means "gesture." The fundamental meaning of the word, as Brecht applied it, implies an actor's physical expression of the social, economic, and political context for the character rather than the physicalization of the character's psychological attitude. The physicalization created to express this context may be as small a gesture as Mother Courage's biting a coin each time she is paid for her wares or as large as Lauffer's exaggeration of a groveling bow to town officials who ignore him in Brecht's adaptation of Jacob M. R. Lenz's 1774 play *The Private Tutor*. Both the centering technique and the movement-types technique explored in chapter 8 are helpful in developing physicalization for the gestus.[7]

Creating a Gestus

For this right-brain exercise, using the scene from *The Good Woman of Setzuan* or *Marat/Sade* in the appendix or from another appropriate play, develop gestures, posture, or movement, that illustrate the social, economic, or political context in which the characters interact. Perform the gestus for the class, first in a larger-than-life size, then life-size.

DISCUSSION

1. How did each person's gestus provide insight into either the social, economic, or political context of the character's life?
2. How does the difference in performance size affect your perception of the comment the gestus makes?
3. How does the difference in performance size affect your awareness of the distance of the actor from the character?

Personal Style and Audience Interaction

One of the characteristics of great drawings is the artist's wholehearted acceptance of his own style and character. It is as if the drawing says for the artist, "here I am."
———*Nathan Goldstein*, The Art of Responsive Drawing

Whatever approach you may take to develop aesthetic distance, your final performance will be colored by the uniqueness of your own individuality.

As you discovered in chapter 8 on the level of unconscious role playing, performers can use only their own experiences, actual or imagined, as resources for creating a character. Likewise, in creating a separation between themselves and their characters, both the personal perceptions and imaginative abilities of the performer are the filters through which the created character must pass. The character, then, is an image, created through the collective efforts of an ensemble of interacting individuals, projected in time and space to the receptors of an audience and then reassembled as a complementary image in the mirror of the audience mind, somewhat in the way that a Rubik's cube is reassembled to its initial design after being scrambled.

The character, like the cube, has a created form. It exists as an extension from its creator. Though it may have had an orderly design in conception, the original design may suffer in the hands of the inept. So it is with the individual audience member. A lack of theatregoing experience or insufficient sophistication may prevent some individuals in an audience from perceiving the actor's design of the role. Even a sophisticated audience member may have personal preferences of style that prevent full appreciation of the actor's personal style of design. This is why a performance reported by five different newspaper reviewers will result in five reviews so widely divergent that one may wonder if the reviewers saw the production on the same night. (Sometimes one wonders if they even attended the same play!)

The actor should not worry, however, about how the character image may or may not be perceived. If the actor has paid attention to the development of the design of the character image and is responsive to the general audience reactions, his or her only other major obligation is to keep that design image fresh. In a college production with a typical three- or four-night performance schedule, this may not be a tremendous problem. Nevertheless, it can be observed that performances of the character image may vary, sometimes considerably, from night to night.

This problem of variability can be overcome partially through sufficient rehearsal and the use of tempo-rhythm as suggested in chapters 6 and 10. But variability can also be reduced by the intelligent discipline of left-brain control, which keeps the designing right brain on track.

Even if the performance of the role does vary somewhat, there is no great loss to the understanding of the play, for many other factors are operating to communicate the interpretation of the play to the audience. The variability of the performance, if played with attention to all the elements you now have at your command, will be an honest expression of your own variability as a human being. It is this live human expression for which audiences attend theatre. As an artist, however, you will want to recreate the image of the character in performance as closely as possible to the image you created in rehearsals, so that for your own satisfaction the character will unfold as rehearsed. As Bruce Wilshire observes:

> . . . we must make a distinction between the actor as artist and actor as character. As artist he controls the extent to which this submission as character occurs.[8]

Other Distancing Techniques

The additional exercises for both sides of your brain that follow may be helpful in achieving both an understanding of the concept of aesthetic distance and the development of it for performance. Please remember, however, that these are primarily learning and rehearsal techniques. In most instances modifications as suggested by your directors should be used during actual performance. Several of these exercises have specific applications to some of the scenes of specific genres offered in the appendix. Where applicable you may wish to try the exercises with those scenes or with other scenes of a similar genre.

Distancing with Narrator/Character: Story Theatre

A. Fairy Tales. The class divides into small groups, which improvise well-known fairy tales, updating them to contemporary settings (as for example, "Goldilocks and the Three Bears Meet in Acid Rain Forest," "Little Red Riding Hood Helps a Wolf with a Vitamin Deficiency," "Alice in Computerland," "Cinderella from the Pizzaria"). Members of the group should narrate themselves into the scene, describing the setting, where they're coming from, why they're there, how they are reacting internally while dealing with the situation externally. There should be a clean separation between actor as self-narrator, speaking directly to the audience (presentationally), and actor as character, speaking to the other characters (representationally).

B. Self Narration. Class members apply the same technique to the scene from *Marat/Sade* in the appendix. Initially, in addition to the dialogue in the script, each one narrates himself or herself in his or her own persona into the scene (as actor) and narrates the internal character reactions (as character) before delivering each line of dialogue.

Distancing with Caricature

A. Human Caricature. With a partner each performer develops a caricature of a well-known personality and places the caricatures in a plausible but unusual situation. (For example, Dolly Parton takes a personal problem to Dr. Ruth Westhiemer or to Dr. Joyce Brothers; Michael Jackson takes Diana Ross to Coney Island.) In developing the caricature, focus on three or four strong personality traits—voice qualities, tempo-rhythms, physical mannerisms, or energy centers.

B. Animal Caricature. Use the image of an animal (either a real animal or a cartoon animal) as the basis for developing a caricature approach to the characters in the scene from *Hotel Paradiso* or another broad comedy of your own choice. In developing your animal image consider items such as the animal's movements, vocal qualities, size, weight, color, and surface texture. After you have divided the scene into motivational beats, play several of the beats using only appropriate animal noises instead of lines.

Lastly, retain the textures of the movements and vocal qualities you have developed, and transfer them into the action and dialogue of the scene.

Distancing with Burlesque

A. Melodrama. Work on a scene from *Night Must Fall* to exaggerate the melodramatic qualities of the characters and the dramatic tension of the scene. Rehearse the scene with physical broadness and vocal exaggeration as if it were a 19th century melodrama. Then try the scene with an urbane, sophisticated approach as if you were playing a comedy by Noel Coward or A. R. Gurney, Jr. Now try the scene realistically, as you might see it on a television soap opera.

DISCUSSION
1. How has your perspective of the scene changed?
2. Is the shape of the scene clearer?
3. Are the characters more vividly etched?

B. Sex-Role Reversal. Rehearse the scene from *Crimes of the Heart* with men playing the roles. Use physical and vocal exaggeration that create stereotypes, with the male actors playing such types as the "helpless, dumb blonde," "the catty gossip," "the earthy mother." Then rehearse the scene with women playing the roles, but as stereotypical male types, "the effete artist," "the rugged macho," "the dapper salesman."

DISCUSSION

1. What did you observe in playing the stereotypes of the opposite sex?
2. Why are stereotypes amusing?
3. Is there any validity for using stereotypes for comedy today in the theatre?
4. What are some of the stereotypes you see on television, in films, and on the stage?

Trifurcating the Character

Use a two-character scene you have worked on from the appendix or from your own choice. Set six chairs in two rows of three, angled toward each other. (See fig. 11.3.) The object of this exercise is to separate each character into three layers:

1. the observer
2. the planner
3. the doer

Each pair of chairs represents one phase—the upstage chairs, the observers; the middle chairs, the planners; the downstage chairs, the doers. At the beginning of the exercise both characters sit in their own upstage chairs. The actor with the first line in the script begins by observing the stage environment as actor. The same actor then moves to the middle chair, where he or she as character describes the relationship with the partner's character, and plans how as character to deal with the partner's character.

The second actor goes through the same two steps: observes the environment as actor, and then as character describes the relationship with the partner's character and how to deal with the partner's character.

The first actor moves to the downstage (third) chair and in character gives the first line of dialogue. The second actor moves to the downstage chair opposite the first actor, and in character gives the second line of dialogue. The process is repeated before each line of dialogue. This exercise is particularly helpful to clarify character actions when the characters are dishonest with other characters as they are in the scenes from *The Good Woman of Setzuan* and *Hotel Paradiso* in the appendix.

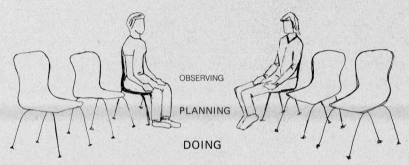

OBSERVING

PLANNING

DOING

Figure 11.3.   Three Chair Exercise. Each actor has a chair for the separation of three aspects of the character: the observer, the planner, the doer.

DISCUSSION

1. What were some character objectives the three-chair process helped clarify for you in your scene?
2. How do you feel now about the skills used for internal and external characterization?

Summary of Part 3

In part 3 of this text you have discovered how right-brain and left-brain functions may be used in the creative processes of the craft of acting in its six levels of operation—from identifying and performing actions, to exploring and interpreting language, to developing both unconscious and conscious role playing, to enhancing emotional expression, and lastly to shaping artistic objectivity toward aesthetic expression.

In part 4 you will consider the additional problems of developing a role in the contexts of rehearsal (chapter 12) and performance (chapter 13). In the final chapter you will examine some of the specific characteristics of popularly performed, contemporary genres, which may be used in developing scenes in the appendix or other scenes of such genres.

Notes

1. Antonin Artaud, *The Theater and Its Double*, Translated by Mary Caroline Richards (New York: Grove Press, 1958), p. 62. Used by permission of the publisher.
2. Michael Chekhov, *To the Director and Playwright* (New York: Harper & Row, 1963), p. 107.
3. Frederick Frank, *The Zen of Seeing* (New York: Vintage Books, 1973), pp. x–xi.
4. "A Short Organum for the Theatre," *Brecht on Theatre*, Translated by John Willet (New York: Hill & Wang, 1964), pp. 179–205.
5. "Appendices to the Short Organum," *Brecht on Theatre*, pp. 276–281.
6. John Gassner, *Directions in Modern Theatre and Drama* (New York: Holt, Rinehart & Winston, 1967), pp. 309–310.
7. For further explanation of this approach with some additional excellent examples, see John Rouse, "Brecht and the Contradictory Actor," *Theatre Journal* 36, no. 1 (March 1984): 32–34.
8. Bruce Wilshire, *Role Playing and Identity* (Bloomington, Ind.: Indiana University Press, 1982), p. xv.

For Further Reading

Booth, Wayne C. *The Rhetoric of Fiction*. Chicago: The University of Chicago Press, 1961. Chapter 6, "Types of Narration," pp. 155–158.
Chaim, Daphna Ben. *Distance in the Theatre: The Aesthetics of Audience Reponse*. Ann Arbor, Mich.: UMI Research Press, 1984.
Chekhov, Michael. *To the Director and Playwright*. New York: Harper & Row, 1963. Ch. 15.
Cohen, Robert. *Acting Power*. Palo Alto, Calif.: Mayfield, 1978. Ch. 5.
Hayman, Ronald. *Techniques of Acting*. London: Methuen, 1969. Ch. 5.
Rouse, John. "Brecht and the Contradictory Actor." *Theatre Journal* 36, no. 1 (March 1984): pp. 25–41.

Part Four

The Perspective of
Role Development

Introduction

Pursue The Process

Is it not monstrous that this player here,
But in a fiction, in a dream of passion
Could force his soul to his own conceit?

————*Shakespeare*, Hamlet

In the first three sections of this text you have been introduced to the right-brain/left-brain concept of the creative processes; developed your sensitivity to your self, your environment, and your fellow performers; and worked on techniques for each of the six levels of the performer's craft. So far you have laid the foundations of your work, which can now be built upon by applying these principles to roles from plays.

In chapter 12 you will find guidelines for developing roles through the rehearsal process. These steps may be applied to the creation of full-length roles as well as to the portrayal of characters in scenes for classroom work. Subsequently, in chapter 13 you are offered suggestions for sustaining your characterizations during performances, dealing with stage fright, and refreshing your creative energies during the run of a play. Together these two chapters offer practical right- and left-brain approaches to role development.

Chapter 12
The Role in Rehearsal

There is another, better self within all of us, but unfortunately it is mostly hidden beyond the threshold of our consciousness. . . . When working upon the characters, try giving this other self the benefit of the doubt by appealing to it for assistance. . . . For this higher self is the voice of the true artist within us, the bearer of our talent, the creator of our genuinely aesthetic endeavors.

———*Michael Chekhov*, To the Director and Playwright

Basic Principles of Role Development

Now that you are familiar with the six levels of craft, you are ready to apply those techniques to the development of characters in plays. Though the primary focus here is on character work in scenes performed for the classroom, the principles apply equally to the full-length role. The major differences between your work on a full-length role and your work for a scene are the complexities of characterization and the depth of emotional discovery achievable in a full-length role, which can only be touched upon in scene work. Nevertheless, you should walk before you run, or you will find yourself floundering with generalities in attempting the complexity of full-length role challenges when you may not yet be prepared to tackle them.

If you develop a sound approach to scene work, then the structures of full-length roles can be both intelligent and exciting. Take your time with the development of each of the six levels of every scene:

1. clear actions
2. insightful delivery of the words
3. believable character relationships with unconscious role playing
4. appropriate conscious role playing
5. emotional honesty
6. an appropriate aesthetic distance for the character

If you will pursue excellence at this stage of your development, then later in your work you will find it easier to master the complexity of a full-length role.

Zero Line

Every role is a challenge. You always start from scratch. Nothing you've done before can prepare you.

————Jessica Tandy

As Jessica Tandy suggests in this observation, made while she was in rehearsals for the highly acclaimed revival of Tennessee Williams's *The Glass Menagerie*, each new role should begin without preconceptions.[1] The performer should begin work on a new role without mannerisms carried over from previous roles and without his or her personality imposing on the new characterization.

A major purpose in the earlier exercises on the four tensions of movement (floating, flying, molding, and radiating), relaxation, and personal mannerisms was to prepare you for role work by returning your mind and body to a natural, uncluttered, balanced condition, from which you may develop whatever physical and mental traits are necessary for a character. This natural, relaxed but alert condition is what we mean by the term zero line. The exercises you performed to achieve it did not erase your own individuality but rather made you more aware of yourself, so your mind and body can serve you and the roles that you will create more effectively.

If you will begin at the zero line with each new scene, each new role, and each new play, you will find the creative experience of developing characterizations challenging and rewarding. Each characterization will be unique. There is nothing that will stunt a performer's creative growth more than falling back on traits developed for previously played characters—a summer stock closet of quickie, clichéd stereotypes that can grow only more stale when recycled as leftovers.

To make your characterizations add up to something, start with nothing— nothing except your craft, your imagination, and your determination to explore and develop the truthfulness of the character and its relationship to the other characters in the play. In the rest of this chapter we will examine and practice some of the techniques for building on the zero line.

Economy

The beautiful movement is the one that accomplishes the greatest effect with the least effort.

————Plato

Many sincere, dedicated, industrious students work too hard at trying to achieve instant results. The inner creative bird is a shy one that cannot be beaten from the bushes but must be coaxed out. The quotation from *Hamlet* at the beginning of this part of the text reflects Hamlet's perplexity at those actors who attempt to force emotions and actions. It is far more honest and eventually stronger to use a small truthful character action on stage than to impose a large action that does not arise from either you or the character in the script.

This observation does not in any way suggest that on stage you should use television-sized behavior. Rather it suggests that whatever the size of the emotional or physical response, it should be a natural result of the circumstances given for the character within the script, with this additional qualification: The performer's response must be adjusted for viewing and hearing, whatever the distance between the performer and the audience.

You may have heard someone in theatre use the expression, "the less—more." As you grow in maturity and in inner and outer technique, you will understand more fully the wisdom of this adage. The precept is a warning against overacting, forcing emotions beyond the character's justification and belaboring the details of individualizing the character at the expense of slowing down the momentum of the character's actions. Nothing can be more distracting in a scene than activity without a purpose. But on the other hand, nothing is more exciting than carefully developed, carefully selected, purposeful action that enlivens and individualizes characterization.

Design and Development: Horizontal and Vertical

As you develop and design a role in rehearsals you will be integrating the six levels of craft. Characterization in either a scene or a full-length role develops both horizontally in time and vertically in depth. Horizontally, facets of the character are revealed as the action of the scene or play unfolds in time. The three levels of craft that are most useful for the horizontal development of character facets are the action level, the word level, and the conscious role-playing level. These levels keep the characters moving toward achievement of their goals. The actor makes varying character adjustments as obstacles to the character's goals are met and dealt with in the forward progression of the play.

Vertically, the greater depth of the character's inner nature is revealed as the complexities of the situations and relationships develop. The unconscious role-playing level and the emotional level are the major contributors to the vertical dimension. The sixth level of craft (aesthetic distance) is usually a constant of the horizontal development, though occasionally the distance of identification between actor and character may become less as the role reaches its climactic moments in vertical development. The following chart (fig. 12.1.) summarizes the use of the six levels in the development of characterization.

For rehearsal purposes it is helpful to focus development on one level of craft at a time. Then additional levels will be merged into your work as you develop the characterization.

The graph provided here (fig. 12.2.) shows an example of the application of this approach to the many facets, or "roles," of Tracy Lord in the popular romantic com-

Horizontal Development	Vertical Development
Action Level Word Level Conscious Role-Playing Aesthetic Distance	Unconscious Role-playing Emotional Level

Figure 12.1.   Levels in Role Development

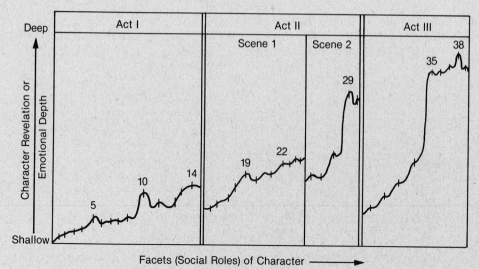

Figure 12.2. Horizontal and Vertical Role Development. Throughout the performance of the play, the character unfolds in two dimensions: the vertical dimension of emotional depth, and the horizontal dimension of personality facets.

edy *The Philadelphia Story*. Horizontal character facets (roles) are indicated on the chart by the small vertical lines. The major character facets are numbered, separated by acts, and correspond to the list below. All roles are unconscious except those marked "conscious." The higher the position of the facet on the graph, the greater the depth of character revelation or emotion in the vertical dimension.

Act I

1. social butterfly
2. condescending sister
3. flippant divorcee
4. social secretary
5. outraged socialite
6. private detective
7. consumate actress (conscious role)
8. teasing niece
9. gracious hostess (conscious role)
10. catty hostess
11. fawning fiancee
12. gushing daughter (conscious role)
13. spurned 'ex' (conscious role)

Act II

Scene 1:
15. avid fan
16. art patroness
17. distraught hostess
18. self-righteous evangelist
19. disdainful goddess
20. bossy sister
21. sentimental lover
22. unmasked pretender
23. determined suppressor
24. disillusioned daughter
25. helpless beggar
Scene 2:
26. eager conspirator

Act III

31. unsteady survivor
32. puzzled amnesiac
33. recuperating patient
34. humble penitent
35. remorseful lover
36. soul-searcher
37. stern judge
38. flustered socialite
39. delirious bride

14. sober heroine	*27.* giddy flirt
	28. desperate gambler
	29. lonely tart
	30. fallen idol

By careful development of a character's multifaceted role in both its horizontal and vertical dimensions, you can achieve more imaginative and exciting performances.

The Design of a Scene

You recall from chapter 6 that you worked on objectives and beats in the action level of performing. Now you should put those techniques into practice as you begin to develop a scene for performance.

Determining Objectives and Beats

Choose a two-character scene from one of those provided in the appendix or from a play of your own selection. (At this point you do not need to concern yourself with the problems of genre, which you will take up in chapter 14.) Divide the scene into beats (that is, into small logical units with a single topic or character objective). Decide what active objectives your character is pursuing. Without discussing your partner's character objectives, improvise the scene on a beat-by-beat basis. Then see if you can identify what objectives your partner's character was pursuing and if your partner can identify your character's objectives.

DISCUSSION
1. What can each of you do to sharpen the playing of the objectives?
2. What adjustments must you make to each other's objectives?
3. What props can you use to develop progressive activities for the character?
4. What other ways can you use space to manifest the dynamic relationship between the characters?

In general you will find that a scene develops with five recognizable sections. At the beginning of most scenes there will be A) exposition, a summary of the relationship of the characters at that point. Then an incident or challenge occurs that increases the tension between characters. This segment is called B) the inciting moment or overt act. The tensions or suspense factors increase between characters through C) rising action until there is D) a climax in the form of a confrontation, a decision, a revelation, or a reversal. Lastly, there is a return to some form of stability with E) a resolution of the differences or a reduction of the tensions. When you find these movements, you will discover the dynamic dramatic development of the scene. Most scenes are similar in form to the traditional structure pictured in the chart. (See fig. 12.3.) The example is from the scene from *Ah, Wilderness!* in the appendix.

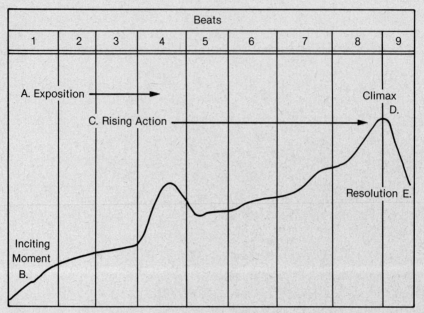

Figure 12.3.   Scene Dramatic Development. Most scenes follow the traditional form pictured here for the scene from *Ah, Wilderness!* in the Appendix.

A. **opening exposition** (Beats #1–3): Richard reveals he has been to a "low dive." Muriel explains that her father made her write a letter to Richard disavowing her love for him.

B. **inciting moment** (Beat #1): Richard arouses Muriel's ire by taunting her with his adventures with a chorus girl he met in the bar. Muriel reminds Richard of the letter that she was forced to send him. Both problems must be overcome before the characters can achieve their objectives.

C. **rising action** (Beat #3–7): Richard protests his faithfulness to Muriel despite his encounter with the chorus girl. Muriel defends her innocence in regard to the offending letter.

D. **climax** (Beat #8): Richard forgives Muriel, and Muriel forgives Richard.

E. **resolution** (Beat #9): The two celebrate their reconciliation with a kiss.

Determining Obstacles

Examine both internal and external obstacles for your character. (If necessary, review the section on obstacles in chapter 6.)

DISCUSSION

1. What internal reservations or inhibitions does your character have that stand in the way of achieving the objectives?

2. How does your partner's character prevent or delay the achievement of your character's objectives?

3. Are there any aspects of the environment that present obstacles to the achievement of character objectives? The weather? The temperature? The humidity? The defined space of the setting? The furniture or other physical objects? The physical discomfort of clothing?

Identifying Moments

In chapter 6 you were introduced to the smallest unit of a scene, the moment. You will recall that a moment is a brief, emotionally charged segment within a beat, which comes from a character realization, a surprise, a decision, or a reversal. With your partner, identify these moments for your character and your partner's character. When you reach these moments in the scene, take your time to let the full impact of the realization, surprise, decision, or reversal affect either or both characters.

DISCUSSION
1. What use may be made of props to expand the moment?
2. What use may be made of space?
3. What use may be made of silent body language?

Identifying Peaks and Valleys

Finding the peaks and valleys in scenes helps to establish a rhythm in the character relationships. With your partner, examine those beats in the scene when the tension between characters is at its highest peak. Find those beats where the tension is at its lowest level.

DISCUSSION
1. What can each of you do to increase the tension in beats of highest intensity? Increase activity? Intensify your voice? Create stronger internal images? Play stronger objectives? Can you find more internal and external obstacles to character objectives that you can attempt to overcome?
2. What can you do to reduce the tensions in beats intended for the least tension? Change spatial relationships? Lower vocal intensity?
3. In which beats is the emphasis on your character and in which beats is the emphasis on your partner's character?

Role Development through Rehearsal

QUINCE: . . . here are your parts. And I am to entreat you, request you, and desire you, to con them by tomorrow night; and meet me in the palace wood, a mile without the town, by moonlight. There will we rehearse, for if we meet in the city, we shall be dogged with company, and our devices known. In the meantime I will draw a bill of properties such as our play wants. I pray you, fail me not.

BOTTOM: We will meet, and there we may rehearse most obscenely and coura-
geously. Take pains, be perfect. Adieu.

———*Shakespeare*, A Midsummer Night's Dream

Preparation for Rehearsals: Actor's Homework

The bottlenose dolphin puts only half its brain to sleep at a time, switching to the
other half after about an hour.

———*Jane Brody*

Productive rehearsals, either for a scene or a production, begin with solid preparation prior to the rehearsal. The primary value of working on your role before the
scheduled rehearsal is that your unconscious mind will begin gathering useful ideas
for later conscious development. Both left-brain and right-brain preparations as suggested below may be helpful.

Exploring Character with the Right Brain

Apply several of the exercises you tried in chapter 2 of this text:

1. Make a drawing of lines that express your feelings about your character in the
   scene. Use a crayon or a pastel for the drawing so that you can vary the width and
   the texture of the lines. Are the lines thin and clear or heavy and complex? Smooth
   or jagged?
2. With crayons, felt markers, or pastels make a drawing of the emotional colorations
   in the scene. Are the colors sharply separated or blurred and overlapped? Are the
   colors light tints or deep in saturation?
3. Using shape, color, and texture, decorate a container with the exterior reflecting
   the way your character thinks others perceive him and the interior reflecting the
   way the character perceives himself.
4. Clap out a tempo-rhythm study for the character, reflecting the actions and atmosphere of the scene.
5. Develop an abstract movement and nonverbal sound study of the behavior of your
   character in the scene. This should be like a self-accompanied modern dance,
   which reflects the objective of the character and the character's relationship with
   the other character(s) in the scene.

Analyzing Character with the Left Brain

First read and study the entire play. Decide what superobjective your character
is pursuing. Next reread and study the scene you are to rehearse. Decide on the
character's objective vis-a-vis the other character(s). Divide the scene into beats, and
decide on tentative beat objectives. Jot down on paper brief, telegraphlike answers to
the following basic questions.

1. Who is my character? What are the relationships between my character and the other character(s) onstage or referred to in this scene?
2. Where is this scene taking place? How does my character respond to this place?
3. Where is my character coming from? Why is my character coming to this location at this particular time?
4. What expectations does my character have about this encounter with other characters? What is the tension level between my character and the other character(s)? What surprises my character about this encounter?
5. How serious or how playful is my character?
6. How vulnerable or impervious is my character?
7. How rational or irrational is my character?
8. How expressive or stoic is my character?
9. How is the character like myself, and how is the character unlike myself?
10. How does my character change from the beginning to the end of the scene?

Writing a Character Biography

You may further develop your left-brain knowledge of the character by writing a brief character biography using both information given in the playscript and incidents created by your imagination or suggested by the character's actions in the play. A written biography may help build up the details of a character's life for your increased understanding and belief in present character actions. You can use the "Personality Profile" form in chapter 8 for specific details to explore.

Adaptation to the Director's Methods

If you are rehearsing for a production and are working with the guidance of a director, you may have to adapt your preferred working methods to the director's creative ways during the rehearsals themselves. Some directors like to give actors broad general outlines of direction first, leaving many of the details up to the actors. Other directors may prefer starting work on small details, which are gradually built up into larger units. Some directors may bounce between the extremes.

The director may wish to block the movement first, read through the script several times before getting you on your feet, or spend time discussing the significance of the ideas in the play. In such situations continue your own creative work on your characterization as homework. Your personal work will add to the excitement of rehearsals when your director eventually reaches the more creative part of the rehearsal sequence.

Whatever method of work the director establishes, you can find a way to make your own contribution of creative characterization to the production. If a director should demand something of you that you do not feel your characterization is yet ready for, it will help both of you to request additional work on the matter. More frequently than not, however, you may be more ready than you think you are, and if you will attempt the action suggested by the director the problem will take care of itself. Sometimes you may ask the director to let you try different approaches to deal with the development of a particular aspect of your characterization. I have never heard yet a director turn down the request from a performer in rehearsal, "May I try something else there?" Directors are delighted to have performers willing and eager to test different creative ideas.

Ultimately, however, in rehearsing for a production, the director's final choices should be followed. The director is responsible for the entire production, and as an actor your viewpoint is limited by the perspective of your character and by your location on stage. From your position you cannot perceive all of the interrelationships of artistic elements evident from the director's perspective in the auditorium.

Rehearsal of Scenes for the Classroom

When you and a partner are rehearsing scenes for classroom presentation, you probably do not have the help of an objective third person, but you both have your left brains to provide some guidance. You will find more value in exploring the reactions of your characters to each other than in trying to direct each other. Use all the techniques now at your disposal. The following approaches offer suggestions to try at rehearsals.

Rehearsing Scenes with Right-Brain Techniques

1. Clap your way through the scene, using only the clapped tempo-rhythms and pantomimed movement to attempt to achieve your characters's objectives.

2. Dance your way through the scene, using only movement to attempt to achieve your objectives.

3. Sing gibberish lines through the scene, using only tempo-rhythms and vocal qualities to attempt to achieve your objectives.

4. Work your way through the scene using only one word per person and movement to attempt to achieve your objectives. Choose a word that crystallizes your character's objective for the scene. You may repeat the one word as many times as you wish.

5. Rehearse the scene as if one character did not understand the language of the other. Only one character may speak English; the other may use an unknown foreign gibberish.

Rehearsing Scenes with Integrated-Brain Techniques

1. Improvise the scene on a beat-by-beat basis, using your own words rather than the author's.

2. Rehearse the scene in the dark, so that the words and voice without the nonverbal means of communication must convey your objectives.

3. Try any of the suggestions under the earlier section in this chapter on obstacles and peaks and valleys.

The Use of Costume

What's most poignant about the getup [for Dustin Hoffman as Willy Loman in Arthur Miller's *Death of A Salesman*] may be the costume (designed by Ruth Morley). Mr. Hoffman's Willy is a total break with the mountainous Lee J. Cobb image. He's a trim, immaculately outfitted go-getter in a three-piece suit—replete with bright matching tie and handkerchief. [See fig. 12.4.] Is there anything sadder than a nobody dressed for success, or an old man masquerading as his younger self?

———*Frank Rich*

Not every performer in a production will have the opportunity to select his or her own costume for a role, but for scenes in class you are your own costumer, and you can certainly enhance the believablity of the character for yourself and the class observers if you use whatever resources are available to you for costuming. If your theatre department does not have a costume collection available for classroom use, you can find amazing bargains in contemporary clothes, and frequently clothes of the last few decades, at Salvation Army and Goodwill budget shops.

An entire costume may not be necessary for class work or rehearsals; perhaps an item or two or a single accessory will be sufficient to help you develop the character. The actress Peggy Wood, who played the leading role on the television series "I Remember Mama," once told a group of acting students at the Dallas Theatre Center that if she could find the right pair of shoes for a character, the rest of the character would soon follow. Any unusual clothing or accessory that requires special handling (such as a long skirt or top hat) should be acquired early enough in rehearsals for you to develop your character's actions with such items.

Coats, skirts, shoes, hats, gloves, and other costume accessories may be just as necessary for the rehearsal of contemporary plays as for period plays where their usefulness may be more apparent. The actor-director Gary Sinise, playing the character of Dopey in a highly acclaimed revival of Lanford Wilson's *Balm in Gilead*, speaks of using an old coat as a stimulus for the development of his characterization: "I didn't really define the character until I found that coat in a pile of junk, and then I started feeling like I had a personality."[2]

Not only can the right costume or accessories help you develop and convey the character, but you also can find character traits by abstracting from costume elements.

Creating Character from Costume

Select a garment or accessory for a character from a scene you are working on. When you make the choice, you may not know why you think it is appropriate, but go with your instincts. Then use the qualities of the item to stimulate other traits of the character. Consider the following about the costume or accessory.

Right-brain considerations

1. What is the texture? Rough or smooth? Shiny or dull?
2. What is the color? Loud or subdued? Pretty or ugly?

Figure 12.4.   Dustin Hoffman in *Death of A Salesman* by Arthur Miller. Costume serves as a stimulus to both actor and audience in suggesting characterization. (Photograph: © 1984 by Inge Morath. Used by permission of Magnum.)

3. Is the item new or worn? What wear is evident?
4. How resilient is the item? Does it bounce back to shape when crushed, or does it stay crushed?

   Left-brain considerations

1. How comfortable is the item? Does it fit tightly or loosely?
2. Where did the item come from? What will happen to it when it is no longer useful to the character?
3. How does the character regard the item? Does the character treasure it or take it for granted?
4. How does the character expect others to regard the item? Admire it? Ignore it?

From the four right-brain considerations, develop character traits through an improvisation of the character performing a typical activity (a progressive activity). From the four left-brain considerations, develop an improvisation featuring the costume item itself. Perform both improvisations for the class.

DISCUSSION
1. What character traits did the class observe in your improvisation based on the abstract qualities of the item?
2. What unusual or strikingly characteristic actions did the class see in your improvisation that featured the item?

At your next rehearsal for class or for a production use costume in some way to enhance your character portrayal.

The Use of Props

When you rehearse for a class scene or a production, you should use props as similar as possible to the ones you will use in performance. Not only will this practice make it easier to adjust to production props, but the props themselves will suggest imaginative uses. You can encourage these uses by spending some rehearsal time on the types of prop exercises you practiced with the action level of craft in chapter 6.

The Use of Makeup

Those photographs of women [Walker Evans's photos of women of the Great Depression] who look out from porches. Those are the faces that arrest me. Some of the faces are beautiful, but these are people who've lived outside like animals all their lives. . . . I want my makeup and I want my face to look like a face that hasn't been inside a house except to sleep at night.

————*Kate Nelligan*

In addition to costumes and props, makeup will enhance your external characterization for the audience, but you may also use makeup to develop and individualize the character for yourself. (See fig. 12.5.)

Figure 12.5. *Hedda Gabler* by Henrik Ibsen. Make-up and costume combine to assist in the characterization of Judge Brack and Hedda Gabler. (Montclair State College, Major Theatre Series. Set and lights: W. Scott MacConnell; costumes: Joseph F. Bella.)

Developing Character with Makeup

While you are still in the early stages of rehearsing a scene or a play, experiment with changing the appearance of your face with makeup. After you have put on a neutral stick or greasepaint base, try the following in a manner appropriate for your character:

1. Block out your own eyebrows, and draw in eyebrows suitable for your character.
2. Use lip rouge to widen or narrow, lengthen or shorten, the lips.
3. Use highlights and shadows to broaden or narrow the nose.
4. Use cheek rouge to widen or narrow the cheekbones.
5. Use highlights and shadows to make the eyes appear larger or smaller.
6. Powder your work.

Then spend several minutes adjusting the muscles of your face to the makeup you have applied. Try to make your face assume the physical characteristics the makeup has suggested.

DISCUSSION
1. Does the makeup suggest something about the character that you had not considered before?
2. How much can you do with your facial muscles to achieve the effect the makeup has given you?
3. How would it help or hinder your characterization to attempt to sustain muscular adjustment of the face during performance?

Aids to Memorization

For most people there is no way to avoid hard work in learning lines. The photographic memory is so rare a gift that in more than 25 years of teaching, I have encountered only two students who could look at a script a couple of times and know the lines securely.

It helps memorization enormously to study the beat development of a scene first, then to improvise the scene exploring the possible actions of the character, using movement and props in an imaginative, story-telling way. But even after a careful understanding of the scene is achieved, repetition is usually required to master the playwright's dialogue. For most people, memorization becomes easier with practice, and there are a few techniques that may lighten your task.

Left-Brain Memorization

One left-brain method of memorizing lines is to divide the scene (or the entire role when you are in a play), into smaller units. If these units coincide with beats, or a change of the character's attack on objectives, you will find the going easier. Become familiar with one unit before you go on to the next. After each successive unit, go back to the beginning of the entire section to get the sequence of development.

Another helpful way to learn lines is with a tape recorder. Put your own lines on tape, and listen to them repeatedly. After you have mastered your own lines, record only the cues, that is, the last few words of each speech previous to yours. Leave enough blank space between cues for you to recite your response, or stop the tape recorder between cues while you say your line.

Right-Brain Memorization

One way the right brain can help memorization is by associating the lines (supplied by the left brain) with movement and use of props. Walking through the spatial patterns you have found in improvising the scene as you repeat your lines helps you coordinate words and movement, each reinforcing the other. Associating progressive activities (as, for example, the purposeful use of props) with lines has a similar reinforcement effect on the right brain.

Another aid to memorization is to allow your subconscious to work for you overnight. If you will review a scene at night just before you go to sleep, your subconscious will work for you effortlessly. You may awake the next morning to discover that you know the scene much better than you did the night before.

You may find that the meditation techniques you developed earlier can be a third right-brain way to help you memorize. If you meditate before you work on lines, you will find your mind clearer and your energy renewed for focusing on learning the character's objectives and the words. Meditating after you study the lines may help you visualize yourself performing the scene.

With each of the methods suggested above you should repeat your lines aloud. The more senses you can involve in memorization, the quicker your mastery of the lines and the characterization. Repeating lines aloud will involve the sense of hearing and the kinesthetic sense of your speech muscles. Remember, your right brain is training your speech muscles to the habits of the character's use of them while your left brain is learning to recall the words.

Summary

In this chapter on the role in rehearsal, you have explored techniques for using the creative processes in developing a character for a scene or a play. You have found right-brain and left-brain ways to analyze a scene, plus right-brain and left-brain ways to explore the characterization and action possibilities in rehearsing a scene. Lastly, you considered some hints on memorization. In the next chapter you will find a few additional suggestions for sustaining your creative processes for performances.

Notes

1. Cited by Carol Lawson, "Broadway," *New York Times*, 29 July 1983, p. C 2.
2. Cited by Enid Nemy, "Broadway," *New York Times*, 3 August 1984, p. C 2.

For Further Reading

King, Nancy R. *A Movement Approach to Acting*. Englewood Cliffs, N. J.: Prentice-Hall, 1981. Ch. 12.

Toporkov, V.O. *Stanislavski in Rehearsal: The Final Years*. New York: Theatre Arts Books, 1979. "Tartuffe," pp. 152–201.

Chapter 13
The Role in Performance

Go to the theatre early on the first night and get made up well in advance of the curtain. Then walk on to the stage and imagine that the curtain is already up and that you are facing the audience. Look out at them and shout, "You are about to see the greatest fucking performance of your entire theatre-going lives. And I will be giving it. You lucky people."

Tell them that once or twice. Then go back to your dressing room and relax, and you'll find that when the curtain does go up you'll have the necessary confidence.

———*Laurence Olivier*

Stage Fright

As you can see from the account above, stage fright can be a problem for professional actors as well as for beginners.[1] The pressure of a new audience every night and the challenge of keeping the creative process alive despite minor aches and pains, depressing weather, and personal problems create stress on actors at all levels of experience. There are stories of professionals who vomit nightly before performances to relieve the tension. There are others who relax all day hoping to condition themselves to take the evening's work in stride.

But the majority of professionals have learned to manage their keyed-up responses with less drastic measures, employing physical and vocal warm-ups for both relaxation and tuning of their physical instrument.

A simple warm-up routine such as the one suggested in chapter 2, singly or with the entire cast, half an hour before performances can go a long way toward relaxing tensions. The exercises also will focus your alertness toward the task at hand.

Ensemble Playing

Ensemble playing is achieved in performances of plays in which each actor appears to behave, listen, and react spontaneously with the focus shifting appropri-

Figure 13.1. *Marat/Sade* by Peter Weiss. Ensemble playing on both the unconscious and conscious role-playing level is demanded in a multi-dimensional play such as *Marat/Sade.* (Photograph: Kent Neely. Courtesy of University Theatre, University of Minnesota, Minneapolis. Director: Stephen G. Hults; set and costumes: J.C. Farris.)

ately from character to character without the intrusion of special attention on star performers. In such performances each actor is equally important and evenly matched with the rest of the cast in sensitivity and accomplishment.

One play popular with college groups that demands the highest achievement of ensemble acting is *The Persecution and Assassination of Jean-Paul Marat as Performed by the Inmates of the Asylum at Charenton Under the Direction of the Marquis de Sade [Marat/Sade]* by Peter Weiss. (See fig. 13.1.) In this play most members of the cast not only must blend in as the characters of inmates in an asylum but must also achieve rapport on another level as they shift to portray the characters of a play-within-a-play that the inmates present for their invited audience. There can be no stars who stand out as personalities to detract from the impact of a believable ensemble in such a play. Another example available on videotape in many public and college libraries is the Royal Shakespeare Company's production of David Edgar's stage adaptation of Charles Dickens's novel *Nicholas Nickleby.*

Ensemble performances are the ideal you should strive to achieve whether you perform in college, community theatre or professional theatre. The ensemble performances which occur through surrender of personal ego to the character and to the purpose of the play transform your achievements from the six levels of craft into the magic of art. Your attention to three elements you have already worked on will help you achieve a higher degree of ensemble performance:

1. careful adaptation of your character's tactics to the obstacles presented by other characters

2. detailed development of progressive activities that reveal your character's desires and individuality
3. sensitive responses to the physical, psychological, and atmospheric environment of each moment of the play as you come to it, without anticipating what may happen in the next moment

Making these three elements of your craft habitual will carry you a long way toward the worthy goal of ensemble performances.

Short Runs

In the typical college theatre production run of one or two weekends, you are not likely to become tired of the same role as you might in a longer run. But you can, nevertheless, lose the edge of excitement of opening night as the production settles into a routine of playing. In addition, you probably have other obligations such as classes or outside work, which take some of the time and energy that you might otherwise expend on further refinement of your role.

Conservation of Your Energy

You can help yourself with the energy problem by avoiding any unnecessary social life such as late cast parties until the run of the play is over. You can also give yourself an extra measure of rest through an additional 15 or 20 minutes of meditation before you report for your makeup call.

The tempo-rhythm study that you used on the development of your character can be one of the best means of insuring that the energy level and pacing of your characterization every night is similar to that on opening night. Before you go on stage, find a quiet place offstage and tap out the tempo-rhythm study that you developed. This right-brain technique will help focus your imagination on the inner and outer life of your character.

Preparation for Your Entrance

Just before you go on stage, close your eyes a moment. With the right brain visualize where your character is coming from, and with the left brain review your objective for entering the scene. Take a couple of deep breaths. Put your fingertips together and press out any remaining unnecessary tension from your shoulders and arms. Then give your hands and fingers a final few, loosening shakes. Check your characterization's posture, walk, and body tensions. Then when you hear your cue, walk on stage with the confidence that your right-brain and left-brain creative processes will take you through the evening just as they have taken you through every rehearsal and previous performance.

Concentration on Second Nights

Second-night performances of many productions are frequently the problem performances, particularly if everyone was keyed up for an exciting, well-received opening night. Second nights can be problems also if the show has been reviewed by an unflattering local critic.

In the event of a successful opening night, on the second night both the cast and crews are going to have to be extra careful not to feel so confident that they make errors with props and the coordination of light cues. The cast is prone to drop well-known lines, slow down the pace, and commit careless omissions of progressive activities or blocking.

A good preventative for the actor is to review both movement and lines nightly before going to the theatre for makeup. No matter how well you think you know what you are doing, a closed-eyed visualization of yourself in character moving through the scenes of the play will heighten your contact with the reality of the relationships your character has with others, deepen your awareness of the complex inner life of the character's objectives, and help you find the perspective to give the entire role the polish it needs to reach the sixth level of craft.

Long Runs

> He's [Hume Cronyn] never satisfied, and neither am I. We both like to perfect our work.
>
> ————*Jessica Tandy*

Jessica Tandy has said on several occasions, including the interview quoted above, that she and her husband, Hume Cronyn, find a long run an opportunity to ferret out the nuances of communication that occur between characters.[2] In the four or five weeks allotted for rehearsal in professional theatre even the seasoned professional finds that there is not enough time to explore fully the possibilities of character behavior or expression. If four or five weeks rehearsal is not enough time for the accomplished professional, then surely the college student, whose hours of rehearsal have been one-half to one-third less than those of the professional, can continue to explore additional nuances, whatever the length of the run.

The international theatre groups that have been universally praised for their work—groups such as Peter Brook's, and earlier, Jerzy Grotowski's and Bertolt Brecht's, as well as Stanislavsky's Moscow Art Theatre group—all spent several months working on new productions. The exquisite detail of their productions attests to the enormous value of ensemble work over a period of time. Obviously, they did not spend their rehearsal time on nonproductive run-throughs but on exploring many possible facets of action and character reaction. You can use a longer run to develop such details yourself as you also work toward the highest levels of excellence.

Create The Illusion of the First Time

> Death from Neglect of the Illusion of the First Time is not confined to matters and methods of speech and mentality, but extends to every part of the presentation, from the most climactic and important action or emotion to the most insignificant item of behavior—a glance of the eye at some unexpected occurrence, the careless picking up of some small object which supposedly has not been·seen or handled before.
>
> ————*William Gillette*

In a long run your lines and progressive activities become so automatic that you may find the spontaneity of your right brain going to sleep on you. At such times you may find it helpful to do improvisations of relationships between the characters outside the play with your fellow actors. Such improvisations an hour or so before the curtain can do wonders to reawaken your listening ability in the play on stage.

Find the Nuances

[Jeremy Irons] keeps an eye and an ear on every night's audience. I've seen him do the part about 30 times now, and each time I could see him changing gears, making small adjustments as he went along without getting out of character.

———*Tom Stoppard*

No performance is exactly like a previous one for several reasons—the differences in the actors from the previous performance, the differences in the collective response of the audience—even the differences in the humidity will make each performance a slightly different work of art.

Those actors who recognize these differences and work within the general framework established by careful rehearsal can always find new shadings of meaning and new attacks on the same objectives, keeping the character fresh for themselves, the other actors, and the new audience. One of Stanislavsky's advocates, I. Sudakov, recognized this in lectures delivered at the Moscow Theatrical University:

Formal uniformity can be repeated from performance to performance but a live, resourceful actor will always have new adaptations or new shadings.[3]

Reexamine Your Role with Replacements

In a long run when new cast members replace departing ones, new energy is brought into a production. You will find this a fine time to reexamine your character's relationships with the characterizations of new cast members. As Tom Porter, production stage manager of the long-running musical *A Chorus Line* observes, "Everybody brings something different—their own personality—and that helps keep it fresh. . . ."[4] Even with the same basic movements and progressive activities, the inner resources of the new players will stimulate additional insights for the possibilities of your own characterization. Use such opportunities to find fresh nuances of action and reaction.

Protect Your Energy

Actress Carol Channing has spoken often of her care in conserving her energy for the evening's performance. She regards service to each new audience as the highest of callings as she plans to be at her best for each person who has come to the theatre.

A mid-afternoon nap, an early light snack of high-protein foods, and an extra 10 minutes of meditation before reporting for makeup call are three good ways to insure your highest energy level for the evening's performance. (See fig. 13.2.)

The tough days are two-performance days. Giving a matinee and evening performance of a long role can be a draining experience, but extra meditation and a brisk walk or run between performances will do wonders to revive your energy.

Figure 13.2.   *My Three Angels* by Sam and Bella Spewack. A high energy level is reflected in the physicalization of characterization in this popular mystery-comedy. (Photo by Kent. Courtesy of Florida Summer Theatre, Stover Theatre, Stetson University. Director: Pat Ritter; set: Byrne Blackwood; costumes: Toni Thompson, Ann Travers.)

Experiment Only with the Consent of Others

The suggestions made here that you continue to develop your characterization and find additional nuances to your role should not be misunderstood as advocacy for wholesale experimentation with your role or violation of the established direction of the production. You have a responsibility to maintain the work established in rehearsals. But with the consent of all concerned, you can continue to try things as ambitious as new blocking and progressive activities—if they will help further to manifest the objectives of the character and the intended interpretation of the play.

Find New Images for Old

Another way of renewing the life of your character is through finding new inner images for emotional moments or new physical responses for sensuous moments. Different parallel experiences may be substituted for ones that you may have used for so long that they have become weak touchstones for your responses.

Quiet Secrets of Accomplished Performers

I think the most difficult equation to solve is the union of the two things that are absolutely necessary to an actor. One is confidence, absolute confidence, and the other an equal amount of humility toward the work. That's a very hard equation.

———*Laurence Olivier*

Sir Laurence Olivier expresses here what most successful performers have learned.[5] The confidence he speaks of comes from having done a thorough, honest job of developing every aspect of characterization. The humility comes from knowing that even with a thorough, honest job there are always more possibilities that can be tried.

Excellent performers know that no matter how good the present performance, the same challenges must be met in the next performance with just as much awareness and responsiveness. This knowledge keeps them humble. But knowing that both the right brain and the left brain are creatively active gives them the confidence to continue meeting those challenges in slightly new and different ways.

Summary

In this chapter you have examined some of the problems of dealing with the role in performance. You have seen that professionals, like neophytes, face the same problems in performance. And you have been introduced to some pointers on dealing with stage fright, ensemble playing, keeping your roles fresh and vital in short and long runs, and exploring the nuances of your character throughout the run of a production.

Using the suggestions made here in your continuing development as an actor will show you the value of the right-brain and left-brain creative processes of acting.

Notes

1. Cited by Logan Gourlay, *Olivier* (New York: Stein & Day, 1974), p. 11.
2. Jessica Tandy in an interview with Arlene Francis, "The Prime of Your Life," New York: WNBC, 28 April 1984.
3. I. Sudakov, "The Creative Process," in *Acting: A Handbook of the Stanislavski Method*, compiled by Toby Cole, p. 84 (New York: Crown, 1955).
4. Cited by Eleanor Blau, "How 'Chorus Line' Keeps Its Kicks After 9 Years," *New York Times*, 7 August 1984, p. C 11.
5. Cited by Gourlay, *Olivier*, p. 11.

For Further Reading

Gillette, William. "The Illusion of the First Time in Acting," with an introduction by George Arlis. Reprinted in *Papers on Acting*. Edited by Brander Matthews, pp. 115–135. New York: Hill & Wang, 1958.
Ratliff, Gerald Lee. *Combating Stage Fright*. New York: Rosen Press, 1984.

Part Five

The Perspective
of Genre

Introduction _____
Capture the Style

The best actors in the world, either for tragedy, comedy, history, pastoral, pastoral-comical, historical-pastoral, tragical-historical, tragical-comical-historical-pastoral, scene individable or poem unlimited. Seneca cannot be too heavy, nor Plautus too light.

——*Shakespeare*, Hamlet

In this part you will consider the variations of acting styles in the genres of plays popularly performed in colleges and schools of theatre. The scenes from such plays reprinted in the appendix contain roles within the typical age-range capabilities of most college students. Suggestions for other plays containing additional usable scenes are listed with each genre. Many of the listed plays contain middle-aged and older characters as well as younger ones. A few 19th century plays have been listed under some genres for your consideration after you have worked on contemporary plays.

Scenes from plays of earlier historical periods such as the Greek, the Elizabethan, and the Restoration are not listed or included because most performers undertake period styles as advanced work after they have mastered the contemporary styles. Period plays also may require special skills such as fencing, historical manners and movement, and facility with verse, which should be studied separately before integrating them with the six levels of the basic acting craft.

Chapter 14 _____
_____*Performing the Genres*

Ceremonies are the outward expression of inward feeling.

———*Lao-Tze*

Style

The Style of the Play

The major consideration in the development of appropriate performing styles for the various genres is the degree of emphasis given to each of the six levels of craft. Later in this chapter you will find listings of the relative emphasis of each of the six levels of craft as it applies to each genre of the scenes reprinted in the appendix.

Though you may not think about the realistic performances in film and television as having a style of acting, their lifelike realism is the dominant style of the present day. The minute detail and small scale of film and television performances have so affected the perceptions of theatre students that they frequently have difficulty adapting to the larger-scale demands of the stage.

Most of your first performance experiences are in the intimate confines of a classroom, and there you may emphasize an honest use of your own experiences in life as the basis for expression. But confining your performances to an imitation of life-size behavior severely limits your ability to act in the range of contemporary styles, even those styles that may seem realistic in dialogue and character portrayal. If you have worked through the exercises presented in earlier sections of this text, you are aware that performance requirements are enlargements and adaptations of communication techniques used in daily life. Theatre performances may seem lifelike, but they are not like life! The important thing to remember as you push beyond the narrow limits of the behavior of daily life is that your belief in the enlarged movement or projected voice will carry the honesty of your conviction even more effectively than a performance that is too small to carry beyond the stage.

The illustration in figure 14.1 suggests the relationship of each genre in its departure from life and its relationship to other genres.

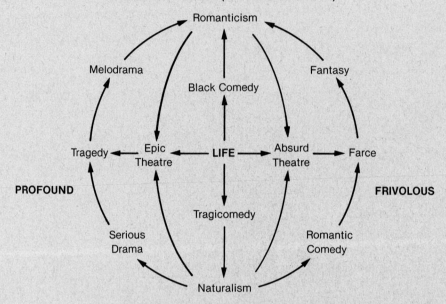

ARTIFICIAL WORLD (ABSTRACTED DETAIL)

Romanticism

Melodrama   Fantasy

Black Comedy

Tragedy ← Epic ← LIFE → Absurd → Farce
        Theatre   Theatre

PROFOUND   **FRIVOLOUS**

Tragicomedy

Serious   Romantic
Drama   Comedy

Naturalism

SCIENTIFIC WORLD (CONCRETE DETAIL)

Figure 14.1   Genre Wheel

Taking Life as the central point, you encounter black comedy and romanticism; as you move upward toward the Artificial World of Abstracted Detail. You find tragicomedy and naturalism as you move down toward the Scientific World of Concrete Detail. As you move left toward the Profound, you find epic theatre and tragedy, and on the right you find theatre of the absurd and farce as the material moves toward the Frivolous. Between tragedy and romanticism is the genre of melodrama, and fantasy lies between farce and romanticism. On the Frivolous side romantic comedy falls between farce and naturalism. On the Profound side, serious drama lies between the heavier more abstract tragedy and the more detailed naturalism.

For the actor the value of identifying the genre of the material is not in fitting plays into Procrustean beds of definition but rather in helping to find performing techniques that most clearly convey the nature of the script. Furthermore, each play has its own unique characteristics, which may not be fully accounted for in a genre definition. Therefore, the descriptions of the various genres that follow later in this chapter should be taken as suggestive guideposts only, for no one play is a pure example of any left-brain categorization. Most plays contain a combination of elements from more than one genre, though each play fits more strongly into one category than another.

With these precautions in mind, you can approach both the definitions and the performances of the various types of material with greater freedom and experimentation than otherwise might be implied. The discussions of each contemporary genre for the scenes you'll find in the appendix include brief suggestions on how to approach the acting style for that type of play. Indications are given of the relative importance of each of the six levels of craft for each particular style. The accompanying photographs also contain many visual suggestions of the appropriate style of performance, so you will find them to be helpful right-brain guides.

The Style of the Actor

Olivier is a great actor partly because he shows us so much of himself in all his performances, partly because he is unafraid to reveal those elements in his personality that most of us are trained to keep hidden. Men are taught from childhood to be ashamed of their femininity: Olivier exploits his brilliantly and therefore enables all of us to come to terms with a part of ourselves.

————*Michael Billington*

Not only does each genre and play have its individual characteristics, but the uniqueness of each performer gives individual style and texture to the playing of the same scene. Even if everyone in the class worked on the same scene, each scene would have different qualities depending on the personalities and sensitivities of the individuals presenting it.

Nevertheless, there are characteristics of each type of material that everyone should strive to understand. Developing your ability to communicate these characteristics to the audience is a necessary part of your work as a performer.

The Performer in the Service of the Play

When you are cast in a production, not only do you have your knowledge of the play and its style to guide you, but you also have the assistance of a director to shape your work toward particular character objectives and stylistic goals. In the classroom, however, you and your partners are usually your own directors, and you must make stylistic choices as well as choices of objectives for your characters.

Your obligation to the script (and to the director if you have one) is to fulfill the playwright's intentions as clearly as you understand them. Your work on scenes from plays is different from the earlier improvised scenes where you were your own author as well as performer. When you perform a scene from a play, you are an interpretative artist as well as a creative artist.

Though your responsibility to the playwright is to be truthful to the representations of the intentions of the play, you have much freedom to develop characterization within the framework supplied by the playscript. To understand this framework most fully, you should, of course, read and study the entire play before working on a selected scene.

Genre for Analysis and Performance

The scenes from full-length plays reprinted in the appendix for analysis and practice represent the genres popular with contemporary audiences and playwrights. These scenes were selected specifically for youthful performers ranging in age from 18 to 22. Most of you should begin performing scenes with characters near your own age, and indeed, in the professional theatre you would not be cast in older roles except in rare circumstances.

Of course many productions presented in college theatres require young performers to portray older characters, but since there are so many vocal and physical adjustments required for the characterization of age, scenes with older characters are not included in the appendix as part of this beginning level of study. If you are an older student, you will find that some of the other plays listed under each genre contain mature roles more suitable than those in the scenes printed in the appendix. Each of the genres to be described should be studied in relation to the relative focus on each of the six levels of craft.

Romantic Comedy

The genre of romantic comedy is a perennial staple of the commercial and college theatre. It features the romantic vicissitudes of a couple in love. (See fig. 14.2 and fig. 7.3.) The course of true love does not run smoothly because of opposition by parents, conflicts with rivals, or compatibility problems. Sometimes there is a combined opposition by all three of these obstacles. The world of romantic comedy is a personal one, though differences in social class may play some part in the obstacles the lovers must overcome to find their happiness.

1. **Action level.** At the action level the objectives are fairly clear and straightforward.
2. **Word level.** At the word level the dialogue may reflect accurately a social class or the slang of the day. The dialogue is frequently witty, and the exact word choice is necessary to convey the wit.
3. **Unconscious role-playing level.** The unconscious role-playing level is frequently less important than the conscious role-playing level, for the lovers are often playing games with those they wish to mislead or with each other.
4. **Conscious role-playing level.** The conscious role-playing level may be used when lovers are deceiving those who oppose their relationship or each other in scenes of flirtation.
5. **Emotional level.** The emotional level is relatively shallow (compared with drama, for example), for the issues in romantic comedies are petty when compared to the life-threatening issues of other genres.
6. **The level of aesthetic distance.** The aesthetic distance between the actor's personality and the role is small, for personal charm and warmth are qualities that endear the characters of romantic comedy to an audience. Scripts of romantic comedies only rarely suggest that the actors should make a social political judgment on the characters.

The scene from *Ah, Wilderness!* by Eugene O'Neill reprinted in the appendix will illustrate these principles of romantic comedy and demonstrate some of the reasons for the popularity of plays of this type.

Other romantic comedies for acting scenes include the following:

A Taste of Honey by Shelagh Delaney
Barefoot in the Park by Neil Simon

Figure 14.2. *Ah, Wilderness!* by Eugene O'Neill. In O'Neill's romantic comedy Muriel and Richard meet secretly to express their love. (Photograph: Joe Meyer. Courtesy of Montclair State College, Major Theatre Series. Director: Clyde McElroy; set and lights: W. Scott Mac-Connell; costumes: Joseph F. Bella.)

The Real Thing by Tom Stoppard
Gemini by Albert Innaurato
The Philadelphia Story by Philip Barry
The Rainmaker by Richard Nash
Design for Living by Noel Coward
Talley's Folly by Lanford Wilson

Same Time, Next Year by Bernard Slade
Home by Samm-Art Williams
A Little Holy Water by Ramon Delgado
La Ronde by Arthur Schnitzler

Serious Drama

Serious drama depicts important issues or serious relationships from a sober, mature viewpoint. Frequently, the problems in such plays deal with relationships between members of a family or a tightly knit group who are threatened either by outside influences or by differing objectives within the unit itself. The resolution of the problem (if indeed there is one) may have serious consequences for some individuals and reward others, but social and personal values suggested by the characters and situations depicted are usually upheld.

1. **Action level.** At the action level objectives are complex and important, and both internal and external obstacles are formidable.
2. **Word level.** Language is usually of less importance than the subtext and character relationships, though occasionally dialogue may border on the sparely poetic.
3. **Unconscious role-playing level.** Unconscious role playing usually predominates over conscious role playing, and frequently characters are forced to recognize traits within themselves that impede progress to their objectives.
4. **Conscious role-playing level.** The level of conscious role playing is relatively unimportant unless characters are trying consciously to manipulate one another to achieve their goals.
5. **Emotional level.** The emotional level is deep and complex. Characters are involved in difficult webs of relationships and situations, which place heavy emotional demands on them.
6. **The level of aesthetic distance.** The actor's personal experience and emotions are closely identified with the character portrayed. The actor does not judge or frame the character of serious drama by distancing herself or himself apart from the role but, rather, identifies closely with the role.

The example in the appendix comes from Paul Zindel's *The Effect of Gamma Rays on Man-in-the-Moon Marigolds.* (See fig. 14.3.)

Other serious dramas for acting scenes include the following:

Orpheus Descending by Tennessee Williams
The Runner Stumbles by Milan Stitt
The Fifth of July by Lanford Wilson
"MASTER HAROLD" . . . *and the boys* by Athol Fugard
The Children's Hour by Lillian Hellman
The Hot l Baltimore by Lanford Wilson
A Raisin in the Sun by Lorraine Hansberry
A Soldier's Play by Charles Fuller
The Awakening of Spring by Frank Wedekind
Miss Julie by August Strindberg
The Seagull by Anton Chekhov
The Wild Duck by Henrik Ibsen

Figure 14.3. *The Effect of Gamma Rays on Man-in-the-Moon Marigolds* by Paul Zindel. Emphasis on the unconscious role-playing level of characterization is strong in serious drama. (Photograph: Owen Fogleman's Studio, Deland. Courtesy Stover Theatre, Stetson University. Director: Marjorie Gilbert; set: Bruce Griffiths.)

Tragicomedy

In the genre of tragicomedy the playwright presents a situation or a set of relationships that is serious and confronts important issues, but the material is treated with moments of humor (frequently grim) that lighten the tone of the play. The humor is usually more prevalent in the earlier portions of a tragicomedy, while the final segments are more tragic as relationships fall apart or objectives have dire consequences or fail to be achieved.

1. **Action level.** At the action level superobjectives are important and serious, but frequently scene objectives for characters are trivial. This triviality provides a humorous contrast to the major issues.
2. **Word level.** The word level is often stressed. With characters frequently unable to exercise their wills toward achieving serious goals, they may babble away the time with striking dialogue.
3. **Unconscious role-playing level.** The level of unconscious role playing usually predominates over conscious role playing, for the characters are engaged in serious relationships and pursuits that do not require hypocrisy or duplicity.
4. **Conscious role-playing level.** The level of conscious role playing is occasionally used to demonstrate the fantasy life of characters in tragicomedy.
5. **Emotional level.** The emotional level varies tremendously from character to character and from scene to scene within the same character as the tone of the play switches from emotional detachment in the lighter scenes to emotional involvement in the heavier scenes.
6. **The level of aesthetic distance.** The distance between actor and character varies

Figure 14.4. *Curse of the Starving Class* by Sam Shepard. Tragicomedy juxtaposes serious issues and events with frivolous ones, but contains a strong emphasis on the unconscious role-playing level with occasional conscious role-playing. (Photograph: Joe Meyer. Courtesy of Montclair State College, Major Theatre Series. Set and lights: John Figola; costumes: Joseph F. Bella.)

with the tone of the scene. In lighter moments there is greater distancing and in heavier moments less distance. But even so, tragicomedy is most effective with actors working at a high level of intensity.

The example offered in the appendix is from Christopher Durang's *Sister Mary Ignatius Explains It All For You*. For illustrations of other tragicomedies see figure 14.4, *Curse of the Starving Class* and refer back to figure 6.5, *The Birthday Party*. Other tragicomedies for acting scenes include the following:

Curse of the Starving Class by Sam Shepard
Buried Child by Sam Shepard
True West by Sam Shepard
The Birthday Party by Harold Pinter
The Killing of Sister George by Frank Marcus
Waiting for Godot by Samuel Beckett
Endgame by Samuel Beckett
When You Coming Back, Red Ryder? by Mark Medoff

Melodrama

A typical melodrama has sharply drawn distinctions separating the persecutors, the persecuted, and the rescuers. Audience sympathies are quickly drawn, and high levels of suspense are created to intensify life-threatening situations. (See fig. 14.5.)

Figure 14.5. *Ten Little Indians* by Agatha Christie. Melodrama is characterized by life-threatening situations and high levels of suspense and tension with the action level and emotional level predominant over character complexity and subtlety. (Photograph: Christopher Focht. Department of Theater, State University of New York-Binghamton. Director: Richard G. Smith; set: John Bielneberg; costumes: Barbara Wolfe.)

The characters tend toward broad types, but actors can provide some variety with unexpected traits. However, if you try to overcomplicate characters in melodrama, you may detract from the focus on fast-paced action and the high level of suspense required for this genre.

1. **Action level.** At the action level bold objectives are required to rescue victims in life-threatening situations. Suspense is built and sustained by withholding outcomes as long as possible.
2. **Word level.** Usually the word level is relatively unimportant except to state clearly the opening situation and occasionally to summarize the complexity of the plot or relationships.
3. **Unconscious role-playing level.** The unconscious role-playing level may be subordinated to the conscious role-playing level as clever criminals and detectives play cat-and-mouse with one another. Unconscious roles are usually obvious to the audience and are uncomplicated, with few internal obstacles.
4. **Conscious role-playing level.** Conscious role playing may be a featured means of concealing identities or ferreting out villains.
5. **Emotional level.** The emotional level of characters in melodramas usually is uncomplicated and basic. Fear dominates as characters are placed in life-threatening situations by forces apparently beyond their control.
6. **The level of aesthetic distance.** If the melodrama is played straight (that is, without the burlesque approach frequently imposed on older melodramas), then the actors should identify closely with the characters and not step outside them to make value judgments.

The scene from this genre in the appendix comes from Emlyn Williams's melodrama *Night Must Fall*.

Other melodramas for acting scenes include the following:

The Little Foxes by Lillian Hellman
Nightwatch by Lucille Fletcher
Ten Little Indians by Agatha Christie
Deathtrap by Ira Levin
Arsenic and Old Lace by Joseph Kesselring
The Bad Seed by Maxwell Anderson
Angel Street by Patrick Hamilton
Rope by Patrick Hamilton

Farce

Farce usually focuses on small personal problems, petty vices grown to excess, and frequently deals with the trivialities of love affairs gone awry. The humor in farce is active and physical and makes great demands on the agility and timing of the performer. Characters are seldom more than cardboard caricatures manipulated by the circumstances of plot and outside events. Farce frequently has the same trio of types found in melodrama: the persecutor, the persecuted, and the rescuer.

1. **Action level.** At the action level character objectives are extremely important to the enlarged egos of the self-centered characters of farce. Large scaled progressive activities are extremely important to the plot and humor.
2. **Word level.** The dialogue is usually composed of simple, short sentences. While lines in romantic comedy may have elegance and wit, those of farce are not usually funny in themselves but only as they extend the humor of the actions. The verbal pace like the action pace begins moderately but accelerates with the passage of time and the complications of the plot.
3. **Unconscious role-playing level.** The unconscious role-playing level is frequently overshadowed by the conscious role-playing level as characters deceive one another and sometimes the audience for major portions of the play.
4. **Conscious role-playing level.** The conscious role-playing level is featured as characters self-consciously try to achieve their objectives and fool other characters along the way toward self-indulgent or selfish goals.
5. **Emotional level.** The emotional level may appear exaggerated on the surface, but the emotions are shallow. Apparent discomfort and suffering must seem intense, while internally the actor is cool with a high energy level.
6. **The level of aesthetic distance.** On the level of aesthetic distance there is frequently a great distance between the actor and the character, for the farcical characters are responding almost puppetlike to the demands of their egos and the outside circumstances that prevent the accomplishment of their trivial pursuits.

The example from *Hotel Paradiso* in the appendix is by that fantastic French farceur Georges Feydeau. (Refer to figure 9.4 for illustration of this scene. Figure V at the beginning of this section shows a broadly humorous moment in another scene from *Hotel Paradiso*.)

Other farces for acting scenes include the following:

A Flea in Her Ear by Georges Feydeau
Black Comedy by Peter Shaffer
Noises Off by Michael Frayn
Cloud 9 by Caryl Churchill
Bad Habits by Terrence McNally
The Ritz by Terrence McNally
The Importance of Being Earnest by Oscar Wilde

Black Comedy

QUINCE: Marry, our play is, *The Most Lamentable Comedy, and Most Cruel Death of Pyramus and Thisby*

————*Shakespeare*, A Midsummer Night's Dream

There are some similarities between tragicomedy and black comedy. In both genres serious situations are depicted with moments of levity. But while tragicomedy focuses on the inescapable consequences of situations or relationships, black comedy looks on the brighter hope for escape. Both tragicomedy and black comedy are very popular with contemporary playwrights, and if you fail to practice these genres, you will have neglected two styles of major contemporary works.

1. **Action level.** Usually the action level of black comedy is more important than in tragicomedy, particularly if the material borders on farce. Character objectives are taken seriously by the characters themselves, but they may seem rather trivial when compared to the life-threatening situations in drama and melodrama.
2. **Word level.** The word level in black comedy is usually not remarkable but supports the action level. In this respect the word level has the same relative importance as it does in farce.
3. **Unconscious role-playing level.** The unconscious role-playing level in black comedy, like that in farce, may take a back seat to the conscious role-playing level.
4. **Conscious role-playing level.** The conscious role-playing level of black comedy may be indulged in by characters seeking to escape from their own sense of being ordinary, as they fantasize in pipe dreams or nostalgia as an escape from the serious problems they should be engaged in solving.
5. **Emotional level.** The emotional level provides a major difference between the playing of farce and black comedy. The characters of black comedy have greater depth and complexity than those of farce. In contrast to the emotional level of characters in tragicomedy, which are frequently as deep as those in serious drama, the emotional level of characters in black comedy is more closely akin to that of romantic comedy. The characters of black comedy do not suffer deeply, but they may complain chronically.
6. **The level of aesthetic distance.** On the level of aesthetic distance the actor may be somewhat separated from close personal identification with the characters of black comedy, but actor comment on the behavior of the characters is minimal to nonexistent.

The black comedy scene in the appendix comes from Beth Henley's Pulitzer Prize script, *Crimes of the Heart.* (See fig. 14.6.)

Other black comedies for acting scenes include the following:

The House of Blue Leaves by John Guare
Entertaining Mr. Sloane by Joe Orton
What the Butler Saw by Joe Orton
Oh Dad, Poor Dad, Mama's Hung You in the Closet, and I'm Feeling So Sad by Arthur Kopit
Uncommon Women and Others by Wendy Wasserstein

Epic Theatre

We have explored the nature of epic theatre in greater detail in the chapter on the level of aesthetic distance, but to review briefly here, you will recall that epic theatre uses highly theatrical means to draw audience attention to social issues. It breaks the actor's identification with the character (after having established it) to comment on the character's behavior and on the situation the character sees in both the play and the world outside the theatre.

Figure 14.6. *Crimes of the Heart* by Beth Henley. Black comedy shares with farce an emphasis on action, but the emotional depth of characterization is deeper. (Photograph: Matt Anderson. Courtesy of Tulane Center Stage. Director: Ron Gural; set: Hugh Lester; lights: John Steele; costumes: Ysan Hicks.)

A less political application of the highly theatrical performance and production style of epic theatre may be seen in such plays as David Edgar's stage adaptation of Charles Dickens's *Nicholas Nickleby*. Other novels adapted for the stage such as Thomas Wolfe's *Of Time and the River* (fig. I) have been influenced by the acting and production style of epic theatre.

1. **Action level.** Within the epic theatre play, at the action level the characters pursue socially important objectives, or they may be ironically criticized if they do not. Character actions are viewed as related to political and social events in the lives of the members of the audience.
2. **Word level.** Words are used in the service of ulterior social ends and tend not to be decorative or poetic but pedestrian. Occasionally, however, rhetorical devices are used to harangue the audience.
3. **Unconscious role-playing level.** The unconscious role-playing level may be the only level on which the characters in the play exist except when they are involved in deceiving other characters or when actors deliberately step out of character.
4. **Conscious role-playing level.** The conscious role-playing level for characters is used only for deception and for characters who are consciously acting roles in plays-within-plays.
5. **Emotional level.** The emotional level may be quite deep and complex initially, so that the audience may be jarred when the actor deliberately distances herself or himself from the character.
6. **The level of aesthetic distance.** The level of aesthetic distance is most important to the playing of epic theatre, for at specific moments the actor deliberately steps aside from the character to comment on either the character's behavior or on the social situation reflected by it.

The example in the appendix comes from Bertolt Brecht's *The Good Woman of Setzuan*. (See fig. 14.7.)

Other epic theatre plays for acting scenes include the following:

The Caucasian Chalk Circle by Bertolt Brecht
A Man for All Seasons by Robert Bolt
Mother Courage by Bertolt Brecht
Marat/Sade by Peter Weiss
Indians by Arthur Kopit
The Elephant Man by Bernard Pomerance
Nicholas Nickleby by Charles Dickens (adaptation by David Edgar)

Plays with Actor-Characters

Plays with actor-characters do not constitute a separate genre, but the technique required for such characters is needed so frequently in contemporary plays of several genres, that you will find it useful to work on actor-character scenes. Any character in a play deliberately creating another characterization—not just a deceptive social role like the consciously role-playing characters discussed in chapter 9, but an entirely different persona—may be considered an actor-character. Such characters

Figure 14.7.   *The Good Woman of Setzuan* by Bertolt Brecht. In Brechtian epic theatre, character behavior makes social and political statements both directly and indirectly. (Photograph: Christopher Focht. Department of Theater, State University of New York-Binghamton. Director: Sue Ann Park; set: Robert Little; costumes: Fran Blau.)

Figure 14.8.   *Marat/Sade* by Peter Weiss. The actor-character role demands that the actor create distinct personae for two levels of characterization. In *Marat/Sade* the inmates impersonate characters of the French revolution in the play-within-the-play. (Courtesy of Tulane Theatre Department, Tulane University. Director: Ron Gural; set: Gary Gaillard.)

may appear in any genre from romantic comedy through epic theatre. (See fig. 14.8 and fig. 9.3.)

The relationship to the six levels of craft will vary with the genre of the play in which the actor-character appears.

The example offered in the appendix comes from Peter Weiss's *Marat/Sade*. Other actor-character scenes are in such plays as the following:

The Real Thing by Tom Stoppard
Charley's Aunt by Brandon Thomas
La Cage aux Folles by Harvey Fierstein
Noises Off by Michael Frayn
Benefactors by Michael Frayn
'Dentity Crisis by Christopher Durang
Sleuth by Anthony Shaffer
The Balcony by Jean Genet
The Maids by Jean Genet

Summary

In this chapter you have explored some of the differences among the genres of contemporary plays. The genres you considered included romantic comedy, serious drama, tragicomedy, melodrama, farce, black comedy, epic theatre, and plays with actor-characters. Applying the techniques you learned in the six levels of craft to these genres and using the principles you studied to rehearse and to perform roles, you can apply your right-brain and left-brain creative processes to create characters in scenes and plays from various contemporary styles.

For Further Reading

Bentley, Eric. *The Life of the Drama*. New York: Atheneum, 1964. Bentley's book offers an excellent discussion of the genres and their relationships to one another.

Crawford, Jerry L. *Acting in Person and in Style*. Dubuque, Iowa: William C. Brown, 1983. Chs. 16–20.

Harrop, John, and Sabin Epstein. *Acting with Style*. Englewood Cliffs, N.J.: Prentice-Hall, 1982.

Epilogue
— The Adventure Continues

To have the gift is one thing, but to sharpen it and hone and perfect it over your whole life is something which now I am prepared to do. I am now able—perhaps only now—to realize what it is I do.

———*Jerome Kilty*

The work that you have begun in developing both sides of your brain for the creative process of acting is only a beginning. If you wish to prepare for a career in professional theatre, you should expect to spend a minimum of four to six years of concentrated work on refining your physical and vocal instrument, learning about the rich heritage of your profession—its history and its plays—and developing auditioning and marketing skills to sell yourself as an actor.

Stay in Shape

Physical Conditioning

You should keep your body healthy with a balanced diet, sufficient sleep, and a regular exercise program. Running and swimming are fine activities to keep your circulation system in good condition and your body flexible and responsive.

Vocal Tuning

Your vocal instrument also should be tuned through practice. Charles Laughton once told students at the Dallas Theater Center that not until he was past 50 years old did he feel that his voice was fully responsive to his will. Even then he worked with his voice 15 or 20 minutes daily, practicing with any printed matter at hand, from the morning newspaper to *The Reader's Digest*. He admonished students to do no less.

Craft Honing

I spend ten or twenty minutes on such exercises in the most varied circumstances I can imagine. . . .

Your subconscious, your intuition, your experiences from life, your habit of manifesting human qualities on the stage will all go to work for you, in body and soul, and create for you.

———*Konstantin Stanislavsky*, Creating a Role

Just as you need to keep your body and voice in shape through exercise and practice, so the creative skills of craft should be maintained with performing experiences in the theatre. Many professional actors periodically take classes that refresh their creative energies and help mature the development of their craft. Stanislavski himself recognized this need to exercise one's craft in the observation above.

If you have difficulty finding opportunities to continue the development of your craft in professional or community theatre, then organize your own group and do improvisations and scenes in your home. If you are more ambitious, you can rent a loft or basement and establish your own theatre. Several of my former students have done just that and are continuing to grow as creative performers.

Other Areas for Advanced Work

Period Styles and Musical Theatre

If you pursue professional work, you will need to study period styles, stage combat, and the manners, decorum, and values of past historical eras. Equally important today, you should acquire special skills such as dancing and singing, and practice them for use in musical theatre.

Film and Television

Most of the techniques you have worked on, except the adaptations to larger spaces, will transfer easily to film and television work. You will find, however, that the technical demands of the media initially require more external adaptation to space while subtle facial expressions become extremely important. Nevertheless, with the sound principles of the creative approach you have studied here, you will be able to make the transitions between the stage and the other media smoothly.

Professional Pride

At various times in the past, actors have been regarded as rogues, vagabonds, and slaves. They even have been denied religious burial because of their profession. Today many stars are glamorized and adulated, but the majority of actors in the theatre do not receive a living wage from acting, and most actors do not find as much challenging work as they deserve. Yet any performer who has followed the difficult road to even modest success in the theatre should carry the title "actor" with pride. We can say with Jessica Tandy, "When I see something on stage really well done, I'm very proud of my profession."[1]

Break a Leg!

An apocryphal story tells of the opening night of a play in a bygone era when the leading actor broke his leg. His leg was put in a cast, and he played opening night anyway. The play received rave reviews and broke records for consecutive performances. Since then "Break a leg!" has been the traditional salutation for wishing actors good luck on opening night.

As the curtain rises on your own use of the principles offered in this right-brain/left-brain approach to the creative processes of acting, may you also, "Break a leg!"

Notes

1. From a television interview with Arlene Francis, "The Prime of Your Life," New York: WNBC, 28 April 1984.

For Further Reading

Cohen, Robert. *Acting Professionally*. 3d ed. Palo Alto, Calif.: Mayfield, 1981.
Shurtleff, Michael. *Audition*. New York: Walker, 1978.

Appendix

Scenes for Analysis and Practice

Here in the appendix you will find scenes representative of the eight types discussed in chapter 14. You will find these scenes useful also for other exercises as suggested throughout earlier parts of the text. For example, the scene from *Ah, Wilderness!*, used to illustrate the concepts in chapter 6 on the level of action, has been divided into beats and analyzed with three levels of objectives: superobjective, scene objective, and beat objectives; four moments are also indicated.

The scene from *The Effect of Gamma Rays on Man-in-the-Moon Marigolds* has been divided into beats with unconscious roles suggested for Ruth and Tillie, as you studied in chapter 8 on the level of unconscious role playing.

Romantic Comedy ─────────────

Ah, Wilderness!
by Eugene O'Neill*

(Richard Miller meets his girlfriend, Muriel McComber, at a quiet beach by an overturned rowboat on a summer evening in 1906.)   BEAT #1

RICHARD: *(Darkly again)* After it was dark, I sneaked out and went to a low dive I know about.

MURIEL: Dick Miller, I don't believe you ever!

RICHARD: You ask them at the Pleasant Beach House if I didn't! They won't forget me in a hurry!

MURIEL: *(Impressed and horrified)* You went there? Why, that's a terrible place! Pa says it ought to be closed by the police!

RICHARD: *(Darkly)* I said it was a dive, didn't I? It's a "secret house of shame." And they let me into a secret room behind the barroom. There wasn't anyone there but a Princeton Senior I know—he belongs to Tiger Inn and he's fullback on the football team—and he had two chorus girls from New York with him, and they were all drinking champagne.

MURIEL: *(Disturbed by the entrance of the chorus girls)* Dick Miller! I hope you didn't notice . . .

RICHARD: *(Carelessly)* I had a highball by myself and then I noticed one of the girls—the one that wasn't with the fullback—looking at me. She had strange-looking eyes. And then she asked me if I wouldn't drink champagne with them and come and sit with her.

*Excerpt from *Ah, Wilderness!*, by Eugene O'Neill. Copyright 1933 by Eugene O'Neill and renewed 1961 by Carlotta Monterey O'Neill. Reprinted from *The Plays of Eugene O'Neill*, by permission of Random House, Inc.

MURIEL: She must have been a nice thing! *(Then a bit falteringly)* And did—you?

BEAT #2

RICHARD: *(With tragic bitterness)* Why shouldn't I, when you'd told me in that letter you'd never see me again?

MURIEL: *(Almost tearfully)* But you ought to have known Pa made me . . .

RICHARD: I didn't know that then. *(Then rubbing it in)* Her name was Belle. She had yellow hair—the kind that burns and stings you!

MURIEL: I'll bet it was dyed!

RICHARD: She kept smoking one cigarette after another—but that's nothing for a chorus girl.

MURIEL: *(Indignantly)* She was low and bad, that's what she was or she couldn't be a chorus girl, and her smoking cigarettes proves it! *(Then falteringly again)* And then what happened?

RICHARD: *(Carelessly)* Oh, we just kept drinking champagne—I bought a round—and then I had a fight with the barkeep and knocked him down because he'd insulted her. He was a great big thug but . . .

MURIEL: *(Huffily)* I don't see how he could—insult that kind! And why did you fight for her? Why didn't the Princeton fullback who'd brought them there? He must have been bigger than you.

RICHARD: *(Stopped for a moment—then quickly)* He was too drunk by that time.

MURIEL: And were you drunk?

RICHARD: Only a little then. I was worse later. *(Proudly)* You ought to have seen me when I got home! I was on the verge of delirium tremens!

MURIEL: I'm glad I didn't see you. You must have been awful. I hate people who get drunk. I'd have hated you!

RICHARD: Well, it was all your fault, wasn't it? If you hadn't written that letter—

MURIEL: But I've told you I didn't mean— *(Then faltering but fascinated)* But what happened with that Belle—after—before you went home?

BEAT #3

RICHARD: Oh, we kept drinking champagne and she said she'd fallen in love with me at first sight and she came and sat on my lap and kissed me.

MURIEL: *(Stiffening)* Oh!

RICHARD: *(Quickly, afraid he has gone too far)* But it was only all in fun, and then we just kept on drinking champagne, and finally I said good night and came home.

MURIEL: And did you kiss her?

RICHARD: No, I didn't.

MURIEL: *(Distractedly)* You did, too! You're lying and you know it. You did, too! *(Then tearfully)* And there I was right at that time lying in bed not able to sleep, wondering how I was ever going to see you again and crying my eyes out, while you—! *(She suddenly jumps to her feet in a tearful fury)* I hate you! I wish you were dead! I'm going home this minute! I never want to lay eyes on you again! And this time I mean it! *(She tries to jump out of the boat but he holds her back. All the pose has dropped from him now and he is in a frightened state of contrition)* BEAT #4

RICHARD: *(Imploringly)* Muriel! Wait! Listen!

MURIEL: I don't want to listen! Let me go! If you don't I'll bite your hand!

RICHARD: I won't let you go! You've got to let me explain! I never—! Ouch! *(For Muriel has bitten his hand and it hurts, and, stung by the pain, he lets go instinctively, and she jumps quickly out of the boat and starts running toward the path. Richard calls after her with bitter despair and hurt)* All right! Go if you want to— BEAT #5 if you haven't the decency to let me explain! I hate you, too! I'll go and see Belle!

MURIEL: *(Seeing he isn't following her, stops at the foot of the path—defiantly)* Well, go and see her—if that's the kind of girl you like! What do I care? *(Then as he only stares before him broodingly, sitting dejectedly in the stern of the boat, a pathetic figure of injured grief)* You can't explain! What can you explain? You owned up you kissed her!

RICHARD: I did not. I said she kissed me.

MURIEL: *(Scornfully, but drifting back a step in his direction)* And I suppose you just sat and let yourself be kissed! Tell that to the Marines!

RICHARD: *(Injuredly)* All right! If you're going to call me a liar every word I say . . .

MURIEL: *(Drifting back another step)* I didn't call you a liar. I only meant—it sounds fishy. Don't you know it does?

RICHARD: I don't know anything. I only know I wish I was dead!

MURIEL: *(Gently reproving)* You oughtn't to say that. It's wicked. *(Then after a pause)* And I suppose you'll BEAT #6 tell me you didn't fall in love with her?

RICHARD:	*(Scornfully)* I should say not! Fall in love with that kind of girl! What do you take me for?
MURIEL:	*(Practically)* How do you know what you did if you drank so much champagne?
RICHARD:	I kept my head—with her. I'm not a sucker, no matter what you think!
MURIEL:	*(Drifting nearer)* Then you didn't—love her?
RICHARD:	I hated her! She wasn't even pretty! And I had a fight with her before I left, she got so fresh. I told her I loved you and never could love anyone else, and for her to leave me alone.
MURIEL:	But you said just now you were going to see her . . .
RICHARD:	That was only bluff. I wouldn't—unless you left me. Then I wouldn't care what I did—any more than I did last night. *(Then suddenly defiant)* And what if I did kiss her once or twice? I only did it to get back at you!
MURIEL:	Dick!
RICHARD:	You're a fine one to blame me—when it was all your fault! Why can't you be fair? Didn't I think you were out of my life forever? Hadn't you written me you were? Answer me that!
MURIEL:	But I've told you a million times that Pa . . .
RICHARD:	Why didn't you have more sense than to let him make you write it? Was it my fault you didn't?
MURIEL:	It was your fault for being so stupid! You ought to have known he stood right over me and told me each word to write. If I'd refused, it would only have made everything worse. I had to pretend, so I'd get a chance to see you. Don't you see, Silly? And I had sand enough to sneak out to meet you tonight, didn't I? *(He doesn't answer. She moves nearer)* Still I can see how you felt the way you did—and maybe I am to blame for that. So I'll forgive and forget, Dick—if you'll swear to me you didn't even think of loving that . . .
RICHARD:	*(Eagerly)* I didn't! I swear, Muriel. I couldn't. I love you!
MURIEL:	Well, then—I still love you.
RICHARD:	Then come back here, why don't you?
MURIEL:	*(Coyly)* It's getting late.
RICHARD:	It's not near half-past yet.
MURIEL:	*(Comes back and sits down by him shyly)* All right— only I'll have to go soon, Dick. *(He puts his arm*

BEAT #7

BEAT #8

around her. She cuddles up close to him) I'm sorry—I hurt your hand.

RICHARD: That was nothing. It felt wonderful—even to have you bite!

MURIEL: *(Impulsively takes his hand and kisses it)* There! That'll cure it. *(She is overcome by confusion at her boldness)*

RICHARD: You shouldn't—waste that—on my hand. *(Then tremblingly)* You said—you'd let me—   BEAT #9

MURIEL: I said, maybe.

RICHARD: Please, Muriel. You know—I want it so!

MURIEL: Will it wash off—her kisses—make you forget you ever—for always?

RICHARD: I should say so! I'd never remember—anything but it—never want anything but it—ever again.

MURIEL: *(Shyly lifting her lips)* Then—all right—Dick. *(He kisses her tremblingly and for a moment their lips remain together. Then she lets her head sink on his shoulder and sighs softly)* The moon *is* beautiful, isn't it?

Objectives and Moments for *Ah, Wilderness!*

I. Superobjectives

Richard: to obtain Muriel's love
Muriel: to prove her love for Richard despite her father's opposition and Richard's doubts (external obstacles)

II. Scene Objectives

Richard: to win a token of Muriel's affection
Muriel: to prove her loyalty to Richard

III. Beat Objectives

Beat #1
Richard: to titillate Muriel's curiosity
Muriel: to challenge Richard's moral behavior
Beat #2
Richard: to arouse Muriel's jealousy
Muriel: to scorn Richard's judgement
Beat #3
Richard: to boast of his faithfulness
Muriel: to play on Richard's sense of guilt

Beat #4
Richard: to calm Muriel's outburst
Muriel: to punish Richard's disloyalty
Beat #5
Richard: to spite Muriel's disdain
Muriel: to reconcile her own misgivings
Beat #6
Richard: to prove his loyalty to Muriel
Muriel: to open the door for reconciliation
Beat #7
Richard: to test Muriel's faithfulness
Muriel: to tender her excuses
Beat #8
Richard: to gain physical reassurance of Muriel's love
Muriel: to reassure Richard of her love
Beat #9
Richard: to express his passion for Muriel
Muriel: to demonstrate her love for Richard

IV. Moments

1. Muriel's reaction to Richard's revelation that the chorus girl kissed him (in Beat #3)
2. Richard's reaction to Muriel's biting his hand (in Beat #4)
3. Richard's reaction to Muriel's kissing his hand (in Beat #8)
4. Both Muriel's and Richard's reactions to the kiss on the lips (end of Beat #9)

Serious Drama _____

The Effect of Gamma Rays on Man-In-The-Moon Marigolds
by Paul Zindel*

(Tillie works on her display. Ruth is brushing her hair)

[Unconscious Roles]
BEAT #1

RUTH: The only competition you have to worry about is Janice Vickery. They say she caught it near Princess Bay Boulevard and it was still alive when she took the skin off it.

(RUTH: Condescending Royalty)

TILLIE: *(Taking some plants from Ruth)* Let me do that, please, Ruth.

(TILLIE: Responsible Care-taker)

RUTH: I'm sorry I touched them, really.

TILLIE: Why don't you feed Peter?

RUTH: Because I don't feel like feeding him . . . Now I feel like feeding him.

(She gets some lettuce from a bag)

I heard that it screamed for three minutes after she put it in because the water wasn't boiling yet. How much talent does it take to boil the skin off a cat and then stick the bones together again? That's what I want to know. Ugh. I had a dream about that, too. I figure she did it in less than a day and she ends up as one of the top five winners . . . and you spend months growing atomic flowers.

TILLIE: Don't you think you should finish getting ready?

BEAT #2
(TILLIE: Efficiency Expert)

RUTH: Finish? This is it!

(RUTH: Superior Big Sister)

TILLIE: Are you going to wear that sweater?

RUTH: Look, don't worry about me. I'm not getting up on any stage, and if I did I wouldn't be caught dead with a horrible bow like that.

TILLIE: Mother put it—

RUTH: They're going to laugh you off the stage again like when you cranked that atom in assembly . . . I didn't mean that . . . The one they're going to laugh at is Mama.

BEAT #3
(RUTH: Know-it-all)
(TILLIE: Shocked Innocent)

TILLIE: What?

RUTH: I said the one they're going to laugh at is Mama . . . Oh, let me take that bow off.

TILLIE: It's all right.

RUTH: Look, just sit still. I don't want everybody making fun of you.

TILLIE: What made you say that about Mama?

RUTH: Oh, I heard them talking in the Science Office yesterday. Mr. Goodman and Miss Hanley. She's getting $12.63 to chaperon the thing tonight.

TILLIE: What were they saying?

RUTH: Miss Hanley was telling Mr. Goodman about Mama . . . when she found out you were one of the five winners. And he wanted to know if there was something wrong with Mama because she sounded crazy over the phone. And Miss Hanley said she *was* crazy and she always has been crazy and she can't wait to see what she looks like after all these years. Miss Hanley said her nickname used to be *Betty the Loon.*

TILLIE: *(As* Ruth *combs her hair)* Ruth, you're hurting me.

RUTH: She was just like you and everybody thought she was a big weirdo. There! You look much better!

BEAT #4
(RUTH: Outraged Possessor)
(TILLIE: Silent Martyr)

(She goes back to the rabbit)

Peter, if anybody stuck you in a pot of boiling water I'd kill them, do you know that? . . .

(Then to Tillie)

What do they call boiling the skin off a cat? I call it murder, that's what I call it. They say it was hit by a car and Janice just scooped it up and before you could say *bingo* it was screaming in a pot of boiling water . . . Do you know what they're all waiting to see? Mama's feathers! That's what Miss Hanley said. She said Mama blabs as though she was the Queen of England and just as proper as can be, and that her idea of getting dressed up is to put on all

BEAT #5
(RUTH: Mocking Peasant)

the feathers in the world and go as a bird. Always trying to get somewhere, like a great big bird.

TILLIE: Don't tell Mama, please. It doesn't matter.   (TILLIE: Trepidant Peace-maker)

RUTH: I was up there watching her getting dressed and sure enough, she's got the feathers out.

TILLIE: You didn't tell her what Miss Hanley said?

RUTH: Are you kidding? I just told her I didn't like the feathers and I didn't think she should wear any. But I'll bet she doesn't listen to me.

TILLIE: It doesn't matter.

RUTH: It doesn't matter? Do you think I want to be laughed right out of the school tonight, with Chris Burns there, and all? Laughed right out of the school, with your electric hair and her feathers on that stage, and Miss Hanley splitting her sides?

TILLIE: Promise me you won't say anything.   BEAT #6

RUTH: On one condition.   (TILLIE: Cautious Negotiator)

TILLIE: What?

RUTH: Give Peter to me.   (RUTH: Ruthless Bargain-hunter)

TILLIE: *(Ignoring her)* The taxi will be here any minute and I won't have all this stuff ready. Did you see my speech?

RUTH: I mean it. Give Peter to me.

TILLIE: He belongs to all of us.

RUTH: For me. All for me. What do you care? He doesn't mean anything to you anymore, now that you've got all those crazy plants.

TILLIE: Will you stop?

RUTH: If you don't give him to me I'm going to tell Mama that everybody's waiting to laugh at her.

TILLIE: Where are those typewritten cards?

RUTH: I MEAN IT! Give him to me!

TILLIE: Does he mean that much to you?

RUTH: Yes!

TILLIE: All right.   BEAT #7

RUTH: *(After a burst of private laughter)* Betty the Loon . . .   (RUTH: Triumphant Victor)

(She laughs again)

That's what they used to call her, you know. Betty the Loon!

TILLIE: I don't think that's very nice.   (TILLIE: Firm Judge)

RUTH: First they had Betty the Loon, and now they've got Tillie the Loon . . .

(To rabbit)

You don't have to worry about me turning you in for any old plants . . .

Tragicomedy _____

Sister Mary Ignatius Explains It All For You
by Christopher Durang*

(While presenting a lecture on her beliefs, Sister Mary Ignatius [assisted by her pupil Thomas] has been interrupted by former students Gary, Diane, Philomena, and Aloysius.)

PHILOMENA: You used to hit me, too.

SISTER: You probably said stupid things.

PHILOMENA: I did. I told you I was stupid. That was no reason to hit me.

SISTER: It seems a very good reason to hit you. Knock some sense into you.

PHILOMENA: You used to take the point of your pencil and poke it up and down on my head when I didn't do my homework.

SISTER: You should have done your homework.

PHILOMENA: And when I didn't know how to do long division, you slammed my head against the blackboard.

SISTER: Did I ever break a bone?

PHILOMENA: No.

SISTER: There, you see! *(To Gary)* And what about you?

GARY: You didn't do anything to me in particular. I just found you scary.

SISTER: Well, I am scary.

GARY: But my lover Jeff doesn't like you cause you made him wet his pants, too.

SISTER: All this obsession with the bladder. *(To Diane)* And you, the nasty one, why did you want to embarrass me?

DIANE: *(Said simply)* Because I believed you. I believed how you said the world worked, and that God loved us, and the story of the Good Shepherd and the lost sheep; and I don't think you should lie to people.

SISTER: But that's how things are. I didn't lie.

DIANE: When I was sixteen, my mother got breast cancer, which spread. I prayed to God to let her suffering be small, but her suffering seemed to me quite extreme. She was in bad pain for half a year, and then terrible pain for much of a full year. The ulcerations on her body were horrifying to her and to me. Her last few weeks she slipped into a semi-conscious state, which allowed her, unfortunately, to wake up for a few minutes at a time and to have a full awareness of her pain and her fear of death. She was able to recognize me, and she would try to cry, but she was unable to; and to speak, but she was unable to. I think she wanted me to get her new doctors; she never really accepted that her disease was going to kill her, and she thought in her panic that her doctors must be incompetent and that new ones could magically cure her. Then, thank goodness, she went into a full coma. A nurse who I knew to be Catholic assured me that everything would be done to keep her alive—a dubious comfort. Happily, the doctor was not Catholic, or if he was, not doctrinaire, and they didn't use extraordinary means to keep her alive; and she finally died after several more weeks in her coma. Now there are, I'm sure, far worse deaths—terrible burnings, tortures, plague, pestilence, famine; Christ on the cross even, as Sister likes to say. But I thought my mother's death was bad enough, and I got confused as to why I had been praying and to whom. I mean, if prayer was really this sort of button you pressed—admit you need the Lord, then He stops your suffering—then why didn't it always work? Or ever work? And when it worked, so-called, and our prayers were supposedly answered, wasn't it as likely to be chance as God? God always answers our prayers, you said, He just sometimes says no. But why would He say no to stopping my mother's suffering? I wasn't even asking that she live, just that He end her suffering. And it can't be that He was letting her suffer because she'd been bad, because she hadn't been bad and besides suffering doesn't seem to work that way, considering the suffering of children who've obviously done nothing wrong. So why was He letting her suffer? Spite? Was the Lord God actually malicious? That seemed possible, but far fetched. Maybe He had no control over it, maybe He wasn't omnipotent as you taught us He was. Maybe He created the world sort of by accident by belching one morning or getting the hiccups, and maybe He had no idea how the whole thing worked. In which case, He wouldn't be malicious, just useless. Or, of course, more likely than that, He didn't exist at all, the universe was hiccupped or belched into existence all on its own, and my mother's suffering just existed like rain or wind or humidity. I became angry at myself, and by extension at you, for ever having expected anything beyond randomness from the world. And while I was thinking these things, the day that my mother died, I was raped. Now I know that's really too much, one really loses all sympathy for me because I sound like I'm making it up or something. But bad things sometimes happen in clusters, and this particular day on my return from the hospital I was raped by some maniac who broke into the house. He had a knife and cut me up some. Anyway, I don't really want to go on about the experience, but I got very depressed for about five years. Somehow the utter randomness of things—my mother's suffering, my attack by a lunatic who was either born a lunatic or made one by cruel parents or perhaps by an imbalance of hormones or whatever, etc. etc. —*this randomness seemed intolerable.* I found I grew to hate you, Sister, for making me once expect everything to be ordered and to make sense. My psychiatrist said he thought my ha-

tred of you was obsessive, that I just was looking for someone to blame. Then he seduced
me, and he was the father of my second abor-
tion.

SISTER: I think she's making all this up.

DIANE: He said I seduced him. And maybe that's so.
But he could be lying just to make himself feel
better. *(To* Sister*)* And of course your idea that I
should have this baby, either baby, is prepos-
terous. Have you any idea what a terrible
mother I'd be? I'm a nervous wreck.

SISTER: God would have given you the strength.

DIANE: I suppose it is childish to look for blame, part
of the randomness of things is that there is no
one to blame; but basically I think everything
is your fault, Sister.

SISTER: You have obviously never read the Book of Job.

DIANE: I have read it. And I think it's a nasty story.

SISTER: God explains in that story why He lets us suffer, and a very lovely explanation it is, too. He
likes to test us so that when we choose to love
Him no matter what He does to us that proves
how great and deep our love for Him is.

DIANE: That sounds like "The Story of O."

SISTER: Well there's obviously no talking to you. You
don't want help or knowledge or enlighten-
ment, so there's nothing left for you but an
unhappy life, sickness, death, and hell.

DIANE: Last evening I killed my psychiatrist and now
I'm going to kill you. *(Takes out a gun)*

GARY: Oh, dear. I thought we were just going to
embarrass her.

SISTER: *(Stalling for time)* And you have, very much so.
So no need to kill me at all. Goodbye, Diane,
Gary, Aloysius . . .

DIANE: You're insane. You shouldn't be allowed to
teach children. I see that there's that little boy
here today. You're going to make him crazy.

SISTER: Thomas, stay offstage with the cookies, dear.

DIANE: I want you to admit that everything's your
fault, and then I'm going to kill you.

PHILOMENA: Maybe we should all wait outside.

SISTER: Stay here. Diane, look at me. I was wrong. I
admit it. I'm sorry. I thought everything made
sense, but I didn't understand things properly.

There's nothing I can say to make it up to you but . . . *(Seeing something awful behind* Diane's *head)* LOOK OUT! *(*Diane *looks behind her,* Sister *whips out her own gun and shoots* Diane *dead.* Sister *like a circus artist completing a stunt, hands up)* Ta-da! For those non-Catholics present, murder *is* allowable in self-defense, one doesn't even have to tell it in confession. Thomas, bring me some water.

GARY: We didn't know she was bringing a gun.

(Thomas brings water)

SISTER: I remember her now from class. *(Looks at her dead body)* She had no sense of humor.

ALOYSIUS: I have to go to the bathroom.

SISTER: *(Aims gun at him)* Stay where you are. Raise your hand if you want to go to the bathroom, Aloysius, and wait until I have acknowledged you. *(She ignores him now, though keeps gun aimed at him most of the time)* Thomas, bring me a cookie. *(He does)* Most of my students turned out beautifully, these are the few exceptions. But we never give up on those who've turned out badly, do we, Thomas? What is the story of the Good Shepherd and the Lost Sheep?

THOMAS: The Good Shepherd was so concerned about his Lost Sheep that he left his flock to go find the Lost Sheep, and then He found it.

SISTER: That's right. And while he was gone, a great big wolf came and killed his entire flock. No, just kidding, I'm feeling lightheaded from all this excitement. No, by the story of the Lost Sheep, Christ tells us that when a sinner strays, we mustn't give up on the sinner. *(*Sister *indicates for* Thomas *to exit, he does)* So I don't totally despair for these people standing here. Gary, I hope that you will leave your friend Jeff, don't even tell him where you're going, just disappear, and then I hope you will live your life as a celibate. Like me. Celibate rhymes with celebrate. Our Lord loves celibate people. And you, Philomena, I hope you will get married to some nice Catholic man, or if you stay unmarried then you, too, will become a celibate. Rhymes with celebrate.

ALOYSIUS: Sister, I have my hand up.

SISTER: Keep it up. And you, Aloysius, I hope you'll remember not to kill yourself, which is a mortal sin. For if we live by God's laws even though we are having a miserable life, remember heaven and eternal happiness are our reward.

Melodrama

Night Must Fall
by Emlyn Williams*

(The stagger of footsteps; Olivia stands in the doorway to the sun-room. She has been running through the forest; her clothes are wild, her hair has fallen about her shoulders, and she is no longer wearing spectacles. She looks nearly beautiful. Her manner is quiet, almost dazed. Dan lowers the chair slowly and sits on the other side of the table. A pause.)

OLIVIA: I've never seen a dead body before . . . I climbed through the window and nearly fell over it. Like a sack of potatoes or something. I thought it was, at first. . . . And that's murder. *(As he looks up at her)* But it's so ordinary . . . I came back . . . *(As he lights his cigarette)* . . . expecting . . . ha *(Laughing hysterically)* . . . I don't know . . . and here I find you, smoking a cigarette . . . you might have been tidying the room for the night. It's so . . . ordinary. . . . *(After a pause, with a cry)* Why don't you *say* something!

DAN: I thought you were goin' to stay the night at that feller's.

OLIVIA: I was.

DAN: What d'you come back for?

OLIVIA: *(The words pouring out)* To find you out. You've kept me guessing for a fortnight. Guessing hard. I very nearly knew, all the time. But not quite. And now I do know.

DAN: Why was you so keen on finding me out?

OLIVIA: *(Vehemently, coming to the table)* In the same way any sane, decent-minded human would want—would want to have you arrested for the monster you are!

DAN: *(Quietly)* What d'you come back for?

OLIVIA: I . . . I've told you. . . .

(He smiles at her slowly and shakes his head. She sits at the table and closes her eyes)

> I got as far as the edge of the wood. I could see the lights in the village . . . I came back.

(She buries her head in her arm. Dan rises, looks at her a moment regretfully, puts away his cigarette, and stands with both hands over the invalid chair)

DAN: *(Casually)* She didn't keep any money anywhere else, did she?

OLIVIA: I've read a lot about evil—

(Dan realizes his hands are wet with paraffin and wipes them on his trousers)

DAN: Clumsy. . . .

OLIVIA: I never expected to come across it in real life.

DAN: *(Lightly)* You didn't ought to read so much. I never got through a book yet. . . . But I'll read you all right. . . . *(Crossing to her, leaning over the table, and smiling at her intently)* You haven't had a drop of drink, and yet you feel as if you had. You never knew there was such a secret part inside of you. All that book-learnin' and moral-me-eye here and social-me-eye there—you took that off on the edge of the wood same as if it was an overcoat . . . and you left it there!

OLIVIA: I hate you. I . . . hate you!

DAN: *(Urgently)* And same as anybody out for the first time without their overcoat, you feel as light as air! Same as I feel, sometimes—only I never had no overcoat— *(Excited)* Why—this is my big chance! You're the one I can tell about meself! Oh, I'm sick o' hearin' how clever everybody else is—I want to tell 'em how clever *I* am for a change! . . . Money I'm going to have, and people doin' what they're told, and *me* tellin' them to do it! There was a 'oman at the Tallboys, wasn't there? She wouldn't be told, would she? She thought she was up 'gainst a soft fellow in a uniform, didn't she? She never knew it was *me* she was dealin' with— *(Striking his chest in a paroxysm of elation)* —Me! And this old girl treatin' me like a son 'cause I made her think she was a chronic invalid—ha! She's been more use to me tonight *(Tapping the notes in his jacket pocket, smartly)* than she has to any other body all her life. Stupid, that's what people are . . . stupid. If those two hadn't been stupid they might be breathin' now; you're not stupid; that's why I'm talkin' to you. *(With exaggerated self-possession)* You said just now murder's ordinary. . . . Well it isn't ordinary at all, see? And I'm not an ordinary chap. There's one big difference 'tween me and other fellows that try this game. I'll *never be found out.* 'Cause I don't care a— *(Snapping his fingers, grandly)* The world's goin' to hear from me. That's me. *(Chuckling)* You wait. . . . *(After a pause)* But you can't wait, can you?

OLIVIA: What do you mean?

DAN: Well, when I say I'll never be found out, what I mean is, no living soul will be able to tell any other living soul about me. *(Beginning to roll up a sleeve, nonchalantly)* Can you think of anybody . . . who can go tomorrow . . . and tell the police the fire at Forest Corner . . . wasn't an accident at all?

OLIVIA: I—I can.

DAN: Oh no, you can't.

OLIVIA: Why can't I?

DAN: Well, I'm up against a very serious problem, I am. But the answer to it is as simple as pie, to a fellow like me, simple as pie. . . . *(Rolling up the other sleeve a little way)* She isn't going to be the only one . . . found tomorrow . . . in the fire at Forest Corner. . . . *(After a pause)* Aren't you frightened? You ought to be! *(Smiling)* Don't you think I'll do it?

OLIVIA: I know you will. I just can't realise it.

DAN: You know, when I told you all that about meself just now, I'd made up my mind then about you. *(Moving slowly after her, round the table, as she steps back towards the window)* That's what I am, see? I make up me mind to do a thing, and I do it. . . . You remember that first day when I come in here? I said to meself then, There's a girl that's got her wits about her; she knows a thing or two; different from the others. I was right, wasn't I? You— *(Stopping abruptly, and looking round the room)* What's that light in here?

OLIVIA: What light?

DAN: There's somebody in this room's holdin' a flash-light.

OLIVIA: It can't be in this room. . . . It must be a light in the wood.

DAN: It can't be.

(A flashlight crosses the window-curtain. Olivia turns and stares at it)

OLIVIA: Somebody's watching the bungalow. . . .

(He looks at her, as if he did not understand)

DAN: *(Fiercely)* Nobody's watching! . . .

(He runs to the window. She backs into the corner of the room)

I'm the one that watches! They've got no call to watch me! I'll go out and tell them that, an' all! *(Opening the curtains in a frenzy)* I'm the one that watches!

(The light crosses the window again. He stares, then claps his hands over his eyes. Backing to the sofa)

Behind them trees. *(Clutching the invalid chair)* Hundreds back of each tree. . . . Thousands of eyes. The whole damn world's on my track! . . . *(Sitting on the edge of the sofa, and listening)* What's that? . . . Like a big wall fallin' over into the sea. . . . *(Closing his hands over his ears convulsively)*

OLIVIA: *(Coming down to him)* They mustn't come in. . . .

DAN: *(Turning to her)* Yes, but . . . *(Staring)* You're lookin' at me as if you never seen *me* before. . . .

OLIVIA: I never have. Nobody has. You've stopped acting at last. You're real. Frightened. Like a child *(Putting her arm about his shoulders)* They mustn't come in. . . .

DAN: But everything's slippin' away. From underneath our feet. . . . Can't you feel it? Starting slow . . . and then hundreds of miles an hour. . . . I'm goin' backwards! . . . And there's a wind in my ears, terrible blowin' wind. . . . Everything's going past me like the telegraph-poles. . . . All the things I've never seen . . . faster and faster . . . backwards— back to the day I was born. *(Shrieking)* I can see it coming . . . the day I was born! . . . *(Turning to her, simply)* I'm goin' to die. *(A pause. A knock at the front door)* It's getting cold.

(Another knock; louder. She presses his head to her)

OLIVIA: It's all right. You won't die. I'll tell them I *made* you do it. I'll tell lies—I'll tell—

(A third and louder knock at the front door. She realises that she must answer, goes into the hall, opens the front door, and comes back, hiding Dan *from view)*

Farce _____

Hotel Paradiso
by Georges Feydeau and Maurice Desvallieres
translation by Peter Glenville*

(Max is alone with Victoire)

MAX:	*(Sitting on high stool, reading)* "Passion is an emotion of the soul, moved by the impulses of one's animal nature, impelling one to consort with objects that appear suitable." *(Deeply convinced)* That's exactly it!
VICTOIRE:	Exactly what, Master Max?
MAX:	I beg your pardon?
VICTOIRE:	What are you doing there?
MAX:	Studying Passion.
VICTOIRE:	*(Skeptical—moves to left of Max and leans on trestle table)* Really! In that position? *(Moving towards him)* If you like I'll help you with your work.
MAX:	*(Earnest)* Have you studied the centres of emotional life?
VICTOIRE:	*(Naturally)* Same as most people!
MAX:	In Spinoza?
VICTOIRE:	No, in the palm of my hand. *(Moves to left of trestle table)*
MAX:	I'm afraid you don't quite understand.
VICTOIRE:	*(Tickles his ear with quill)* Are you sure I can't help with your work?
MAX:	*(Imperturbable)* That tickles.
VICTOIRE:	Don't you like it?
MAX:	I didn't comment on the nature of the sensation.

*Excerpt from Act I, *Hotel Paradiso*, © Copyright 1957 by Peter Glenville. Published by Samuel French. Used by courtesy of Peter Glenville.

I stated a fact. It tickles. *(Aside, as he swivels around on the stool)* What a curious girl!

VICTOIRE: You're not very friendly, are you?

MAX: I am working! *(Gets up)* I cannot study Passion with a woman next to me! *(He moves to sofa, sits. Reading aloud)* "There is a distinction between idealistic love and sensual love. The passion of a lover for his mistress and that of a kind father for his children.

(Victoire crosses to him above sofa)

They have certain emotional impulses in common, but—

(He looks at Victoire and moves to the other end of the sofa. She sits left of Max)

—in the first case love is aimed at the *possession* of the object rather than the object itself."

(She tickles his leg)

(Looking up) That is a distinctly pleasant sensation!

VICTOIRE: *(Behind him, coiling a lock of his hair round her finger)* Think so?

MAX: Undoubtedly! *(Reading)* "A father seeks the well-being of his children—"

VICTOIRE: *(Up to Max's shoulder)* You're a big, big, beautiful baby. *(She continues to play with his hair)*

MAX: Please, M'selle! You may tickle but don't talk.

VICTOIRE: Yes, M. Max.

MAX: A father seeks the well-being of his children—

VICTOIRE: *(She leans over sofa)* Has anyone ever told you you're quite a good looker? *(She tickles)*

MAX: Me? I've no idea. Oh, yes. Once.

VICTOIRE: Who?

MAX: A photographer. He advised me to order three dozen copies.

VICTOIRE: Oh!

MAX: *(Continuing to read)* "A father seeks the well-being of his children—" *(He pauses. His eyes are raised furtively)*

VICTOIRE: *(Finger on Max's knee)* What is it, M. Max?

MAX: Nothing! Nothing at all! It's just that—well, in some perplexing way—that movement of the hand—it was rather agreeable. I can't think why!

VICTOIRE: Really?—Why not ask Spinoza? *(Takes hand away)*

MAX: He is silent on the subject!

VICTOIRE: Well, then, I'd shut that silly old book if I were you. *(She takes the book and shuts it; get up, crosses above sofa left of Max)* How can a young man find out about passion in a book! Like learning to swim on a cushion! No good if you're tossed in the sea. *(She sits down beside him)*

MAX: *(To front)* What is the matter with this girl?

VICTOIRE: *(Hands on his shoulders)* Look at you. *(Left of Max)* Those awful glasses. *(She takes them off)* Can't you see without them?

MAX: Oh yes!—In fact, rather better!

VICTOIRE: *(Going behind sofa)* And just look at your hair! You ought to try a different style. You've got to give nature a helping hand, you know! *(Rumples hair)*

MAX: *(Closing his eyes, with concentration)* Do that again!

(She rumples hair again)

Again. Oh yes.

(Her hands to ears, to chin and down front of chest)

That's very, very good! Oh yes, indeed! *(Breaks and grabs book from left end of sofa)* "Passion is an emotion of the soul—"

VICTOIRE: M. Maxime.

MAX: Au revoir, M'selle.

VICTOIRE: Au revoir!

MAX: M'selle?

VICTOIRE: *(Goes to the door up left)* It's unbelievable! It's like getting blood from a stone. *(Exits)*

MAX: *(Reading)* "The affection of honourable men—"

Black Comedy _____

Crimes of the Heart
by Beth Henley*

(Meg, Lenny, and Babe are in the kitchen)

LENNY: Hey, I have an idea—

BABE: What?

LENNY: Let's play cards!!

BABE: Oh, let's do!

MEG: All right!

LENNY: Oh, good! It'll be just like when we used to sit around the table playing hearts all night long.

BABE: I know! *(Getting up)* I'll fix us up some popcorn and hot chocolate—

MEG: *(Getting up)* Here, let me get out that old black popcorn pot.

LENNY: *(Getting up)* Oh, yes! Now, let's see, I think I have a deck of cards around here somewhere.

BABE: Gosh, I hope I remember all the rules—Are hearts good or bad?

MEG: Bad, I think. Aren't they, Lenny?

LENNY: That's right. Hearts are bad, but the Black Sister is the worst of all—

MEG: Oh, that's right! And the Black Sister is the Queen of Spades.

BABE: *(Figuring it out)* And spades are the black cards that aren't the puppy dog feet?

MEG: *(Thinking a moment)* Right. And she counts a lot of points.

BABE: And points are bad?

MEG: Right. Here, I'll get some paper so we can keep score. *(The phone begins to ring)*

LENNY: Oh, here they are!

MEG: I'll get it—

LENNY: Why, look at these cards! They're years old!

BABE: Oh, let me see!

MEG: Hello . . . No, this is Meg Magrath . . . Doc. How are you? . . . Well, good . . . You're where? . . . Well, sure. Come on over . . . Sure, I'm sure. Yeah, come right on over . . . All right. Bye. *(She hangs up)* That was Doc Porter. He's down the street at Al's Grill. He's gonna come on over.

LENNY: He is?

MEG: He said he wanted to come see me.

LENNY: Oh. *(After a pause)* Well, do you still want to play?

MEG: No, I don't think so.

LENNY: All right. *(Lenny starts to shuffle the cards, as* Meg *brushes her hair)* You know, it's really not much fun playing Hearts with only two people.

MEG: I'm sorry; maybe after Doc leaves, I'll join you.

LENNY: I know; maybe Doc'll want to play, then we can have a game of bridge.

MEG: I don't think so. Doc never liked cards. Maybe we'll just go out somewhere.

LENNY: *(Putting down the cards.* Babe *picks them up)* Meg—

MEG: What?

LENNY: Well, Doc's married now.

MEG: I know. You told me.

LENNY: Oh. Well, as long as you know that. *(Pause)* As long as you know that.

MEG: *(Still primping)* Yes, I know. She made the pot.

BABE: How many cards do I deal out?

LENNY: *(Leaving the table)* Excuse me.

BABE: All of 'em, or what?

LENNY: Ah, Meg? Could I—could I ask you something? *(Babe proceeds to deal out all the cards)*

MEG: What?

LENNY: I just wanted to ask you—

MEG: What? *(Unable to go on with what she really wants to say,* Lenny *runs up and picks up the box of candy)*

LENNY: Well, just why did you take one little bite out of each piece of candy in this box and then just put it back in?

MEG: Oh. Well, I was looking for the ones with nuts.

LENNY: The ones with nuts.

MEG: Yeah.

LENNY: But there are none with nuts. It's a box of assorted cremes—all it has in it are cremes!

MEG: Oh.

LENNY: Why couldn't you just read on the box? It says right here, "Assorted Cremes," not nuts! Besides this was a birthday present to me! My one and only birthday present; my only one!

MEG: I'm sorry. I'll get you another box.

LENNY: I don't want another box. That's not the point!

MEG: What is the point?

LENNY: I don't know; it's—it's—You have no respect for other people's property! You just take whatever you want. You just take it! Why, remember how you had layers and layers of jingle bells sewed onto your petticoats while Babe and I only had three apiece?!

MEG: Oh, God! She's starting up about those stupid jingle bells!

LENNY: Well, it's an example! A specific example of how you always got what you wanted!

MEG: Oh, come on, Lenny, you're just upset because Doc called.

LENNY: Who said anything about Doc? Do you think I'm upset about Doc? Why, I've long since given up worrying about you and all your men.

MEG: *(Turning in anger)* Look, I know I've had too many men. Believe me, I've had way too many men. But it's not my fault you haven't had any—or maybe just that one from Memphis.

LENNY: *(Stopping)* What one from Memphis?

MEG: *(Slowly)* The one Babe told me about. From the— club.

LENNY: Babe!!!

BABE: Meg!!!

LENNY: How could you?!! I asked you not to tell anyone! I'm so ashamed! How could you?! Who else have you told? Did you tell anyone else?

BABE: *(Overlapping, to* Meg*)* Why'd you have to open your big mouth?!

MEG: *(Overlapping)* How am I supposed to know? You never said not to tell!

BABE: Can't you use your head just for once?!! *(Then to* Lenny*)* No, I never told anyone else. Somehow it just slipped out to Meg. Really, it just flew out of my mouth—

LENNY: What do you two have—wings on your tongues?

BABE: I'm sorry, Lenny. Really sorry.

LENNY: I'll just never, never, never be able to trust you again—

MEG: *(Furiously, coming to* Babe's *defense)* Oh, for heaven's sake, Lenny, we were just worried about you! We wanted to find a way to make you happy!

LENNY: Happy! Happy! I'll never be happy!

MEG: Well, not if you keep living your life as Old Granddaddy's nursemaid—

BABE: Meg, shut up!

MEG: I can't help it! I just know that the reason you stopped seeing this man from Memphis was because of Old Granddaddy.

LENNY: What—Babe didn't tell you the rest of the story—

MEG: Oh, she said it was something about your shrunken ovary.

BABE: Meg!!

LENNY: Babe!!

BABE: I just mentioned it!

MEG: But I don't believe a word of that story!

LENNY: Oh, I don't care what you believe! It's so easy for you—you always have men falling in love with you! But I have this underdeveloped ovary and I can't have children and my hair is falling out in the comb—so what man can love me?! What man's gonna love me?

MEG: A lot of men!

BABE: Yeah, a lot! A whole lot!

MEG: Old Granddaddy's the only one who seems to think otherwise.

LENNY: Cause he doesn't want to see me hurt! He doesn't want to see me rejected and humiliated.

MEG: Oh, come on now, Lenny, don't be so pathetic! God, you make me angry when you just stand there looking so pathetic! Just tell me, did you really ask the man from Memphis? Did you actually ask that man from Memphis all about it?

LENNY: *(Breaking apart)* No; I didn't. I didn't. Because I just didn't want him not to want me—

MEG: Lenny—

LENNY: *(Furiously)* Don't talk to me anymore! Don't talk to me! I think I'm gonna vomit—I just hope all this doesn't cause me to vomit! *(Lenny exits up the stairs sobbing)*

MEG: See! See! She didn't even ask him about her stupid ovary! She just broke it all off 'cause of Old Granddaddy! What a jackass fool!

BABE: Oh, Meg, shut up! Why do you have to make Lenny cry? I just hate it when you make Lenny cry! *(Babe runs up the stairs)* Lenny! Oh, Lenny— *(Meg takes a long sigh and goes to get a cigarette and a drink)*

MEG: I feel like hell. *(Meg sits in despair—smoking and drinking bourbon)*

Epic Theatre ————————————

The Good Woman of Setzuan
by Bertolt Brecht
translated by Eric Bentley*

(Shen Te and Yang Sun are in the park)

YANG SUN: Well, what are you staring at?
  SHEN TE: That rope. What is it for?
YANG SUN: Think! Think! I haven't a penny. Even if I had, I
            wouldn't spend it on you. I'd buy a drink of
            water.

(The rain starts)

  SHEN TE: *(Still looking at the rope)* What is the rope for? You
            mustn't!
YANG SUN: What's it to you? Clear out!
  SHEN TE: *(Irrelevantly)* It's raining.
YANG SUN: Well, don't try to come under this tree.
  SHEN TE: Oh, no. *(She stays in the rain)*
YANG SUN: Now go away. *(Pause)* For one thing, I don't like
            your looks, you're bowlegged.
  SHEN TE: *(Indignantly)* That's not true!
YANG SUN: Well, don't show 'em to me. Look, it's raining.
            You better come under this tree.

(Slowly, she takes shelter under the tree)

  SHEN TE: Why did you want to do it?
YANG SUN: You really want to know? *(Pause)* To get rid of
            you! *(Pause)* You know what a flyer is?
  SHEN TE: Oh yes, I've met a lot of pilots. At the tearoom.

YANG SUN: You call *them* flyers? Think they know what a machine is? Just 'cause they have leather helmets? They gave the airfield director a bribe, that's the way *those* fellows got up in the air! Try one of them out sometime. "Go up to two thousand feet," tell him, "then let it fall, then pick it up again with a flick of the wrist at the last moment." Know what he'll say to that? "It's not in my contract." Then again, there's the landing problem. It's like landing on your own backside. It's no different, planes are human. Those fools don't understand. *(Pause)* And I'm the biggest fool for reading the book on flying in the Peking school and skipping the page where it says: "We've got enough flyers and we don't need you." I'm a mail pilot with no mail. You understand that?

SHEN TE: *(Shyly)* Yes. I do.

YANG SUN: No, you don't. You'd never understand that.

SHEN TE: When we were little we had a crane with a broken wing. He made friends with us and was very good-natured about our jokes. He would strut along behind us and call out to stop us going too fast for him. But every spring and autumn when the cranes flew over the villages in great swarms, he got quite restless. *(Pause)* I understand that.

(She bursts out crying)

YANG SUN: Don't!

SHEN TE: *(Quieting down)* No.

YANG SUN: It's bad for the complexion.

SHEN TE: *(Sniffing)* I've stopped.

(She dries her tears on her big sleeve. Leaning against the tree, but not looking at her, he reaches for her face)

YANG SUN: You can't even wipe your own face. *(He is wiping it for her with his handkerchief. Pause)*

SHEN TE: *(Still sobbing)* I don't know *anything*.

YANG SUN: You interrupted me! What for?

SHEN TE: It's such a rainy day. You only wanted to do . . . *that* because it's such a rainy day.

(To the audience)

> In our country
> The evenings should never be somber

> High bridges over rivers
> The gray hour between night and morning
> And the long, long winter:
> Such things are dangerous
> For, with all the misery,
> A very little is enough
> And men throw away an unbearable life.

(Pause)

YANG SUN: Talk about yourself for a change.

SHEN TE: What about me? I have a shop.

YANG SUN: *(Incredulous)* You have a shop, have you? Never thought of walking the streets?

SHEN TE: I did walk the streets. Now I have a shop.

YANG SUN: *(Ironically)* A gift of the gods, I suppose!

SHEN TE: How did you know?

YANG SUN: *(Even more ironical)* One fine evening the gods turned up saying: here's some money!

SHEN TE: *(Quickly)* One fine morning.

YANG SUN: *(Fed up)* This isn't much of an entertainment.

(Pause)

SHEN TE: I can play the zither a little. *(Pause)* And I can mimic men. *(Pause)* I got the shop, so the first thing I did was to give my zither away. I can be as stupid as a fish now, I said to myself, and it won't matter.
I'm rich now, I said
I walk alone, I sleep alone
For a whole year, I said
I'll have nothing to do with a man.

YANG SUN: And now you're marrying one! The one at the tearoom by the pond?

(Shen Te is silent)

YANG SUN: What do you know about love?

SHEN TE: Everything.

YANG SUN: Nothing. *(Pause)* Or d'you just mean you enjoyed it?

SHEN TE: No.

YANG SUN: *(Again without turning to look at her, he strokes her cheek with his hand)* You like that?

SHEN TE: Yes.

YANG SUN: *(Breaking off)* You're easily satisfied, I must say. *(Pause)* What a town!

SHEN TE: You have no friends?

YANG SUN: *(Defensively)* Yes, I have! *(Change of tone)* But they don't want to hear I'm still unemployed. "What?" they ask. "Is there still water in the sea?" You have friends?

SHEN TE: *(Hesitating)* Just a . . . cousin.

YANG SUN: Watch him carefully.

SHEN TE: He only came once. Then he went away. He won't be back. *(Yang Sun is looking away)* But to be without hope, they say, is to be without goodness!

(Pause)

YANG SUN: Go on talking. A voice is a voice.

SHEN TE: Once, when I was a little girl, I fell, with a load of brushwood. An old man picked me up. He gave me a penny too. Isn't it funny how people who don't have very much like to give some of it away? They must like to show what they can do, and how could they show it better than by being kind? Being wicked is just like being clumsy. When we sing a song, or build a machine, or plant some rice, we're being kind. You're kind.

YANG SUN: You make it sound easy.

SHEN TE: Oh, no. *(Little pause)* Oh! A drop of rain!

YANG SUN: Where'd you feel it?

SHEN TE: Between the eyes.

YANG SUN: Near the right eye? Or the left?

SHEN TE: Near the left eye.

YANG SUN: Oh, good. *(He is getting sleepy)* So you're through with men, eh?

SHEN TE: *(With a smile)* But I'm not bowlegged.

YANG SUN: Perhaps not.

SHEN TE: Definitely not.

(Pause)

YANG SUN: *(Leaning wearily against the willow)* I haven't had a drop to drink all day, I haven't eaten anything for *two* days. I couldn't love you if I tried.

(Pause)

SHEN TE: I like it in the rain.

Actor-Characters _____

The Persecution and Assassination of Jean-Paul Marat as Performed by the Inmates of the Asylum of Charenton under the Direction of the Marquis de Sade

by Peter Weiss*
SCENE 17. FIRST CONVERSATION BETWEEN CORDAY AND DUPERRET

(Corday is led forward by the two Sisters, supporting her under the arms. Duperret walks behind, supporting Corday's back with his hands)

HERALD: *(Plays a few runs on his Pan-flute)*
           And now nobility meets grace
           Our author brings them face to face
           The beautiful and brave Charlotte Corday

(Turns round in concern, nods in relief and points his staff at Corday)

           The handsome Monsieur Duperret

(With the help of the Sisters, Corday enters the arena. Duperret walks beside her. The Sisters withdraw. Corday and Duperret greet each other with exaggerated ceremony)

           In Caen where she spent the best years of her
             youth
           in a convent devoted to the way of truth
           Duperret's name she heard them recommend
           as a most sympathetic helpful friend

(Duperret *uses the scene to make amorous advances to* Corday. *The* Herald *addresses* Duperret)

> Confine your passion to the lady's mind
> Your love's platonic not the other kind.

(*He gives the* orchestra *a sign with his staff.* Corday *stands with head held back, eyes closed. The* orchestra *plays the Corday theme. The* Herald *withdraws. He waits a few seconds and watches* Corday)

CORDAY: (*With her eyes closed*)
> Ah dearest Duperret

(*She hesitates then starts again as if singing an aria*)
> Ah dearest Duperret what can we do
> How can we stop this dreadful calamity
> In the streets everyone is saying
> Marat's to be . . .

(*She hesitates.* Duperret *gently caresses her hips and back*)

> Marat's to be tribune and dictator
> He still pretends that his iron grip
> will relax as soon as the worst is over
> But we know what Marat really wants
> anarchy and confusion.

(Corday *stands sunk into herself*)

DUPERRET: (*Embracing* Corday, *also as if singing an aria, but with great ardour*)

> Dearest Charlotte you must return
> return to your friends the pious nuns
> and live in prayer and contemplation
> You cannot fight
> the hard-faced enemies surrounding us

(*One of the* Sisters *approaches* Duperret *and pulls back his hand, which he had placed on her bosom.* Corday *stands sunk into herself*)

> You talk about Marat but who's this Marat
> A street salesman a funfair barker
> a layabout from Corsica sorry I mean Sardinia
> Marat the name sounds Jewish to me
> perhaps derived from the waters of Marah in
>   the Bible
> But who listens to him
> Only the mob down in the streets
> Up here Marat can be no danger to us.

*(Duperret embraces Corday's hips. The four singers are filling in
time with all sorts of pranks, throwing dice and showing each other
card tricks)*

CORDAY: *(Suddenly awake and full of power)*
            Dearest Duperret you're trying to test me
            but I know what I must do

*(Tries to free herself from Duperret's embrace. The two Sisters stand-
ing behind the podium interfere and pull back Duperret's hands)*

            Duperret go to Caen
            Barbaroux and Buzot are waiting for you
                there
            Go now and travel quickly
            Do not wait till this evening
            for this evening everything will be too late.

DUPERRET: *(Passionately, in aria style as before)*
            Dearest Charlotte my place is here

(Throws himself on his knees and hugs her legs)

            How could I leave the city which holds you
            Dearest Charlotte
            my place is here.

*(He forgets himself and becomes wilder in his embracing. The Her-
ald pushes him with his staff and then taps on the floor)*

HERALD: *(Prompting)*
            And why should I run . . .
DUPERRET: And why should I run
            now when it can't last much longer

(Stroking Corday vigorously)

            Already the English lie off Dunkirk and Tou-
                lon
            The Prussians . . .
HERALD: *(Prompting)*
            The Spaniards.
DUPERRET: The Spaniards have occupied Roussillon Paris
            . . .
HERALD: *(Prompting)*
            Mayence . . .
DUPERRET: Mayence is surrounded by the Prussians
            Condé and Valenciennes have fallen to the Eng-
            lish . . .
HERALD: *(Correcting)*
            Austrians . . .
DUPERRET: To the Austrians
            The Vendée is up in arms

(With much ardour and vigorous embraces)

> They can't hold out much longer
> these fanatical upstarts
> with no vision and no culture
> They can't hold out much longer
> No dear Charlotte here I stay

(Snuggles up to her and puts his head into her lap)

> waiting for the promised day
> when with Marat's mob interred
> France once more speaks the forbidden word
> Freedom.

(Duperret raises himself, clinging to Corday, tries to kiss her. Corday extricates herself, the two Sisters come to her aid, pushing Duperret away and pulling her back to her bench. The music ends)

SECTION PHOTO CREDITS

Title Page
Earth Spirit by Frank Wedekind
Yale School of Drama, New Haven, Connecticut
Director: Lee Breuer; Set: Kate Edmunds
Costumes: Nancy Thun; Lights: Tom Schraeder
Performers: Joyce Fideor, Brian McEleney
Photographer: Bruce Siddons
Courtesy of *Yale Drama Alumni Newsletter*
Phillis C. Warfel, Editor

Part One: The Creative Perspective
Of Time and the River by Thomas Wolfe
Adapted by Eugene McKinney and Paul Baker
Baylor University Theatre, Waco, Texas
Photographer: Windy Drum
Director: Paul Baker
Set and costumes: Virgil Beavers

Part Two: The Human Perspective
Uncommon Women and Others by Wendy Wasserstein
Major Theatre Series, Montclair State College, Upper
Montclair, N.J.
Set and lights: W. Scott MacConnell
Costumes: Joseph F. Bella

Part Three: The Perspective of Craft
Hamlet by William Shakespeare
Hardin-Simmons University, Abilene, Texas
Set: Gail Ruth Egleston

Part Four: The Perspective of the Role
Madwoman of Chaillot by Jean Giraudoux
Kentucky Wesleyan College, Owensboro, Ky.
Set: Phil Padgett
Costumes: Vivian Parks

Part Five: The Perspective of Genre
Hotel Paradiso by Georges Feydeau
St. Cloud State University, St. Cloud, Minn.
Set: Stephen R. Meyer
Costumes: Harvey Paul Jurik

Appendix
Earnest in Love by Anne Croswell and Lee Pockriss
Montclair State College, Major Theatre Series, Upper
Montclair, N.J.
Set: W. Scott MacConnell
Costumes: Joseph F. Bella
Photographer: Joe Meyer

Additional Credits
Students in exercise photographs: Marisa Altamura, Michelle Begley, Kernan Bell, Thomas Drummer, Gladys DuChantier, Steven Friedman, Paula Goldberg, Carolyn Tonic Robinson, David Scott Saunders, Anna L. Smyre.

Exercise and mask photos by C. Spaccavento.

Graphic illustrations by Nancy Bartlett.

Except where otherwise indicated, production photos were taken by the text author of plays under his direction.

299

Index

W

Warm-up exercises
    physical, 15–16
    vocal, 17–18
Words
    connotations, 130
    denotations, 129–130
    as image makers, 128–129, 129 (fig. 7.2)
    vocal transfer, 127–128

Z

Zero-line base, 203, 216